North Carolina beyond the Connected Age

NORTH CAROLINA BEYOND THE CONNECTED AGE

The Tar Heel State in 2050

MICHAEL L. WALDEN

The University of North Carolina Press
Chapel Hill

The University of North Carolina Press has been a
member of the Green Press Initiative since 2003.

Cover illustration: icons from thenounproject.com;
Milky Way time-lapse image by tobkatrina,
© iStockphoto.com.

Library of Congress Cataloging-in-Publication Data
Names: Walden, Michael L. (Michael Leonard), 1951– author.
Title: North Carolina beyond the connected age : the
Tar Heel state in 2050 / Michael L. Walden.
Other titles: Tar Heel state in 2050
Description: Chapel Hill : The University of North Carolina
Press, [2017] | Includes bibliographical references and index.
Identifiers: LCCN 2017009062 | ISBN 9781469635712 (cloth : alk. paper) |
ISBN 9781469635729 (pbk : alk. paper) | ISBN 9781469635736 (ebook)
Subjects: LCSH: North Carolina—Economic conditions—21st century. |
Industries—North Carolina. | Labor supply—North Carolina.
Classification: LCC HC107. N8 W347 2017 | DDC 330.9756/00112—dc23
LC record available at https://lccn.loc.gov/2017009062

To Mary now,
and to my parents in the past

CONTENTS

FIGURES, TABLES, AND MAPS

Figures

Tables

Maps

PREFACE

North Carolina was a different place in the 1970s. Its population was smaller, younger, whiter, and less educated than it would be at the dawn of the twenty-first century. Although changes were under way, the "Big Three" industries of tobacco, textiles, and furniture still dominated the state's economy. The major trade agreements that would open these industries to international competition—and shrink them in the process—were still to come. Although the standard of living for the state's residents lagged the nation, North Carolinians had made great strides since World War II, and a middle-class lifestyle was now a reality—or a realistic dream—for most households. Most North Carolinians still lived in small towns and rural regions. The future metropolitan giants of Charlotte and Raleigh-Durham were on the cusp of their growth spurt.

By the beginning of the twenty-first century all this had changed. Pushed by both domestic and international migration, the state's population had almost doubled. It had become more diverse racially, ethnically, and culturally. In some big cities, it was difficult to find a native-born North Carolinian. The "Big Three" of tobacco, textiles, and furniture were shadows of their former selves, having been replaced by the "Big Five" of technology, pharmaceuticals, food processing, banking, and vehicle parts firms. Over 60 percent of the state's residents lived in urban counties. Metropolitan areas were ascending, small towns and rural areas struggling. Several counties had lost population. In contrast, the state's two racehorse economies of Charlotte and Raleigh-Durham were adding new households at record rates from both within and outside the state. Charlotte became the nation's second largest banking center, acquired two major league sports franchises, and hosted the 2012 Democratic National Convention. The Raleigh-Durham metro region saw its technology center—the Research Triangle Park—develop to become the model for similar endeavors around the nation and world. But the economic dream had faded for many, with the percentage of households classified as middle class dropping by half in thirty years.[1]

These trends were not unique to North Carolina. Indeed, most southeastern states experienced similar patterns. However, North Carolina was traditionally a state of relatively low population density, with numerous small towns and no dominant big cities. In 1970, it ranked sixth among the states, behind only the Dakotas, Mississippi, Vermont, and West Virginia, with the smallest proportion of its population living in urban areas. By 2010, fourteen states had a lower urbanized population than North Carolina, and the growth in the state's population between 1970 and 2010 was 70 percent greater than for the nation as a whole.[2] As traditional rural industries declined and urban areas boomed, the state's balance of power shifted from the countryside to the cities. For the first time, in 2012 a big-city mayor, Pat McCrory of Charlotte, was elected governor. Symbolizing this change, the new McCrory administration altered the funding formula for state road projects from geographic-based to needs-based; more money would henceforth be spent in fast-growing urban areas and less in rural regions.

The Great Recession was a watershed event for North Carolina, as it was for the nation. Because twice as much of the state's economy as the nation was based on manufacturing and because manufacturing always takes a big hit during recessions, the recession clobbered North Carolina more than most other states. At its peak, the state's jobless rate was almost 1.5 percentage points higher than the national rate and seventh highest among the states. Per capita income relative to the national level, after rising for several decades, began to fall. Even the state's racehorse economies found that they were not immune to the downturn. Charlotte, with its concentration of banking, lost 8 percent of its jobs and 5 percent of its economic output. The tech-heavy Raleigh-Durham region saw almost fifty thousand jobs cut.[3] Regions dependent on tourism and second homes, such as the coastal community of Wilmington, stayed in recession well after the state's economy began to rebound.

The recovery from the Great Recession illustrated the new structure and composition of North Carolina. By 2013, both Charlotte and Raleigh-Durham had recovered the economic output and jobs lost during the previous five years, but the rest of the state lagged behind. During the first five years of the job recovery, 2010–15, these two dominant metropolitan areas generated over 70 percent of net job creation. If the next two largest metropolitan regions (Greensboro and Winston-Salem) are added, the proportion climbs to almost 85 percent.[4] Cranes constructing new high-rises and commercial towers in metro areas stood in contrast to boarded-up, abandoned factories in small towns.

So it is with trepidation, anticipation, and uncertainty that North Carolina looks to the future. Future tellers—those experts who examine trends and anticipate change—are divided on what will come next.[5] Certainly there are many visions, but at the extremes are two polar opposites: the "optimistic future" and the "pessimistic future."

The optimistic future relies importantly on innovation to make our future lives better—just as it has in the past. Standards of living started to rise dramatically as people began to invent, create, and then harness new techniques and machines for the betterment of most. The First Industrial Revolution of the late eighteenth and early nineteenth centuries developed the power and procedures for people to build, produce, and expand beyond levels ever imagined. Employing the steam engine, ironworks, and new machine tools, advances were made in agriculture, clothing, housing, and medicine to raise standards of living from their prior stagnant levels to new heights. The Second Industrial Revolution, spanning the mid-nineteenth to mid-twentieth centuries, saw the developments of electricity, mechanized ground transportation, air flight, radio and television, and new housing and medical advances push living standards even higher for a broader range of people.[6]

What some term the Third Industrial Revolution and others call the Information Revolution began in the late twentieth century and is ongoing. This has been the internet age, in which computers, smartphones, and the worldwide web have placed information and the ability to analyze and use it at the fingertips of virtually everyone in the world. The technologies have effectively shrunk the globe by increasing communication and knowledge. They have also motivated more worldwide trade and, with it, have helped reduce world inflation rates and interest rates. Entire new industries creating, producing, and expanding these technologies have developed and employed millions. World poverty rates have declined while world measures of health and nutrition have grown.

Urban studies theorist Richard Florida sees the stages of innovation in a slightly different way, which he terms "Resets."[7] He argues that societal Resets have followed periods of major economic stress, producing innovations as well as changes not only in how and where people work and live but also, importantly, in educational institutions and transportation methods. The first modern Reset followed the Long Recession of 1873–79 and shifted workers from the farm to the factory, moved families from rural regions to cities, spawned the expansion of K–12 education, and linked the population with railroads and streetcars. The second Reset began after the Great Depression of the 1930s and gradually transferred work from factories to service centers, moved households from cities to suburbia, expanded college education, and connected the economy with interstate highways and airports.

Florida says that we are now in the third great Reset following the Great
Recession of 2007–9. The fastest job growth is in creative jobs that develop
value through ingenuity, problem-solving, and the arts. Cities, suburbs, and
exurbs are merging into megaregions. Rapid economic change has accelerated "creative destruction"—the continuous overhaul and rejuvenation of the
economy—to such a level that workers need to pursue several occupations
over their careers. The need for flexibility is prompting a shift from owning to
renting. High-speed rail both within and across megaregions will eventually
dominate connectivity. The greatest challenge during the third Reset is design-
ing an educational system that can support timely and rapid reskilling of the
labor force.

The optimistic future sees the Third Industrial Revolution continuing and
the current Reset succeeding. Further advances in information technology in
such areas as virtualization, nanotechnology, cloud computing, data analysis,
and applications we cannot even now imagine will result in large gains in
resource efficiencies, safety, predictive powers, and the access and use of information.[8] Even if the development of innovations slows, greater adaptability
of existing technology in the economy will result in improved productivity.[9]
The results will be lower product costs and prices, more affordable medical
care, a healthier environment and healthier citizens, lower energy costs, and
lower education costs, among others—all outcomes that will send standards
of living to record highs.[10] Many innovations will take place in manufacturing,
which—optimists point out—has a rate of innovation twice its relative size in
the economy.[11] One analysis suggests that innovations in the energy field alone,
using new energy sources as well as improved efficiencies in existing sources,
will free up 28 percent of household disposable income for use in other areas.[12]
Although some industries will experience downsized employment through
technology and machines replacing human labor, optimists believe that new
industries will develop—many of them impossible to forecast today—to provide ample jobs with better working conditions and improved earnings. Optimists agree that dynamic economies destroy some industries and jobs even as
they create new industries and jobs. This, they argue, is how gains are made,
and the net result is forward movement.[13] In short, the three-hundred-year
march of improved living standards and an easier life will continue under the
optimistic future.

Demography and expanded international trade are also part of the optimistic future. Although the U.S. population will age and the birthrate will hover
just above replacement level, the nation's demographic outlook looks much
brighter than in China, Japan, and Europe, where both the total population

and people of working age are projected to shrink.[14] By comparison, driven by the large millennial generation, the U.S. total and working-age populations will expand, thereby improving the relative productive capacity of the nation vis-à-vis its major economic competitors.[15]

Internationally, hundreds of millions of individuals worldwide will move from subsistence level to middle-class status, prompting dramatic changes in consumption and spending habits. One estimate puts the gains at 1.8 billion more middle-class people with an eighteen-trillion-dollar increase in spending worldwide by 2025.[16] Developed countries such as the United States should be well positioned to tap these expanding markets for new sales and job creation. Manufacturing, agriculture, and even entertainment—where the United States is the world leader—will be at the top in reaping the rewards of the new global consumers.

So the optimistic future sees innovation, adjustment, and renewal as the keys to a better economic future. Optimists say that the ability to adapt to changing circumstances has been the hallmark of the U.S. economy. Indeed, the core feature of competitiveness in our economy promotes a constant dynamic of adaptation that propels the country forward, and as modern technology continues to lower the fixed costs of businesses, optimists see competitiveness and innovation reaching new levels.[17] Certainly the economic adjustments are not without losers and losses, so a continual challenge is how to cushion these losses without constraining the adjustment. But, optimists believe, the benefits of change exceed the costs from change and thus net gains are made. It has happened in the past, optimists say, and it will happen in the future.

The pessimistic future sees the future much differently. Though they do not deny the benefits of past changes, adjustments, and innovations, pessimists fundamentally believe that this time is different and see a future characterized by "secular stagnation," a period of prolonged slow economic growth.[18]

Perhaps the most forceful advocate for the pessimistic view is economist Robert Gordon.[19] Gordon sees several "headwinds," as he calls them, reducing future economic growth. One negative trend is demographics. The nation's population will continue to age. People are living longer and birthrates have been declining. The result is a population profile that is rapidly becoming more top heavy, with a rising number of older persons per younger—and especially *working* younger—persons.

The demographic trend will create three traumas for the economy. First, Gordon argues, older individuals spend less, so the nation's increased age profile will decrease aggregate spending on goods and services produced by businesses. This will create a subtle, yet significant recession. Second, older households will deplete their savings by selling stocks, bonds, mutual funds, and real estate, thereby putting downward pressure on the values of all these assets and adding to the subtle recession. Third, a rising share of governments' budgets will of necessity be spent on entitlement programs supporting the elderly, including federal contributions to Social Security, Medicare, and Medicaid and state contributions to Medicaid. Taxes on working households will be increased to keep these programs solvent. Higher tax rates could in turn cause slowdowns in private economic activity.

Gordon's second headwind centers on technology, specifically on the lack of significant technological gains. He argues that most of the major inventions and innovations have occurred. Nothing in the future will rival the impact of the steam engine, flight, auto travel, or penicillin. Future inventions will simply be minor add-ons—or tweaks—to existing machines and technology, and therefore none will have the societal improvements brought about by the earlier periods of creativity and discovery.[20]

Furthermore, Gordon sees an educational system and students that are not keeping up with the skills needed to adapt to a modern economy that values cognitive abilities and problem-solving over routine tasks and physical labor. Thus, labor productivity and pay will slide, domestic labor will face stiffer competition from global labor, and income inequality will rise between those with valuable skills and those without them.

Gordon's last headwind comes from the environment and comprises two issues. First, the rising cost of limited energy and other natural resources will not be overcome by gains in efficiency. Higher prices for energy and natural resources will slow economic growth. Second, global warming will reduce economic growth because spending to improve energy efficiency or avert global warming will divert funds that could be used for productivity-enhancing investments. In Gordon's words, such spending simply keeps us "running in place" rather than running ahead.

Gordon has calibrated the adverse impacts of these headwinds on economic growth. He estimates that the average annual long-run growth rate of 2 percent per person will be reduced by one third to 1.3 percent for the economy as a whole. However, for the 99 percent of households who are not the elite in skills, productivity, and income, the average annual growth rate per person will be a dismal 0.2 percent.

Other economists share Gordon's pessimistic predictions for economic growth. Gordon Bjork thinks that all the benefits from specialization and economies of scale in the economy have occurred and that the movement of women into the paid workforce—which boosted economic output—has run its course.[21] Bjork assesses both these factors will slow future economic progress. Likewise, John Fernald and Charles Jones, as well as Canyon Bosler and coauthors, predict that slowing improvements in educational attainment, research and development, and population will shave the annual growth rate from 2 percent to 1.8 percent, while Jacques Bughin and coauthors see these factors depressing corporate and investment returns.[22] Fredrik Erixon and Björn Weigel argue that the structure of modern capitalism is inevitably leading to slower growth.[23]

Other analysts have focused on individual components of Gordon's assessment. Regarding demography, Paul Taylor predicts that the country's dependency rate—defined as the number of children plus the number of elderly as a percentage of the working-age population—will rise from 20 percent in 2010 to 36 percent in 2050.[24] With relatively fewer working-age individuals, Taylor expects lower economic growth. Nicole Maestas, Kathleen Mullen, and David Powell calibrate that aging will subtract between 0.6 and 1.2 percentage points from annual economic growth, and Etienne Gagnon, Benjamin Johannsen, and David Lopez-Salido's estimate is within this range.[25] Similarly, Harry Dent Jr. argues the peak in U.S. spending occurred in the early 2000s.[26] As a result of a lower birthrate and an aging population, he sees fewer funds available for investing leading to falling aggregate spending and price deflation until 2025, with only a modest recover thereafter.[27]

Geneticist Jan Vijg divides innovations into "nonequivalent"—those that represent breakthroughs of fundamentally different products and processes—and "equivalent"—those that simply provide more applications for the same products and processes.[28] Nonequivalent innovations are those that propel the economy to new levels. Unfortunately, Vijg sees more recent innovations falling into the equivalent rather than nonequivalent category, in part because regulatory constraints and social safety nets have increased satisfaction and reduced risk-taking. By Vijg's count, the number of nonequivalent innovations fell by 70 percent between the 1970s and the 2000s. James Pethokoukis and Ryan Decker and coauthors support this conclusion by noting a decline in entrepreneurial activity in the past forty years.[29] For his part, Tyler Cowen contends that most of the "game-changing" technology has already been developed.[30]

Murray and McGowan/Andrews document the growing dichotomy in U.S. households between those with marketable training and skills and those without.[31] They lament that the country will see a large and growing lower class consistently in need of help, thereby requiring continual public support which will siphon funds away from productivity-enhancing investments. Cowen echoes this view by concluding that "average is over."[32] Stiglitz sees growing income inequality as reducing household mobility between income strata and discouraging achievement among those on the lower rungs of the income ladder.[33] Others argue rising income inequality reduces economic growth due to the lower spending rates of upper income households.[34] Nir Jaimovich and Henry Siu document progressive increases in job polarization during recent recessions, and David Autor, David Dorn, and Gordon Hanson; Gregory Clark; Enrico Moretti; and Pol Antràs, Alonso de Gortari, and Oleg Itskhoki all demonstrate class and geographic divisions resulting from the growing income polarization.[35]

Economist William Nordhaus assesses the adverse economic effects of global warming, including reduced agricultural productivity, increased property damage from more intense storms, loss of biodiversity, and health deterioration. He estimates total economic costs between 1 percent and 5 percent of GDP, which in 2015 translated to between $180 billion and $900 billion annually (in 2015 dollars).[36]

Perhaps the most troubling implications of the pessimistic future are for the job market. In the 1930s, John Maynard Keynes talked about "technological unemployment," where innovations and new technology would eventually render many jobs obsolete.[37] Until now the additional income created by innovations combined with the continual upgrading of the educational system have allowed replacement jobs to be created in new industries. However, some economists now see this virtuous cycle of innovations creating new income and new employment as ending.[38] These economists say that we may have reached a point where innovations and technological advances will, on net, destroy jobs and expand inequality between those with and without employment. This may be a major reason for the successively weaker job recoveries from recessions beginning in the 1990s and labor's reduced share of national income.[39] One estimate suggests that almost half of U.S. employment could be at risk of replacement by technology.[40] Whereas in the past technology could complement employment, today technology is more likely to substitute for employment. Paul Beaudry, David Green, and Benjamin Sand see evidence of this even for skilled occupations, and Andrew Weaver and Paul Osterman find little evidence to support a supposed shortage of skilled workers.[41] For his part, Daniel Alpert argues that we are entering a period of sustained excess labor.[42] If this is accurate, some see a need for the public sector to create "virtual" or "make-work" jobs that give displaced workers something to do as well as increased income transfers from the employed and prosperous to the unemployed and struggling.[43]

TABLE P.1 The Optimistic Future versus the Pessimistic Future

Factor	Optimistic Future	Pessimistic Future
Demography	Demographic future better for U.S than for competitors; will give U.S. an edge	Rising dependency ratio and slower population growth will slow economic growth
Innovation	Continued innovative gains, perhaps at an accelerated pace	Game-changing innovative gains are over
Education	Will adapt and improve to reskill the labor force	Educational improvements will lag and perhaps stop
Labor and skills	Reskilling of labor force will increase labor productivity	Increasing technological unemployment
Income inequality	Education will improve opportunities for income mobility	Income inequality will increase; need for "virtual" jobs and increased income transfers
Climate	Improvements in resource efficiency and resource substitutes will address climate challenges	Global warming will impose costs on economy; resources diverted to address global warming will slow economic growth
Net result	Long-run pace of economic growth will continue	Economic growth will slow

The factors that will determine the economic future and the contrasting assessments of the optimistic future and the pessimistic future are presented in table P.1. Both futures foresee an increased demographic dependency rate and slower population growth. The optimistic future evaluates these trends as a plus because they will occur to a lesser extent in the United States compared to other competitor countries. The pessimistic future sees the demographic trends as hurting growth.

The line is clearly drawn on innovation. The optimistic future thinks that major innovative gains will be made, leading to significant economic growth. The pessimistic future believes the opposite: big, innovative gains are over for the foreseeable future, and this will be a major reason for the slide in economic growth.

In the past 150 years U.S. education policy and practices have adapted to the changing economy and workplace by upgrading the skill levels of the workforce, first by expanding K–12 education and then by making college education accessible to more students. The optimistic future holds that the country's educational system will continue to adapt to the changed economic future, through such techniques as massive open online courses and quick reskilling for displaced workers. The pessimistic future questions the ability of the educational bureaucracy to adjust and is skeptical of continued gains in educational attainment.

Both futures predict changes for the labor market and for the types of skills valued by the market. The optimistic future believes that the educational system can be altered to accommodate different skill needs and will be able to guide workers to job categories where demand is growing. That is, in the race between education and technology—the phrase coined by economists Claudia Goldin and Lawrence Katz—education will win, just as it has in the past.[44] The pessimistic future sees technological unemployment as the major labor market trend that will leave a large percentage of the workforce functionally unemployed. Similarly, the optimistic future thinks that educational and employment opportunities will blunt increases in income inequality, whereas the pessimistic future sees an inevitable increase in income inequality between the highly rewarded skilled and creative workers and everyone else. In this pessimistic world, public-sector-supported jobs and generous income transfers will be required.

Both futures accept the possibility of climate issues centered on global warming. The optimistic future argues that these issues can be addressed with innovations in energy and resource efficiencies and with energy and resource substitutes; indeed, the optimistic future sees economic gains as these responses create new industries. Even if these responses are forthcoming, the pessimistic future sees no gain for the economy as the efforts come at the expense of spending in other industries; climate issues, therefore, can only reduce economic growth.

The net result is a stark difference in the future. The optimistic future predicts continued growth at no diminished rate; the pessimistic future sees a future of slower economic growth and declining numbers of jobs, with little ability to control the outcomes.

North Carolina beyond the Connected Age takes these alternative futures and the conditions behind the futures and applies them to North Carolina. The goal is to think about the likely outlook—or outlooks—for the state at midcentury. Where states might fall on the optimistic and pessimistic continuums clearly can vary based on many circumstances. For example, although the nation may be aging, the type and rate of demographic change will not be the same for all states. North Carolina is younger—demographically speaking—than the nation as a whole, and the state has successfully attracted younger households for decades. This means that the adverse consequences that many expect from an aging population may affect North Carolina to a lesser degree.

The industry mix of North Carolina is also different than the mix in the nation overall: the goods-producing sector is larger and the service-producing sector is smaller. This suggests that technologically based drivers, as well as other drivers such as expanding international trade, will be different in North Carolina. Could the state nurture industries that will be game-changers and standard-of-living enhancers? Or will North Carolina's economic structure follow the path dictated by the nation?

It also follows that the future for jobs could be different in North Carolina, importantly because the number and kinds of jobs will be determined largely by future demographic and industry changes. If the state experiences sufficient population growth, spending reversals associated with an aging and asset-depleting society could be moderated.

The study of alternative paths to North Carolina's future applies two models for considering resource use, particularly for public policy: cost-benefit analysis and the definition of private and public goods. Cost-benefit analysis explicitly recognizes that at any time all societies have limited resources, and so comparison of benefits obtained relative to costs incurred for alternative uses of scarce resources is an important consideration for both private and public decision-making. Private goods are products and services developed and delivered by private, profit-seeking firms, whereas public goods are products and services from governmental units.[45] Because of the broad and deep fundamental changes expected in the economy in upcoming decades, products and services considered as either private or public will likely be redefined.

The following eight chapters look at North Carolina's future in depth. Chapter 1, "Will They Still Come?," explores North Carolina's demographic trends and projections for the future. The second chapter, "Hot Places and Open Spaces," examines how and where North Carolinians will live in future decades. "Where's the Growth?" (chapter 3) focuses on the future for technology and innovation in the state and how these forces will shape the industries of the next economy. This is followed by a detailed look at tomorrow's workforce—who will work, where they will work, what kind of training workers will need, and what they will earn (chapter 4, "Winners and Losers in Making a Living") and the implications for the educational and training system (chapter 5, "Resetting Education"). Potential resource limitations in water and energy and associated environmental issues and their effects on the future North Carolina economy are addressed in chapter 6 ("Requiem for Resources?"). The question of the role of government in shaping the economic future—importantly, whether more or less governmental direction is needed—is the topic of chapter 7 ("Government's Role: Lean In or Back Off?"). The book concludes with perhaps the most important question: "Is the Future in Our Hands?" (chapter 8). Can we shape our economic future, or are the determining trends beyond our control?

North Carolina has been a state on the way up for most of the decades since World War II. The population grew, people flocked to the state, the state's economy was retooled, and living standards improved both absolutely and relatively to the nation. The Great Recession and the subsequent slow recovery stopped or reversed many of these trends, and questions are now being raised about the state's economic future. This book accesses whether this turnaround was temporary and the past days of growth and improvement will return or whether North Carolina—like the nation—is looking at a more modest future for all and a bleak future for many.

Indian prime minister Jawaharlal Nehru is reputed to have said, "Life is like a game of cards. The hand you are dealt is determinism; the way you play it is free will."[46] Forces may be moving and shaping our economy in ways that we cannot control. They are the hand we are dealt. If we can identify and understand these forces, then perhaps we can play the cards in a way to give us the best possible future. *North Carolina beyond the Connected Age: The Tar Heel State in 2050* tries to identify both the hand dealt and the available plays.

North Carolina beyond the Connected Age

MAP 1.1 North Carolina Counties.

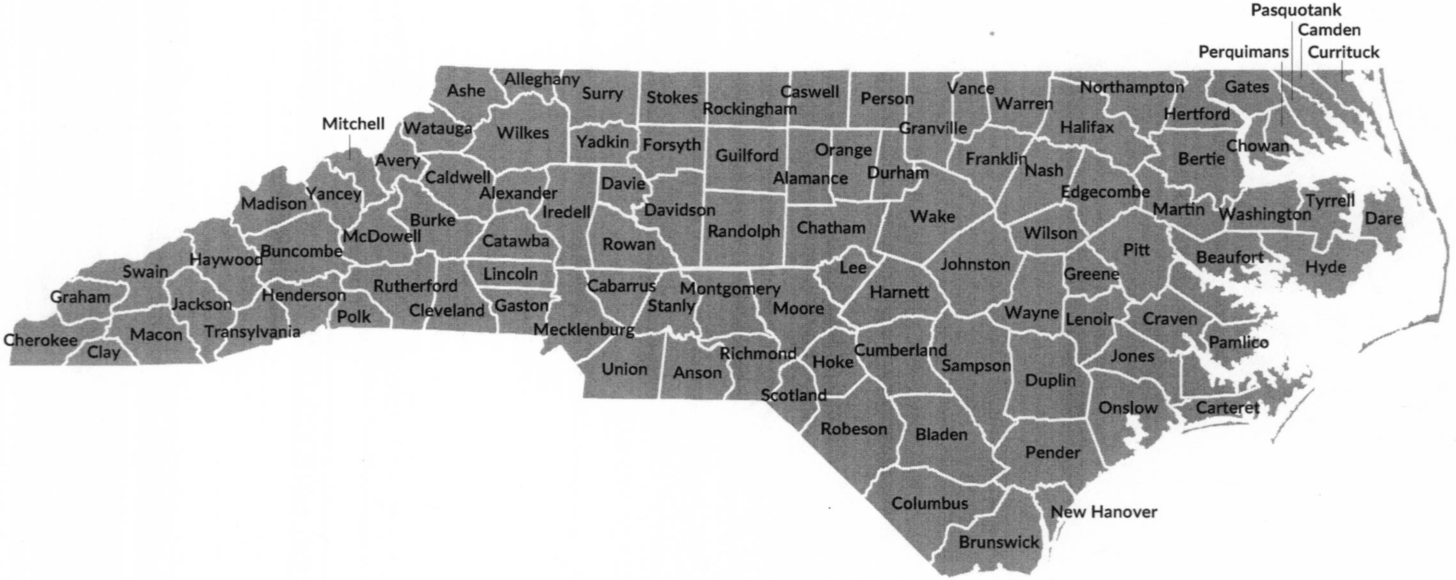

1. WILL THEY STILL COME?

Looking Back

For most of its history, North Carolina lagged the nation in population growth (fig. 1.1). Like the rest of the South, North Carolina in the colonial and antebellum periods was an agricultural and rural region with a low population density. This began to change in the late nineteenth century with the mechanization of farming and the resulting shift to machinery inputs and away from human labor in agriculture. Still, the state's population growth lagged national growth in the early twentieth century due to the out-migration of African American households to northern states and the lack of big city development in the state. The state's population growth beat national growth in the post–World War I 1920s and depression era 1930s but then lapsed in subpar growth for several decades afterward.[1]

The turnaround in North Carolina's population growth came in the 1970s. Several factors led both South and North Carolina to add population at faster rates than the nation as a whole. The spread of air conditioning made the region more hospitable to people wishing to escape harsh northern winters yet not wanting to overheat in summer; this was especially the case for the growing retiree segment. Increased international competitiveness in business and production made the nonunionized South increasingly attractive to factories and companies seeking to reduce labor costs. And the lessening of racial tensions, especially after the turbulent 1960s, reduced this stigma that had long been associated with the region.[2]

There are two fundamental sources of population growth for a state. One is the excess of births over deaths, termed the net birthrate. The other is the excess of individuals moving to the state over individuals moving out of the state (net in-migration) and the net movement of foreign-born individuals moving to the state (immigration).

FIG. 1.1 Difference between North Carolina and U.S. population growth rates by decade.

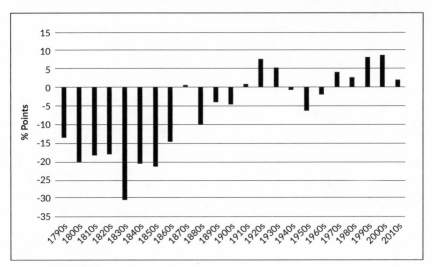

NOTE: 2010s based on 2010–16.
SOURCE: U.S. Census.

North Carolina has relied importantly on people moving to the state from other states for its recent population growth (fig. 1.2). An astounding 70 percent of the state's population growth in the last half of the 1980s was from net in-migration, and the rate remained high in the 1990s (40 percent), 2000s (50 percent), and 2010s (36 percent). Immigration contributed approximately 18 percent to total population growth since the mid-1980s. North Carolina consistently ranked either second or third among all states in net in-migration throughout this period.[3] Indeed, without in-movers from other states and nations, North Carolina would have had 2.4 million fewer people in 2016 than its 10.1 million total.

Where have North Carolina's new residents come from, why have they come, and what characteristics have they brought with them? For in-migrants from other states, the leading "sending" states have been Florida, New York, California, Pennsylvania, and Ohio.[4] In-migrants from Florida have likely been reverse snowbirds, retirees seeking a slightly less humid and warm state as their residence. New York, Pennsylvania, and Ohio are Rust Belt states whose economies have struggled with higher costs and difficult winters compared to their southern neighbors. And although California has been a growth leader since World War II, its economy sputtered during much of the 2000s. For movers from other nations, the dominant sending region has been Latin America (Central America, South America, and the Caribbean), with Mexico being the leading country. Second has been the Asian region.

FIG. 1.2 Relative contributions of the net birthrate, the net in-migration rate, and immigration to North Carolina's population growth by decade (percentage of total population change).

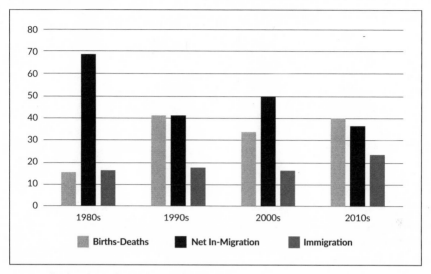

NOTE: 1980s based on 1985–1990, 2010s based on 2010–2015.
SOURCE: U.S. Census.

People have moved to North Carolina primarily for work-related factors. Almost half arrive because of a job transfer, a new job, or retirement. In second place, accounting for about one fourth of moves, is family-related factors, including divorce or separation and children moving away from their parents.[5] Movers are overwhelming young—almost two-thirds are between eighteen and thirty years—and separated, divorced, and widowed adults are more mobile than never-married individuals. Individuals with a college degree move more than those without advanced educational training, and movers have higher incomes than nonmovers.[6] Movers may also be attracted to North Carolina because of its warmer temperatures.[7]

Looking Ahead

Predicting the population of any region, such as a state, requires projections for the sources of population change: change resulting from the difference between births and deaths (labeled natural population change), and change resulting from net in-migration and immigration.

If the age structure of the current population is known, then assumptions for the future birthrate and future death rate can be applied to generate natural

TABLE 1.1 Actual and Predicted U.S. Population Totals and Age Structure

	Number (Millions)			Percentage of Total		
	2010	2030	2050	2010	2030	2050
Total population	308.7	358.5	399.8	100.0	100.0	100.0
Under 18	74.1	80.3	85.9	24.0	22.4	21.5
18–24	30.6	30.5	34.0	9.9	8.5	8.5
25–44	82.1	93.9	101.5	26.6	26.2	25.4
45–64	81.5	81.0	94.8	26.4	22.6	23.7
65 and older	40.4	72.8	83.6	13.1	20.3	20.9

SOURCE: U.S. Census; author's calculations for 2050.

population forecasts. Likewise, if assumptions about net in-migration and immigration are applied, then population change resulting from these factors can be projected.

The U.S. Census is the lead authority in making national and state population forecasts. The forecasts are subject to error, since the four key factors—birthrates, death rates, and net in-migration and immigration rates—cannot be perfectly predicted. Death rates are certainly influenced by conditions of medical care. Birthrates have biological, socioeconomic, and medical determinants. In-migration and immigration rates are perhaps the most difficult to predict, because economic and legal conditions both domestically and overseas have determining influences on these rates.

The population totals and age structures of North Carolina and the United States in 2010 and their predicted values in 2030 and 2050 are compared in tables 1.1 and 1.2, and the relative growth paths of the North Carolina's population components are shown in fig. 1.3.[8] The state's population is expected to continue growing faster than the nation's, by a margin of 40 percent to 30 percent, respectively, between 2010 and 2050. But like the nation as a whole, North Carolina will also dramatically age between 2010 and 2050. The sixty-five and over population will increase over 240 percent, far more than any other age category. By 2050, almost 21 percent of the state's population will be in the "senior citizen" category, up from 13 percent in 2010.

Ethnically, North Carolina will become less white. The percentage of the state's population that is white and non-Hispanic is forecasted to fall from 65 percent in 2013 to 50 percent in 2050. The black and non-Hispanic share will also drop from 21 percent in 2013 to 18 percent in 2050. Conversely, the

TABLE 1.2 Actual and Predicted N.C. Population Totals and Age Structure

	Number (Millions)			Percentage of Total		
	2010	2030	2050	2010	2030	2050
Total population	9.6	11.6	13.4	100.0	100.0	100.0
Under 18	2.3	2.4	2.6	23.9	20.5	19.5
18–24	1.0	1.1	1.2	9.9	9.4	9.0
25–44	2.6	3.0	3.2	26.9	26.1	24.1
45–64	2.5	2.8	3.5	26.3	24.1	26.1
65 and older	1.2	2.3	2.9	13.0	19.9	21.3

SOURCE: U.S. Census; author's calculations for 2050.

Hispanic share of the state's population will more than triple, from 8.5 percent in 2013 to 26 percent in 2050. The Asian population share will also double between 2013 and 2050, from 2 percent to 4 percent.[9]

North Carolina appears to be better positioned than the nation overall in terms of the relative size of the state's working population. Demographers use a concept termed the dependency ratio, defined as the populations under age eighteen plus sixty-five and older as a percentage of the total population. It is called the dependency ratio because it is argued that these two age groups—the very young and the very old—necessitate the largest relative amount of public assistance compared to other age groups. Children require education through the public schools, and senior citizens make use of public programs like Social Security, Medicare, and Medicaid. Although states do not fund Social Security and Medicare, they do share in the costs of Medicaid.

The dependency ratio for the three years 2010, 2030, and 2050 for North Carolina and the nation is shown in fig. 1.4. The trend shows a significant rise in the dependency ratio for both areas as the twenty-first century progresses. Of course, a major driver is the rising population share accounted for by senior citizens. However, in each year the North Carolina dependency ratio is lower than the national dependency ratio. Stated another way, the forecasts indicate the percentage of North Carolina's population in the prime working years (eighteen to sixty-four) will consistently be higher than the nation's through midcentury.[10] This will be a positive indicator for the state, in terms of both business recruiting and lower relative public sector spending compared to the nation overall.

How do these demographic projections for North Carolina—and the nation—compare to expectations for world population changes? United Nations

FIG. 1.3 Projected growth paths of North Carolina age population components
(index numbers with 2010=100).

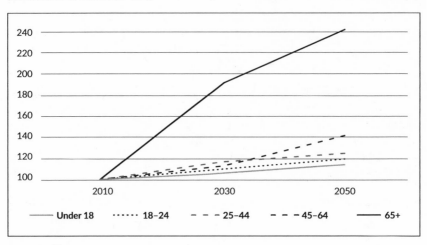

SOURCE: table 1.2.

forecasts indicate that the world's population will grow from 6.8 trillion in
2010 to 8.6 trillion in 2030 and then to 9.5 trillion in 2050.[11] This represents
a 40 percent increase between 2010 and 2050, greater than the expected 30
percent gain in the national population but the same as North Carolina's projected 40 percent increase over the same period. North Carolina's population
growth is thus expected to keep up with world growth.

Also like North Carolina and the nation, the world is becoming older.
Although the United Nations uses a sixty and over age category to define
elderly (as compared to sixty-five and older used for the United States and
North Carolina), the elderly share of the world population is expected to
increase 144 percent between 2010 and 2050, more than twice the increase
for the United States and North Carolina. Although the youth share (nineteen
and under) of the world population will shrink in coming years—just as in the
cases for North Carolina and the United States—it will remain much higher
than in the Tar Heel State and the nation.[12] It thus appears that North Carolina
and the United States will remain competitive with the world at midcentury in
terms of the relative sizes of their prime working populations.

Challenging the Numbers

Any forecast—about economics, demography, or who will win the next Super
Bowl—is open to challenge. The demographic forecasts for North Carolina's
population in the decades ahead are based on assumptions for future birthrates,

FIG. 1.4 Actual and forecasted dependency ratios for North Carolina and the United States.

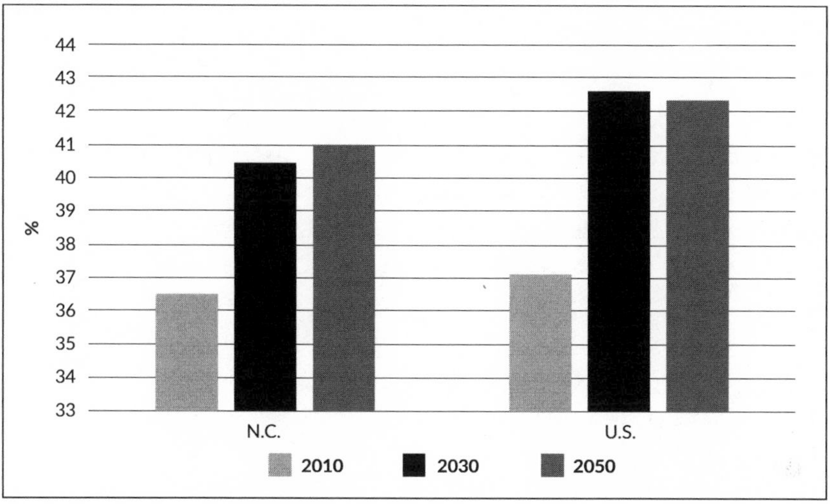

SOURCE: tables 1.1 and 1.2.

future death rates, in-migration from other states, and immigration from other countries. By studying trends and patterns in household size, career choices of households, family planning methods, and medical technology, treatments, and care, demographers have been largely successful in understanding and predicting birthrates and death rates. International migration is less predictable because federal laws and enforcement are key factors in determining this movement, and these laws and enforcement are products of the political system. As related earlier, immigration has accounted for approximately 18 percent of North Carolina's population growth in recent decades. A significant quickening or slowing of immigration to the state could therefore increase or decrease future population projections.

The biggest wild card to the state's population future remains net in-migration, which has accounted for between 35 percent and 50 percent of the state's population growth in the past three decades. Studies show that the two most important factors attracting households to a state are an expanding job market and affordable housing prices.[13] Even including the Great Recession, North Carolina has had stronger job growth and a slower increase in home prices than the nation in the past two decades.[14] The state has also benefitted from its warmer climate, a feature that has been found to attract households.[15] Clearly there will be a large reservoir of potential in-migrants to draw from, particularly retirees: seventy million individuals nationwide will retire in upcoming decades.[16]

Questions can be raised about whether the conditions for attracting households to North Carolina from other states will continue.[17] As the state grows and becomes denser, home prices could rise faster. And a scenario can be developed where the state's lower rate of educational attainment makes it a prime candidate for massive technological unemployment as robots and other modern machinery replace humans in many workplaces. Some even question whether the sunny South will remain attractive if climate change results in significantly higher temperatures. Then, currently colder northern states may become the temperate regions in which to live.[18] Changes in federal immigration laws could either speed or slow the rate of households coming to North Carolina from other countries.[19]

Last, there is the deeper question of whether population growth and economic expansion are desirable. Debate on this issue spans centuries. On one side are growth enthusiasts who contend that population expansion is essential for economic prosperity.[20] An expanding population leads to growing sales, which allow companies to exploit economies of scale and use resources more efficiently. Growth enthusiasts also see population expansion, especially the revitalizing energy brought by youth, as necessary to continue sparking innovation. They argue that an older, aging society, with a corresponding shorter time horizon, is less likely to generate the savings and investments needed for innovations. An older society understandably focuses on spending today rather than spending in the future.

These points are strongly countered by those who don't see a linkage between population growth and economic progress.[21] Most in this group do not advocate absolute population decline, which they agree could set off a host of adverse consequences. Instead, this slow growth group is not alarmed by a moderation in population growth.[22] If smaller increases in population expansion have adverse impacts for the labor supply, then slow growers recommend financial incentives—perhaps via the tax system—to extend the work career of elderly persons. Slow growers also believe that motivations for innovation will always be present, even if markets are expanding slowly, due to the natural competitive desire of entrepreneurs to capture larger market shares. Certainly, a big plus for slower population growth is less strain on limited natural resources and lower environmental costs.

Is More More, or Less?

North Carolina has been moving up the population ladder. In 1970, the state was the twelfth most populous in the nation. By 2013, the Tar Heel State had risen to be the tenth largest in population, and a year later, North Carolina overtook Michigan as the ninth most populous state in the nation.[23] The population rise is not the result of a higher birthrate or a lower death rate than the rest of the nation; rather, it is largely the result of people moving to North Carolina from elsewhere.

Official population projections expect this trend to continue. North Carolina's population growth rate is forecasted to be one-third faster than the nation's through midcentury. The state will have 13.4 million residents in 2050, easily making it the sixth- or seventh-largest state in the country. With this faster population growth will come greater economic clout, larger markets for businesses, and more influence in national politics.

Still, the expected changes in the state's population will present challenges. Like the nation, the fastest growing segment of the population will be residents sixty-five and over. Their percentage of total people will rise from 13 percent in 2010 to over 20 percent in 2050. At the same time, the state's dependency ratio—the percentage of the population under eighteen years of age plus the percentage sixty-five and over—will jump from 36 percent in 2010 to 41 percent in 2050. However, the state's dependency ratio will remain lower than the national ratio. This means that North Carolina will have a higher proportion of its population in the prime working ages (ages eighteen to sixty-four) than the country overall. Also, with the world aging more rapidly than North Carolina, the relatively larger size of North Carolina's prime working population should be a competitive benefit.

Yet even demographic projections must be questioned. With so much of North Carolina's recent past and future population growth dependent on in-migration and immigration, anything that reduces the state's relative attractiveness could lower the projected numbers. Technological inventions reducing future labor usage, residential developments increasing land and housing costs, or even climate change making the state too warm and too sunny are all possibilities that could throw North Carolina's population advances into reverse. Changes in federal immigration laws could also alter the future numbers.

Then there is the viewpoint that such a reverse would not be all bad. Significantly slower population growth would relieve pressure on limited natural resources and the environment, and it would give the state time to pause and make quality-of-life advances in public infrastructure and in skill training. The big question is whether a significant slowdown—or even stagnation—in population growth would diminish the creativity, entrepreneurship, and innovation that drive modern state economies.

Probably the smart money is on a continued increase in North Carolina's population fueled by a desire of people to live in a pleasing, warm climate where economic opportunities and amenities abound. But just where will the new millions live in the state, and how will the state's big cities, small towns, and rural regions grow and be interrelated? These questions are the subject of the next chapter.

2. HOT PLACES AND OPEN SPACES

The Big Move

In 1970, over half (54 percent) of North Carolinians lived in rural areas, making the state the sixth most rural in the nation, behind Vermont, West Virginia, North Dakota, South Dakota, and Mississippi. Even agricultural states like Nebraska and Kansas had a higher percentage of people living in cities.[1] Charlotte, the state's largest city, had fewer than 250,000 residents.[2] The leading industries of tobacco, textiles, and furniture were located largely in rural areas or small towns.

By 2010, the state's population geography had changed completely. The percentage of residents living in rural areas had declined to 33 percent.[3] Urban and surrounding counties, particularly in the Charlotte, Triangle, and Wilmington areas, boomed, while many rural counties lagged in population growth—and a few even lost residents (map 2.1).

North Carolina's geographic population shift in the late twentieth and early twenty-first centuries was not unique. The entire United States grew more urban, and many rural areas lost population. Since the mid-1970s, national population growth in rural—or nonmetropolitan—counties has lagged population growth in metropolitan counties. In 2012, nonmetropolitan counties actually lost residents.[4]

Rural areas have been disadvantaged by trends in education, industry growth, demography, prices, and preferences. Rural counties have traditionally had lower levels of educational attainment than urban areas.[5] For example, 20 percent of the population twenty-five years and older in metropolitan areas of North Carolina had a four-year college degree in 2010, compared to only 9 percent for nonmetropolitan areas. The high school dropout rate has also been significantly lower in metro areas than in nonmetro regions.[6] These differences are important because one of the biggest economic shifts in the past forty years has been the movement away from jobs requiring lesser levels of education to jobs requiring more levels of education.[7] This shift has made urban areas more attractive for job development relative to rural areas. Urban

MAP 2.1 County Population Growth Rates, 1970–2010.

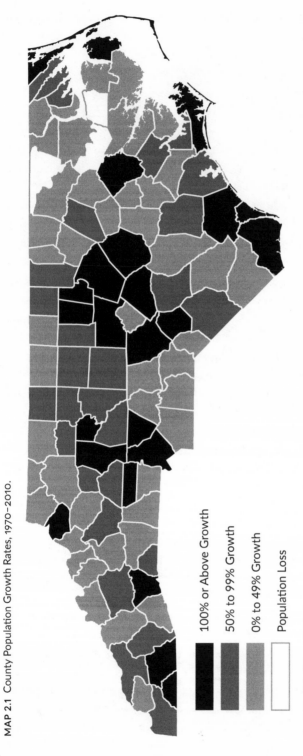

100% or Above Growth

50% to 99% Growth

0% to 49% Growth

Population Loss

SOURCE: U.S. Census Bureau.

areas have become the centers of ideas and creativity, both important ingredients of the Information Revolution.[8]

Education has had another impact on locational choice. The rise of so-called power couples—married or partnered college-educated individuals each with his or her own career—has increased the attractiveness of residing in an urban area. Because urban regions have a denser location of employment opportunities, especially for those requiring higher levels of education, it becomes easier for power couples to find satisfying employment and maintain a single residence in cities.[9]

Rural areas have also been battered by changes in industrial composition. This is especially the case for North Carolina, where industries like agriculture, textiles, forestry, and furniture were mainstays in rural and small town regions. Agriculture continues to mechanize and substitute machinery and technology for labor. Textiles, forestry, and furniture have lost output and employment to foreign competitors, especially since 2000, when the World Trade Organization was instituted. At the same time, new industries such as technology, pharmaceuticals, and finance expanded in urban areas, where they had access to a highly educated workforce.[10] Yet it was not just higher-paying jobs that increased in urban settings. Lower-skilled and lower-paying occupations also grew in consumer service, medical service, personal service, and leisure service firms to serve the growing urban population.

A major demographic trend of the past four decades favoring cities and urban regions has been the declining birthrate. From 1970 to 2010, the U.S. birthrate fell 25 percent.[11] With a lower birthrate has come smaller household sizes and a reduced need for space. By definition, space is more plentiful and cheaper in rural areas than in urban locations. With a reduced desire for space, more households have been willing to trade less space in the city for greater access to jobs, services, and amenities like restaurants.

Similarly, the rise in the cost of driving has worked to the advantage of urban areas. After accounting for general inflation, gasoline prices (per gallon) jumped 75 percent between 1970 and 2010.[12] This increase made commuting from a rural residential location to a job in the city relatively more expensive. Thus, in the tradeoff between lower shelter costs but higher commuting costs in rural areas versus higher shelter costs and lower commuting costs in urban areas, the increase in gas prices tipped the scales closer to urban locations.[13]

Last, an apparent shift in personal preferences has been a factor in the rural to urban move, particularly in recent decades. Perhaps shaped by their educational experiences, their exposure to a broader range of options and opportunities via technological access, a greater concern about environmental issues, or a desire to have a more varied and faster-paced lifestyle with instant social interaction, the millennial generation (those born between 1980 and 2000) has been shunning the countryside and suburbia and choosing to live in central cities.[14] They walk, ride, or use public transportation for work, have eschewed home ownership for renting, and like the "live, work, play" possibilities of the city. There are, however, questions about whether these preferences will be maintained as the millennials age, become married or partnered, and—for at least some—have children.[15]

To compound these advantages of urban locations, there is evidence that many of the best and brightest of rural regions eventually move to urban areas, further lowering the educational skill base of rural locations.[16]

The big move of the past forty years contradicts what many predicted would happen as a result of the Information Revolution. It was formerly thought that computers and the internet would connect the work of people and disconnect them from geography.[17] Rural areas would thrive as households chose the tranquility and beauty of life in the countryside while they telecommuted for their earnings. Certainly, not everyone would—or could—do this, but enough would select this lifestyle to generate a rural revival.

These predictions ignored the value of face-to-face interactions, notably in the business world. To date, nothing—including an internet connection or a teleconference—can perfectly substitute for the physical interactions of looking into someone's eyes, reading physical reactions and body language, or shaking hands. These details are all important to conducting business meetings, organizing strategies, or even delegating and supervising work tasks. By expanding the range of potential contacts, some of which will be taken to the next step of personal meetings, information technology has made denser locations where personal meetings are easier more, not less valuable to workers.[18]

Where to Live?

Four factors helpful in understanding the locational choices of both firms and households are identified in table 2.1.[19] *Income* represents the ability of a household to earn a higher salary or a firm to earn a higher profit as a result of an urban or a rural location. Recent trends in the location of higher-paying industries, the location of creative, highly educated workers, and the ability to interact with a wider range of producers and talent have made this a positive for urban locations and a negative for rural locations. *Amenities* measure the broad range of consumer and business services and activities available at a location. Cities offer personal and health care services, a variety of retail outlets, gyms, and restaurants for households, and support companies for businesses, whereas rural areas provide open space and wildlife. Individual households

TABLE 2.1 Factors Affecting the Location of Economic Activity

	Income	Amenities	Land Costs	Transportation Costs
Urban areas	+	+	−	+
Rural areas	−	−	+	−

NOTE: + indicates early twenty-first-century advantage; − indicates early twenty-first-century disadvantage.

will have different preferences, but for most, the nod recently goes to man-made amenities. Many firms also find benefits in accessing specialized talent and supplies by clustering near similar companies in the same industry. *Land costs*—and by extension the price of space—are lower the farther a site is from centers of economic activity. Lower land costs are thus a benefit of rural regions. In contrast, *transportation costs* are greater in more remote areas, and higher prices of gasoline add to this disadvantage of rural locations.[20]

Urban areas have a clear advantage for both firms and households in the early twenty-first century; only land costs are an advantage for rural sites. This is the reason economic activities with large uses of land, such as agriculture and vehicle assembly plants, continue to be located in rural settings. Also, in the days when households were larger, the lower land (and shelter) costs of a rural location were attractive. But today's smaller households have traded the cheaper costs of shelter in rural regions for the reduced space but lower transportation expenses of cities.

The future locational choices of households and firms will be guided by the same factors presented in table 2.1. If the economy continues to evolve as it has in recent decades, then education, creativity, and idea generation will all become even more important elements of commerce and the workforce. Cities will continue to nurture these activities via face-to-face contact and collaboration. Firms providing both business and personal services will continue to agglomerate in urban areas. Live, work, and play communities will become the prototype for urban living that supports social interaction, limits commuting, and puts physical and natural amenities like parks and water features within easy reach for households.[21]

Or not! One development that could be a geographic game-changer for the location of households and firms is virtualization. Virtualization is a technology that allows a person to have all the sensory and experiential benefits of being in a location and interacting with others but without needing to be there physically. If virtualization is ever developed for widespread use, then the current *income* advantage of cities would be dramatically reduced. Individuals could live and be anywhere and—through the use of virtualization—enjoy all the advantages of personal contact. Creative individuals and business colleagues could meet and interact in virtual space while still physically located in multiple locations, reducing and perhaps eliminating the income-enhancing benefit of cities.[22]

Likewise, if future technology is perfected to deliver consumer products and services easily and cheaply over long distances, then the *amenities* advantage of urban areas will also disappear. We are already seeing examples of this technology with some medical procedures performed remotely and drones delivering packages to rural households.[23]

At the same time, as urban areas grow larger, denser, and more congested, travel within them will become more time-consuming and land prices will rise more quickly. These changes could reduce the relative disadvantage rural areas currently have in *transportation costs* and increase the relative advantage they hold in *land costs*. Supporting this trend could be the development and widespread use of driverless vehicles, which some say would make longer commutes faster and less stressful.[24]

So, a rural renaissance is possible. But is it likely?

The Geography of 2050

The safe bet is that North Carolina's urbanization trend will continue in the coming decades. These trends could result in a growth pattern such as that displayed in map 2.2.[25] The most rapid population growth will be in the urbanized areas of the Triangle, Charlotte, and Wilmington areas. Wake County—the central county of the Triangle region—and Mecklenburg—the main county of the Charlotte area—would both add population at rates approaching 100 percent between 2010 and 2050. The population growth in these two counties alone would account for almost 40 percent of the state's population growth during the four decades. Slightly slower growth is projected in selected counties in the Triad, in Asheville, and in two counties in the east near East Carolina University.

The ring of rapid population growth from the Triangle west through the Triad and south to Charlotte could be expected to merge with similar urban growth in Greenville-Spartanburg (South Carolina), Atlanta, and Birmingham (Alabama) to form a megametropolitan area that some have dubbed "Char-lanta."[26] This megaregion can already be seen prominently in 2012 using the concentration of night lights over the country (fig. 2.1). The megaregion would have an estimated annual economic output of more than a trillion dollars (2014 dollars), making it the fourth-largest megaregion in the country behind Bos-Wash (Boston to Washington, D.C.), Chi-Pitts (Chicago

MAP 2.2 Forecasted County Population Growth Rates, 2010–2050.

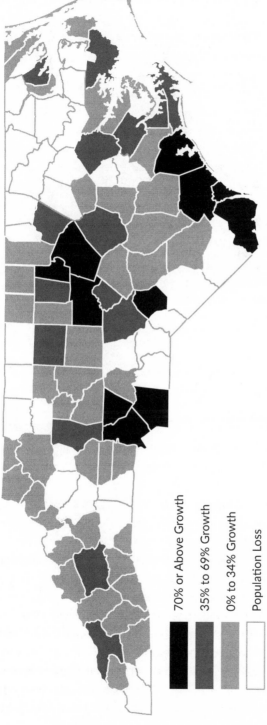

70% or Above Growth

35% to 69% Growth

0% to 34% Growth

Population Loss

SOURCE: North Carolina Office of Budget and Management; author's calculations.

FIG. 2.1 U.S. megaregions in 2012.

SOURCE: courtesy National Aeronautics and Space Administration and National Oceanic and Atmospheric Administration.

to Pittsburgh), and South Cal (southern California).[27] The higher densities of the megaregions could make high-speed rail more economically feasible as an alternative to travel by automobile.[28]

Yet the most striking feature of the forecasts in map 2.2 is the population *loss* projected in one-third of the state's counties. These counties are clustered in the east, foothills, and south-central and north-central borders. If these predictions come true, North Carolina's urbanized population will almost reach 80 percent by 2050. North Carolina will be a state of dense cities and urban areas with wide-open rural regions in between. Rural North Carolina will be dominated by farming, firms requiring substantial acreage (manufacturing assembly plants, solar collectors, and data storage facilities), outdoor recreation, and simply open spaces. There just will not be many permanent residents.

Some do see a strategy to at least slow the rate of population loss in rural counties.[29] This is to attract retirees to rural counties and small towns and to build a consumer service economy around them.[30] As indicated in the previous chapter, retirees (those aged sixty-five and over) will be the fastest-growing population segment in both the nation and North Carolina. Modern retirees are increasingly footloose and financially independent. Research shows that they are attracted to areas with scenic, recreational, and cultural amenities and having reasonable housing costs.[31] These are characteristics that rural areas and small towns—especially in North Carolina—offer. The challenge will be for rural areas to provide ready access to medical care for elderly residents, including access to hospitals with surgical and advanced treatment facilities.

Trend or Tipping Point?

Current socioeconomic trends favor the continued growth and expansion of urbanized regions in North Carolina. Smaller household sizes, the ongoing benefit of higher education degrees, and the development of an economy based on ideas, creativity, and collaboration have been pushing more people and firms to choose urban locations over rural sites. Even the importance of information technology—once thought to reduce, if not eliminate, the consideration of location—has apparently had the opposite effect of elevating the significance of the face-to-face contacts available in urban settings.

If these trends persist, then it is expected that North Carolina's urbanization will also proceed. Between 2010 and 2050, some of the state's urban counties could double in population, while one-third of the state's counties might lose people. The percent of the state's residents living in urban areas could rise from 67 percent to between 75 percent and 80 percent. The area from the Triangle to the Triad to Charlotte might possibly become part of a massive multistate, urban megaregion. North Carolina will become a state of urban hot places and rural open spaces.

In looking almost four decades ahead, however, caveats are always in order. As urban areas become more populous and denser and land prices in cities rise, some firms and households may reverse the trends and head to rural settings. We could reach an urban tipping point, where rural becomes the new "in" and urban is "out." Such a move would be supported by advances in technology providing virtualization of meetings and experiences, telecommuting, online shopping and purchases, driverless vehicles, and rapid delivery of consumer products and services using drones and computer interfaces. These developments could counter the advantages of urban areas in personal contacts and service amenities and could help spark a return of rural living.[32] If this happens, then the geography of North Carolina's population would be more evenly spread across the state's counties and could ultimately eliminate the distinction between urban and rural.

Regardless of where North Carolina's growing population lives, the economy will have to expand to accommodate their lifestyles and living standards. Where exactly will new economic growth take place in North Carolina as the twenty-first century progresses? The next chapter offers some insights and potential answers.

3. WHERE'S THE GROWTH?

Transformation Then and Now

In the past century, the North Carolina economy has undergone two major transformations. The first was the movement off the farm and into the factory. As the Industrial Revolution came to agriculture, tractors and other equipment replaced the work of thousands of farmers. Fortunately, this was just when manufacturing was developing and expanding in the state, with scores of new textile, furniture, and tobacco factories springing up in the state's cities and small towns.[1] Although farm output didn't fall, manufacturing production rose much faster, so the dominance of farming in the state waned while manufacturing's impact rose.[2] Between 1900 and 1940, farming's share of the state economy (measured by gross domestic product, or GDP) was cut in half, while manufacturing's share increased eightfold (fig. 3.1).[3] A similar shift occurred in employment (fig. 3.2).

In North Carolina, manufacturing hit its highest level of GDP share in 1940 and its top of employment share in 1970. From these peaks to 2015, manufacturing's share of GDP in the state was halved and its share of total employment was reduced by over two-thirds.[4] However, from 1940 to 2015 the state economy expanded by 1,000 percent, and between 1970 and 2015 total state employment doubled.[5] Again, the reason was the growth of a new sector—in this case, the service sector. Increasing affluence, the movement of women into the paid workforce, the continuing advancements in the productivity of farming and manufacturing, and increasing urbanization caused output and employment in a wide variety of services—personal, health care, professional, and leisure—to grow at rapid rates. By 2015, the share of state GDP for the service sector had tripled since 1970, and its employment share had more than doubled.[6]

These changes have not been unique to North Carolina; they mirror the national pattern of the declining relative importance of farming and manufacturing and the growing relative importance of services to the economy. Farming

FIG. 3.1 Shares of the aggregate North Carolina economy in farming, manufacturing, and services.

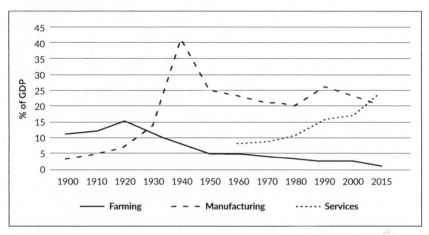

NOTE: incomplete data for services before 1960.
SOURCE: U.S. Census Bureau; U.S. Department of Commerce.

and manufacturing, however, have maintained a higher level of significance in North Carolina than in the nation overall. In 2015, farming's share of state GDP was 8 percent higher than the comparable national share, and manufacturing's share of state GDP was 65 percent higher than the comparable national share.[7]

Even with these transformations in the composition of the North Carolina economy, economic progress has been made over time. Inflation-adjusted GDP per capita from 1900 to 2015 rose 570 percent, translating into an average annual growth rate of 1.6 percent (fig. 3.3).[8] Growth stalled during the 1930s, 1970s, and in the first decade of the 2000s. For the first two slow-growth periods, growth recovered during the following decades. An important question for today's economy is whether growth will quicken in the upcoming decades of the twenty-first century.

Under the Hood

To establish a starting point for projecting where North Carolina's economy might go in the coming decades, it is useful to set the specific status of the state's economic composition at the beginning of the twenty-first century, which some argue marks an acceleration of the next great transformation in the information or digital age. The focus is on industries that sell products or services outside the state and earn revenues for owners and workers in

FIG. 3.2 Shares of total North Carolina employment in farming, manufacturing, and services.

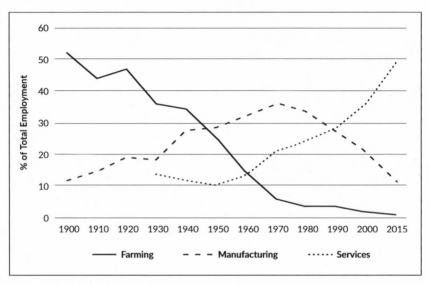

NOTE: incomplete data for services before 1930.
SOURCE: U.S. Census Bureau; U.S. Department of Commerce.

the state. Excluded are industries that primarily serve households within the state, such as retailing, health care, and education. Certainly, these industries focused on within-state markets will expand as the state's population grows, although the way they expand (for example, use of technology versus labor) will likely be different than in the past.[9]

North Carolina's industries are measured in table 3.1 on three dimensions: (1) the industry's output *growth rate* from 1997 to 2012; (2) the *relative productivity* of the industry as measured by output per dollar of labor compensation in North Carolina divided by the same metric for the nation; and (3) the *location quotient* of the industry, which is the industry's percentage of total GDP in North Carolina divided by the industry's percentage of total GDP in the nation.[10] Values above 1 for relative productivity mean that workers in the industry are more productive compared to workers in the country overall, and values above 1 for the location quotient suggest that the industry is more important in North Carolina than the industry is in the nation as a whole.

Six groupings of North Carolina's industries are suggested by the measures. The first grouping is composed of the industries that dominated the state for most of the twentieth century: textiles, tobacco products, furniture, wood products, minerals products, apparel, and paper products. Although they are still

FIG. 3.3 Trends in North Carolina GDP per capita (2015 dollars).

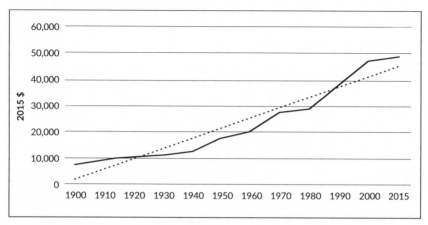

NOTE: trend line is dashed.
SOURCE: fig. 3.1; U.S. Department of Commerce; U.S. Census Bureau.

much more important to the state than to the nation—as indicated by the high location quotients—these industries have rapidly declined in output. Although some are changing—high-tech textiles and apparel are good examples—the industries will likely continue to shrink in the twenty-first century.[11]

The industries in the second group also are relatively more important to the state than to the nation. Unlike the first group of industries, however, they have higher relative productivity, and—crucially—they have experienced recent rapid growth rates. Consequently, these industries (pharmaceuticals, banking, machinery manufacturing, and transportation equipment) move in to the twenty-first century with momentum. If future economic conditions continue to support and improve on these gains, these industries can be a platform for future growth in the state.

The third group (computers and electronics, computer system design, food processing, primary metals production, information, and other transportation equipment) has also had strong recent growth, but unlike the second group, the industries are less important in the state than in the nation, and relative productivity levels are also lower. Still, if national growth in the sectors persists, the opportunities for expansion in North Carolina are there.

The fourth and fifth groups are alike in that their industries have experienced recent slow or negative growth and have relative productivity levels that are near the nationwide average. The difference is that the fourth group (plastics, farming) is relatively more important in North Carolina, whereas the industries in the fifth group (fabricated metals, accommodations and food

TABLE 3.1 North Carolina Industry Groupings at the Start of the Twenty-First Century

	Growth Rate	Relative Productivity	Location Quotient (LQ)
1. Negative growth, average productivity (LQ > 1)			
Textiles	−67.5%	1.02	5.13
Tobacco products	−36.1%	0.99	3.72
Furniture	−50.0%	0.87	2.63
Wood products	−19.4%	0.97	1.57
Minerals products	−34.4%	1.15	1.47
Apparel	−79.5%	0.97	1.37
Paper products	−30.3%	0.82	1.15
2. Strong growth, average to high productivity (LQ > 1)			
Pharmaceuticals	57.5%	1.82	3.13
Banking	178.4%	1.32	1.93
Machinery manufacturing	84.9%	1.50	1.33
Transportation equipment	187.5%	1.11	1.04
3. Strong growth, average to low productivity (LQ < 1)			
Computers and electronics	439.1%	0.83	0.96
Computer system design	258.9%	1.03	0.75
Food processing	241.1%	1.16	0.70
Primary metals production	81.9%	1.04	0.65
Information	97.4%	0.77	0.59
Other transportation equipment	199.4%	1.27	0.44
4. Slow growth, average productivity (LQ > 1)			
Plastics	5.7%	1.15	1.92
Farming	0.8%	1.31	1.04
5. Slow or negative growth, average productivity (LQ < 1)			
Fabricated metals	−3.7%	1.09	0.89
Accommodations and food service	29.9%	0.93	0.85
Printing	19.5%	1.03	0.83
Transportation and warehousing	7.9%	0.96	0.76
6. Other			
Electrical equipment	−0.5%	1.32	2.64
Petroleum and coal products	−32.4%	0.43	0.08

SOURCE: U.S Department of Commerce; author's calculations.

service, printing, and transportation and warehousing) are relatively less important in the state. Growth rates will need to accelerate for these sectors to be major players in North Carolina's future economy.

The sixth group is composed of two industries that do not easily fit into the other categories. Electrical equipment (lighting, appliances) manufacturing is relatively more important in the state than in the nation and has higher relative productivity, but its output has been virtually stagnant in recent years. Petroleum and coal products production is almost nonexistent in the state compared to the nation, but there has been debate over whether the sector has growth potential in North Carolina. The economic possibilities for developing the energy exploration and production market in North Carolina are assessed later in the chapter.

Although North Carolina can certainly develop new economic industries, much of the state's economic growth in coming decades will likely come from existing sectors. For this reason, it is important for the state to have several industries that have competed well during the turbulent years of the early twenty-first century. Three questions arise: How well will these sectors perform in upcoming decades? Can lagging sectors be turned around? Can new sectors can be cultivated and grown?

An Economy Built for the Future?

Where will North Carolina's economy be in 2050, and what economic sectors will get it there? Answering these two questions requires a two-part approach. First, we must assess what economic sectors will lead world growth and what their combination will mean for the aggregate condition of the economy. Second, we must evaluate whether North Carolina is positioned to take advantage of the economic growth created by these leading sectors and, if not, what will have to change in the state for this growth to occur.

Both optimists and pessimists agree on five broad world forces that will shape the future economy for the better (optimists) or for the not-much-better and maybe worse (pessimists). The forces are: (1) an aging population; (2) technological innovation and implementation; (3) access to the growing economic influence of developing countries; (4) changing tastes and preferences; and (5) the quest for affordable energy and natural resources to fuel our economy and lifestyle.

AGING POPULATION

An aging population is perhaps the most obvious world trend of the twenty-first century. How both the nation and North Carolina will become older in upcoming decades has been documented in chapter 1. The reason for an aging population is simple. At the same time that medical technology and treatments as well as better nutrition are expanding lifespans, birthrates are falling. These are worldwide phenomena. As a result, the percentage of the world's population aged sixty-five and older will jump from 7.8 percent in 2011 to 15.6 percent in 2050.[12]

Economists have debated the aggregate impact of the aging population. One side sees a positive for the economy as elderly households reduce savings and increase spending during their remaining years. The other side expects a negative effect from lower investment rates and from older individuals cashing out of the stock market. Japan, which has aged more than other countries, is ground zero for this debate. Pessimists point to Japan's lagging economic growth as evidence of the adverse effects from an older population. Others posit alternative reasons for Japan's lackluster economy, including lack of competition and heavy-handed government control and regulation of key industries, as well as a shortage of appropriate stimulus policies.[13]

North Carolina has two manufacturing industries that should be positively affected by the aging trend: pharmaceuticals and medical equipment and supplies. Pharmaceuticals is among those industries listed in table 3.1 that have had strong growth, relatively high productivity, and a stronger presence in North Carolina than in the nation overall. Although not shown, the medical equipment and supplies sector is part of the machinery manufacturing industry in the same group in table 3.1. Data specifically for medical equipment and supplies show that this industry also has a relatively stronger presence in North Carolina and a high level of productivity.[14]

North Carolina could also benefit economically from the aging trend if retired households continue to migrate to the state from elsewhere. The beach, mountain, and even metropolitan areas of North Carolina have been popular locations for out-of-state retirees wanting to enjoy the state's outdoor amenities or live near children and grandchildren. Out-of-state retirees bring pension income and create a range of spending impacts from residential construction to retail shopping to personal services—all economic activities that tend to be labor intensive and difficult to outsource. Conversely, retirees generally do not have children to educate, meaning that state and local public education budgets are not affected. Elderly households have greater needs for medical spending, but the major government program addressing health costs of the elderly (Medicare) is federally funded with no state contribution.[15]

TECHNOLOGICAL INNOVATION AND IMPLEMENTATION

Economists agree that the pace of technological innovation and implementation is crucial to the rate of economic improvement in a society. A major point of difference between optimists and pessimists about the economic future is over the speed and impact of technological change. Optimists believe that enough game-changing technological developments will continue to be made so as to raise the aggregate standard of living in coming decades.[16] Pessimists believe the opposite. They think that the major technological breakthroughs have been made and, as a result, that technology will not prompt growth as it has in recent decades.

Computers and electronics, computer design systems, and the information sector are three of the most technologically oriented industries. In table 3.1 these industries are in the third category: industries that have experienced strong growth in North Carolina but have average to low relative productivity and location quotients under 1. This means that even though the tech sector in the state has expanded rapidly, it has also done so in other states. In addition, in terms of value of output per dollar spent on labor, North Carolina's tech sectors are average or below average.

Although as a state North Carolina does not look exceptional as a site of technology activity, the Triangle region clearly stands out as a leader in technology research and innovation. Several independent rankings put the Triangle in the top ten of metropolitan areas for both technology jobs and technology companies.[17] The region has a critical mass of activities in rising tech sectors like nanotechnology, informatics (big data), clean technologies, interactive gaming and online learning, biotechnology, and instrumentation.[18]

Nearly all regions and states are chasing technology as an economic driver. Therefore, to participate in the future expansion of the technology sector—on whatever path that expansion will occur—North Carolina will have to work on improving the relative productivity of the sector. Simply put, the state will need to make itself more attractive for firms to locate and expand their tech business in North Carolina as compared to other states. Most states are actively courting tech firms through access and interactions with universities, through business parks geared to technology, and through amenities that appeal to tech workers, who are often very young. North Carolina will have to continue to do the same. The state has the advantage of having several Research I universities (Duke, North Carolina State, UNC–Chapel Hill) with a national profile of research and development and business interactions.[19] Most of the expansion of the tech sector in the state in coming decades will likely take place in its central corridor, beginning from the already tech-rich Triangle and moving west to the Triad (Greensboro–Winston-Salem–High Point metropolitan area) and then south to Charlotte. This corridor contains the aforementioned Research I universities, a steady supply of graduates from STEM (science, technology, engineering, and mathematics) majors, and the highest percentage of workers with a bachelor's degree or above in the state—as well as one of the highest such rates in the country.[20]

New technology may also help some of the industries in category 1 (table 3.1), which are North Carolina's traditional economic sectors but which have experienced negative growth. New high-tech textile products are being developed with applications in machinery and apparel. For example, modern textile technology is being used to develop lightweight but high-strength materials for airplanes, and similar technology has been produced for clothing that can directly heat and cool the wearer (thereby reducing the need to heat and cool large spaces), protect the wearer from airborne bacteria and contaminants, and be self-cleaning.[21] Likewise, there have been recent explorations in potential medicinal uses of tobacco. Although these new applications for North Carolina's traditional industries will likely never revive their past dominance, they have developed—and can continue to develop—niche sectors that will contribute to economic growth and add employment opportunities.[22]

ACCESS TO THE GROWING ECONOMIC INFLUENCE OF DEVELOPING COUNTRIES

The shift of economic influence to developing countries has been occurring since the end of World War II but has accelerated since 2000 with the formation of the World Trade Organization.[23] In just the first ten years of the twenty-first century, developing countries' share of the world economy (GDP) rose from 18 percent to 28 percent.[24] Economic forecasts suggest that developing countries—particularly in Asia and Africa—will experience annual growth rates twice those in the developed countries in coming decades.[25] The implication is that economic growth prospects will increasingly be in developing countries. These prospects include both the sale of goods and services to those countries as well as tourism activity from developing countries to the United States. This adds urgency for states to be internationally connected and aware to take advantage of these opportunities.

How well is North Carolina connected to the rest of the world at the beginning of the twenty-first century? Several measures are indicated in table 3.2. Relative to the size of its economy or population, North Carolina lags the nation in international connectedness for all the measures except one: employment in foreign-owned companies. Both the foreign-born general population and the international student population are lower in the state than in the nation overall. Exports from the state are a smaller share of GDP, and the state's transportation connections—via air flights and the state ports—are far under

TABLE 3.2 Measures of North Carolina's International Connectedness

Measure	North Carolina Rate	U.S. Rate
Foreign-born population as % of total population	7.6	13.1
International college students as % of total students	2.1	3.7
Exports ($ value) as % of GDP	6.2	9.5
Employment in foreign-owned companies, % of all jobs^	6.1	5.0
Daily direct international flights per capita	1.9	4.4
N.C. share of overseas tourists to the U.S., % of total tourists	1.2	16th highest
Port cargo (% of total U.S. port cargo)	0.7	17th highest

SOURCE: Foreign-born population: U.S. Census Bureau, "American Community Survey, 2013," and includes naturalized and non-naturalized citizens (2013 data). International college students: U.S. Department of Education, "Digest of Educational Statistics, 2013," and *Study North Carolina*, www .studynorthcarolina.us (2011–12 academic year data). Exports: U.S. Census Bureau, "Foreign Trade Statistics, 2013" (2013 data). Employment in foreign-owned companies: Brookings Institute, *FDI in U.S. Metro Areas: The Geography of Jobs in Foreign-Owned Establishments* (Washington, D.C., June 20, 2014) (2011 data). Daily direct international flights: U.S. Department of Transportation, Bureau of Transportation Statistics, RDU International Airport, Charlotte-Douglas International Airport (2013 data). N.C. share of overseas tourists: U.S. Department of Commerce, "Overseas Visitation Estimates for U.S. States, Cities, and Census Regions" (2013 data). Port cargo: U.S. Department of Transportation, Bureau of Transportation Statistics, North Carolina Ports Authority (2013 data).

A: Counting employment at suppliers to foreign-owned companies, the rates are 19.1% for North Carolina and 17.1% for the United States. Organization for International Investment, *Global Investment Provides the Jobs We Need* (Washington, D.C., June 3, 2016).

the U.S. rates. North Carolina attracts only 1.2 percent of overseas tourists and is beaten on this measure in the Southeast by both Florida and Georgia. Yet foreign investments have been attracted to North Carolina, as indicated by the higher relative level of employment in foreign-owned companies in the state compared to the nation. This suggests that the state's major issue in international connectedness is the linkages from North Carolina to the rest of the world and not from the rest of the world to the Tar Heel State.

Two ways to address this issue involve the state's international air flights and ports; traffic at both in North Carolina falls short of national standards (table 3.2). Nonstop international flights from North Carolina at the beginning of the twenty-first century were limited to Charlotte's Douglas International Airport and Raleigh-Durham's RDU International Airport. Nonstop international flights are highly coveted but also highly risky from the airlines' perspective. Carriers typically require airports to provide an initial contingency fund—often in the millions of dollars—to cover potential losses in the early rollout of international flights.[26] Nevertheless, studies show that nonstop international flights are associated with significant economic growth between locations, especially if those locations already had strong growth.[27] A study analyzing the economic impact of adding a daily nonstop flight from RDU International Airport to Europe estimated that it could increase annual GDP in the Raleigh-Durham Triangle region by $1.4 billion (2014 dollars) and boost regional employment by fourteen thousand jobs over twenty-five years.[28]

Other researchers have made even stronger arguments about the influence of economic linkages from air flight connections by boldly predicting that cities and regions centered on airports will be the growth nodes of the future.[29] To date it appears that economic growth generated by airports is confined to urban areas with quick access to interstate highways and skilled labor. North Carolina's attempt to jump-start business expansion with an international-quality airport in rural eastern North Carolina (termed the Global Transpark) has had limited success, never employing the number of workers originally forecasted.[30] As one example, a FedEx regional parcel facility chose a site near the Piedmont International Airport in the Triad rather than at the Global Transpark. Whether airport expansion leads economic growth or economic growth generates an airport expansion is also a question.[31]

Airport expansion and enhanced international connections that do occur in the first half of the twenty-first century in North Carolina will likely be at the two international airports in the Charlotte and Triangle metropolitan areas, mainly because these two regions will continue to be the fastest growing in the state and among the fastest expanding in the nation. Rather than public money, private funds will likely be needed to defray any initial losses on the flights. Regional businesses will have to be persuaded that such costs are an investment related to higher future returns.

North Carolina's ports are small and shallow compared to ports in nearby states—especially ports in Charleston, South Carolina, and Norfolk, Virginia—and most shippers in the state use out-of-state ports.[32] The newly expanded Panama Canal allows super cargo carriers from Asia—heretofore precluded from reaching the East Coast—to dock at East Coast ports. Transportation by water is typically the most cost-effective method of moving cargo over long distances.[33] This means that some cargo that was formerly delivered to Long Beach, California, or Seattle and then trucked to the East Coast can more economically arrive at the East Coast via the expanded Panama Canal. Departing ships then offer the opportunity for exporters to transport cargo using via ocean waters. East Coast port trade—including both imports and exports—is thus expected to expand at accelerated rates.

North Carolina's two ports at Wilmington and Morehead City are inadequate to accommodate the super cargo carriers, and there are also major limitations to expanding them.[34] However, as the giant container ships dock at Norfolk, Charleston, and other East Coast ports (Miami, New York–New Jersey), a cascading effect of smaller cargo ships docking at smaller ports is expected. Wilmington and Morehead City have the capacity to increase usage and generate additional jobs (perhaps as many as one hundred thousand additional direct and supplier-induced jobs), but one estimate indicates that the ports could reach capacity by 2035.[35]

To capture even greater economic benefits from both exporting and importing through ports, a new port will likely need to be developed in North Carolina. Studies show high benefit-cost ratios for the state from an enhanced port.[36] A three-billion-dollar modern port was proposed in 2005 for the Southport area south of Wilmington, but the plans collapsed under the weight of the price tag and environmental concerns.[37] Another issue is supporting infrastructure for the ports, primarily rail lines, roadways, and warehouses to carry and store cargo to and from the ports. A study of I-95 in North Carolina, a key component of this supporting infrastructure, showed that it is insufficient to handle the future usage associated with increased port and cargo activity. Again, benefit-cost ratios from improving and expanding I-95 have been calculated to be high, but the stumbling block is raising the funds for the initial investment.[38]

To take full advantage of expected economic opportunities in foreign countries, North Carolina will have to increase its linkages via ocean travel. This will require improved roads, rails, and—most important—better ports. Financing is the major hurdle because the investments will be large, easily approaching ten billion dollars (2015 dollars) if a new port and highway improvements (such as for I-95) are included. There are three funding options: traditional state public financing, innovative state financing, and private financing. Traditional public financing requires the state to issue general obligation bonds, pledge payment of the bonds from general tax revenues or specific tax revenues such as gas taxes, and be authorized by voter approval. A popular form of innovative state financing allows bonds to be issued without voter approval and to be backed by revenues from the funded project. In the case of a port, a portion of revenues earned by the port from users would be earmarked for the bond costs. For roads, revenues from tolls are collected for bond payments. Private financing, which can be done with or without state participation, relies on the standard private model of bond issuance for construction and payment of the bonds from revenue earned from the operation. The model has been used for road construction in conjunction with state participation, whereby the state and private firm share in the construction costs. Importantly, the private investors could be domestic or foreign.[39]

Just as increased direct international flights will be a significant element of economic growth for the state's large metropolitan areas, port development can be a key ingredient in economic development for the state's eastern rural counties, which have lagged in growth during the late twentieth and early twenty-first centuries. As is often the case, financing is the issue, with the most likely answer to be innovative private financing.

CHANGING TASTES AND PREFERENCES

As economic growth has spread to developing countries and greater world trade and communications have enhanced interactions among countries and cultures, there has been a shift in tastes and preferences, especially among consumers in developing countries. Some call this "cultural homogenization" or, more crudely, the "McDonaldization" of consumers.[40] The notion is that the world's consumers, especially those reaching middle-class status, are altering their tastes and preferences to be more similar to Western or American tastes and preferences. For example, China's meat consumption rose an astounding 600 percent between 1980 and 2012, compared to a gain of 45 percent for the United States over the same period.[41] Although China has been expanding its internal meat production, analysts forecast that China and similar countries will continue to rely on meat imports in the twenty-first century.[42]

The United States has long had one of the most productive agricultural sectors in the world. Superior soil quality, ample rainfall, and highly knowledgeable farmers have led to a doubling of farm output in the past sixty years and to farm productivity rates that are among the highest of any industry.[43] North Carolina's farmers have been part of these trends. Indeed, North Carolina farming is 31 percent more productive that national farming (table 3.1).

But what is most noteworthy about North Carolina's agriculture in light of the change in world diets is the transformation of the state's farming sector in recent decades. North Carolina's farming was long based on crops—first cotton, then tobacco. King Cotton and King Tobacco provided the highest returns per acre and the largest revenues per farm. The rise of synthetic fabrics, the decline in smoking, and the emergence of foreign competition all combined to deflate the economic clout of cotton and tobacco. But through a combination of talent, vision, and innovation, just as the crops-based farm economy was downsizing, a meats-based farm economy was developed and expanded in the state.[44] At the beginning of the twenty-first century, North Carolina had one of the largest meat sectors in the country. The state ranked second in hog production and fourth in poultry production among the states.[45] The largest hog processing facility in the world was in North Carolina.[46] The state is thus well positioned to take advantage of changing world diets favoring meat.

Can North Carolina move on this advantage? The knowledge, experience, and capacity are present to ramp up meat production and processing in the state. There are three impediments, however. One is environmental. Pollution from hog waste, in particular, has been an ongoing issue in North Carolina. Regulations instituted in 1999 have curtailed growth in the industry, from an annual average of 12 percent between 1993 and 1998 to -0.5 percent from 1998 to 2015.[47] The hog waste issue will thus need to be addressed before substantial expansion can occur. Three approaches are most likely to be used: breeding of hogs to reduce waste amounts, development of market uses for hog waste, and technology installed at farms to decrease the harmful effects of waste. To be implemented, however, these methods will have to be cost-effective—that is, profitable—for adoption by the farms.[48]

A second impediment is international access via a port. As discussed above, North Carolina's ports have limited capacity, and expansion prospects are limited. A new port, perhaps focused on agribusiness, will be needed to fully capture the opportunities from changing foreign diets.[49] It is certainly conceivable such a port could be financed and operated by private investors, including foreign investors.

A third barrier is continuing trade restrictions on the sale of U.S. agricultural products, particularly in Asian countries. The proposed Trans-Pacific Partnership trade pact would have significantly reduced limits on U.S. exports to many Asian countries—including Japan and potentially China—and allowed North Carolina agricultural exports to grow at a faster rate.[50]

Finally, there is a wild card—probably too speculative to be thought of as a barrier today—but still one that should be considered. This is the possibility of shifting meat production from the farm to the lab. Synthetic meat production, which is the growing of meat from cultures in laboratories, is already possible. Advocates say that the practical perfection of this technique could be revolutionary, by improving the quality and health of meat consumption, reducing the adverse environmental aspects of current farm production methods (waste, high grain consumption), and making meat consumption possible almost anywhere in the world. There are two current downsides: cost (synthetic meat production can cost over 4,000 percent more than conventional farm meat production) and consumer acceptance. If these barriers can be overcome, however, synthetic meat production may become a serious rival to farm production. And if this development occurs, the prospects for expansion of

North Carolina's meat industry—indeed, the prospects for the existence of the industry—may eventually be in doubt.[51]

If environmental issues, transportation and port issues, and international trade issues can be resolved, then meat production and meat exports could lead economic growth in rural North Carolina in the twenty-first century.

AFFORDABLE ENERGY AND NATURAL RESOURCES

The quest for affordable energy and natural resources to fuel our economy and lifestyles has been a defining objective of the twenty-first century. The energy sector in North Carolina at the beginning of the twenty-first century is small (table 3.1). However, with the development of hydraulic fracturing ("fracking") technology for onshore energy recovery and increased interest in off-shore energy exploration in the Atlantic Ocean, discussion about the potential for developing the energy sector has been intense.

How large is this potential? Two academic studies have attempted to answer this question. A study I conducted estimated the potential economic impact for North Carolina from both onshore and offshore energy recovery.[52] Timothy Considine's research focused on an examination of the offshore possibilities.[53]

Based on available estimates of onshore energy reserves—mainly natural gas—in the state, I found very little economic impact from onshore energy recovery. Using current (in 2012) estimates of future natural gas prices and reserve estimates from the U.S. Geological Service, I calculated the most likely annual economic effects (including effects on state suppliers and on state retail sales) from onshore energy development of only $158 million and 1,400 permanent jobs. These numbers are in the context of an annual gross state product of $430 billion and total employment of almost 4 million in 2012. Under optimistic supply estimates and high natural gas prices, the totals could rise to $890 million and 8,000 jobs. But under pessimistic supply estimates and low natural gas prices, the totals are only $15 million and 130 jobs (all dollar amounts are in 2012 purchasing power values).

Both studies found the economic potential for North Carolina from offshore energy recovery to be much greater. The state has the largest estimated reservoir of offshore oil supplies of any state on the East Coast. Using the most likely scenario, I estimated that offshore oil (and some natural gas) exploration and recovery could generate $1.9 billion in annual income (GDP) in the state, 16,910 permanent jobs, and $116 million in annual public revenues. For his medium production scenario, Considine forecasted $1 billion in new annual income, 15,328 permanent jobs, and $171 million in annual public revenues.

Given that the two studies used different estimation methodologies, the results are very similar.

Both studies generated alternative estimates for offshore energy recovery based on the uncertainty of future price forecasts and available supply. My estimates ranged from a low of $10 million in annual income and 118 jobs to a high of $8 billion in annual income and 72,000 jobs. Considine's range was narrower—a low of $339 million in annual income and 5,366 jobs to a high of $1.9 billion and 29,866 jobs.

Each study also considered the possible environmental costs to North Carolina of offshore energy exploration and recovery. I estimated the cost of oil spillage from the recovery work. Although—based on past experience—the likelihood of spills is low, if an accident did occur, I put the cost at $83 million, with the losses concentrated on coastal counties. Considine estimated the adverse environmental effects from the use of the recovered and refined energy and the subsequent emission of additional carbon to the atmosphere. For his moderate scenario, he put the annual cost of this environmental damage at $92 million.

Would offshore energy development in North Carolina put the state on par with North Dakota and Texas, where energy recovery has been a big boost to their economies? Using the most likely or moderate estimates from both studies, the answer appears to be a strong "no." Annual energy output in North Dakota in 2012 accounted for 8 percent of GDP and 14 percent of employment, and in Texas it accounted for 21 percent of GDP and 5 percent of employment. For North Carolina, the numbers are either 0.4 percent (Walden) or 0.2 percent of GDP (Considine) and 0.4 percent of employment (both studies).[54] Even though the numbers would still yield monetary benefits greater than the expected monetary environmental costs, policy makers always must consider the possibility of dramatically altering both the economy and nature of coastal counties if offshore oil recovery became a significant industry—changes that are difficult to monetize.

Thus, while offshore energy development has economic potential for North Carolina, there are doubts about onshore energy recovery. Rather than drilling onshore for natural gas supplies, a more likely scenario is that the state will receive increased supplies of natural gas from external sources (such as Pennsylvania) via a pipeline planned for the eastern part of the state.[55]

How well is North Carolina situated for the development of alternative energy resources, particularly renewable sources like solar and wind power? In the early twenty-first century (2014), renewable energy accounted for 6 percent of the state's net electricity generation, one fourth less than the national share.[56] Solar power advocates think that this source could generate as much as 20 percent of the state's energy needs by 2030.[57] But much will depend on the economics of solar power, including the price of competitive power sources like natural gas and developments in the storage capacity of solar power.[58] Still, there is increasing private sector interest in solar power, as evidenced by a large solar farm planned for the massive seven-thousand-acre Chatham Park mixed-use development in the Triangle region.[59]

The state of North Carolina concluded a comprehensive study of the potential for offshore wind power.[60] Due to its long coastline and extended continental shelf, the state has the largest potential for offshore wind-generated power of any state on the East Coast. The report estimated that, if fully developed, offshore wind power could supply the energy needs of North Carolina and several other East Coast states.[61] However, there are risks with offshore wind power to the coastal bird population as well as to marine life and ecology, and delivering this power to users would require significant transmission infrastructure upgrades.

The most likely scenario for North Carolina's energy sources in the twenty-first century is for reduced reliance on coal-generated power, increased usage of natural-gas-generated power, and modest increases in renewable sources such as solar power. Plans for expanding the state's usage of nuclear power are uncertain. Duke Energy had planned to add to the Shearon-Harris Nuclear Power Plant in central North Carolina, but those plans were later suspended.[62]

Last, although water is sometimes not considered a resource, adequate availability of water is crucial for economic development. One obvious example is agriculture. As a result of the massive and devastating drought in California in the early twenty-first century, many industries have raised the level of importance of water supplies in making location decisions. Because California's long-term water outlook remains uncertain, some see opportunities for attracting portions of that state's fifty-four-billion-dollar annual farm production to states with more reliable water resources, such as North Carolina.[63] Whether this strategy is feasible will depend on whether California's drought is short-lived or decades long.

The New Look of North Carolina

If North Carolina's long-run annual growth rate per capita of 1.6 percent continues, and if the state's population reaches 13.4 million in 2050, then the size of the state economy will reach $1.1 trillion (2015 dollars) by midcentury. This is as large as the current (2015) national economies of Mexico and South Korea and would likely move North Carolina up several notches in state GDP rankings in the country (North Carolina was ninth in 2015).

FIG. 3.4 Economic sector shares in North Carolina regions, 2015.

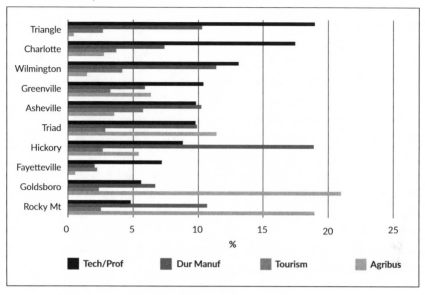

SOURCE: U.S. Department of Commerce; IMPLAN for North Carolina.

Regions of North Carolina will develop differently because the regions vary in their economic structure. Figure 3.4 shows the current (2015) share of aggregate regional production (GDP) in North Carolina's major regions for four economic clusters that are expected to be important for economic growth through the mid-twenty-first century: the technology-professional (or creative) sector, durable manufacturing, tourism, and agribusiness.[64] The technology-professional sector is dominant in the fast-growing Triangle and Charlotte regions and is significant in the Triad, the midsize regions of Asheville and Wilmington, and the university center of Greenville in the eastern part of the state. Durable manufacturing has the highest relative importance in the foothills area of Hickory, where a combination of traditional industries (furniture) exist alongside factories producing technology equipment (electrical and computer equipment). The regions surrounding mountainous Asheville and coastal Wilmington have the largest relative importance of tourism, while agribusiness is dominant in the rural regions of Rocky Mount and Goldsboro. Fayetteville is relatively low on all four sectors because its economy is driven by military spending at Fort Bragg, the largest armed forces base in the world.

If North Carolina can take advantage of the trends expected in the twenty-first century, then the economic geography of the state will look like that depicted in map 3.1. Technology will dominate the economic growth in the metro corridor

MAP 3.1 North Carolina Economic Geography in 2050.

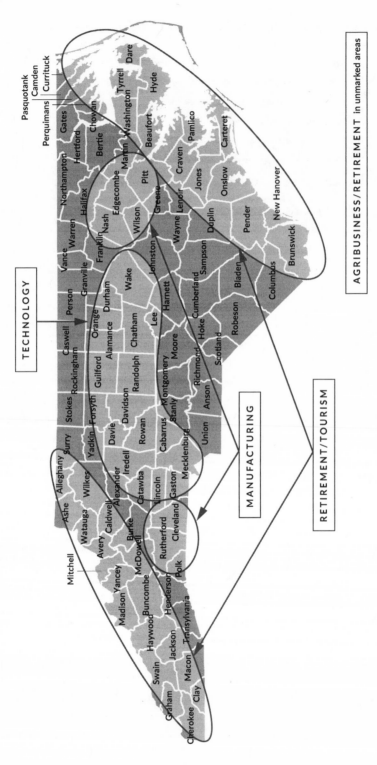

from the Triangle (Raleigh-Durham) to Charlotte, with each region building on its existing competitive industries: technology parts, instruments, and bio-technology in the Triangle; aerospace and pharmaceuticals in the Triad; and communications, packaging, and pharmaceuticals in Charlotte. Manufacturing firms—often tied to technology—will thrive adjacent to the metro corridor, both east of the Triangle and west of Charlotte, taking advantage of access to the bustling metros and low-cost land.[65] Transshipment facilities—or inland ports—will link to the manufacturing firms and move the finished products to final destinations. A combination of retirement living and tourism—much of the latter from foreign countries—will lead growth in both coastal and mountain counties. The rural and small town areas between the coast and the metro corridor on the east and south, between the mountains and the metro corridor on the west, and north of the metro corridor will be dominated by the expansion of retirement communities and agribusiness. In the east agribusiness opportunities will be driven by the meat industry, while in the west crops will be the leader. Prosperity will not be evenly divided between the state's regions—it never will—but there will be strategies and options for economic growth everywhere.

Of course, there are many "ifs" in these projections! North Carolina certainly has the resources, experience, and reputation to take advantage of the expected expansion in the technology sector, but there will be strong competition. Unlike previous industries that were centered on site-specific resources—such as the steel industry locating near iron ore deposits in the North or textile mills being close to cotton fields in the South—the technology industry is unattached and mobile because it is based on ideas developed by humans. Thus, attracting and keeping innovative and creative scientists and entrepreneurs are the keys to growing tech businesses. Fortunately, North Carolina has much to offer with its pleasant and diverse natural environment, world-class universities, and existing critical mass of tech centers in its metropolitan areas and near its universities. But other regions in the nation and in the world have similar advantages, so it will be a continuing challenge for the state to maintain its luster and attractiveness to future generations of technology builders.[66]

Likewise, manufacturing may never expand in the nation or the state, thus making the idea of a manufacturing renaissance an illusion. Or the refinement and spread of 3-D manufacturing may make large-scale factories a figment of the past as making products moves to people's homes. Retirees in northern states might never move if global warming significantly increases winter temperatures, and tourists may go elsewhere or take virtual vacations in their own living rooms. Ports and roads may never get built, and the failure to solve the animal waste problem or the development of synthetic meat production could mean that the state's farmers lose out on the worldwide growth of meat consumption. So, like all forecasts, nothing is guaranteed.

But, at least, we know what is possible. And we know something about what the state's businesses, workers, and public officials need to consider doing to make the possible become a reality. Still, the winds of change will continue to blow across North Carolina's economic landscape. Adjusting to—and with any luck harnessing—these winds to improve the lives of the state's residents will continue to be the ongoing challenge.

Most people judge the progress of the economy by their income earned in the workplace. But as the types of businesses and the nature of work continue to change rapidly in the twenty-first century, how will employment opportunities be different, and how will these opportunities affect salaries, educational requirements, and living standards? These are the important topics of the next chapter.

4. WINNERS AND LOSERS IN MAKING A LIVING

Is Education Enough?

Economists use the term "human capital" as a shorthand for the skills, training, and formal educational levels of the workforce. As economies have progressed in the twentieth century and into the twenty-first century, the development of human capital has become the focus for the economic improvement of states as well as nations.

Human capital has assumed an elevated importance for three reasons. One is the shift from "brawn power" to "brain power" as a worker's major contribution. Since the days of the Industrial Revolution and spanning today's Information Revolution, machines and technology are increasingly accomplishing not only tasks requiring physical power but also routine applications. Workers with talents in management, analysis, problem-solving, and innovation are in increasingly high demand. These skills use cognitive abilities and are usually based on higher levels of formal education.

A second reason for concentrating on the development of human capital is the recognition of the rewards provided to human capital in the marketplace. For workers to achieve better wages and salaries, they will need enhanced levels of human capital. This factor becomes even more important as technological improvements increase the tasks that machines and electronic devices can do in place of workers.[1]

Combining the above two observations leads to the third reason: that for an economy to grow, whether at the national or state level, workers need to be equipped with sufficient human capital. Amounts of human capital are a main—and perhaps *the* main—factor in determining advances in an economy's aggregate economic growth and, by extension, advances in an economy's standard of living.[2]

FIG. 4.1 Gains in North Carolina and U.S. educational attainment, 2000–2015 (percentage point change for adults age 25 and over).

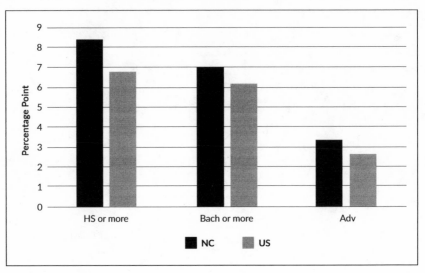

SOURCE: U.S. Census Bureau, "Statistical Abstract," "American Community Survey."

North Carolina has made strides in improving its human capital. The percentage point changes in the early twenty-first century in adults with various levels of educational attainment in the state and the nation are shown in fig. 4.1. For each of the three educational attainment levels examined—high school graduate or higher (HS or more), bachelor's degree or higher (Bach or more), and advanced degree (Adv)—North Carolina's gains have been better than in the nation as a whole.[3] If North Carolina's superior gains continue at the same rate, then the state will catch up to the nation in high school attainment in the early 2020s, in bachelor's degree attainment by the mid-2030s, and in advanced degree attainment by the late 2030s.[4]

North Carolina looks even better when measures of educational performance are compared. The National Assessment of Educational Progress is considered the gold standard for measuring learning achievement at the elementary school level. Beginning in the early 2000s for mathematics, North Carolina fourth graders consistently scored better than their national counterparts, and eighth graders scored either the same or better. For reading, fourth graders have scored better or higher than their national counterparts since the mid-1990s. Only eighth graders taking the reading test have scored lower than their national counterparts in a few years since the late 1990s.[5]

These comparisons are important because a large body of research suggests that workforce training and skill levels are key factors in explaining differences in economic growth among states.[6] Further, some research indicates that these skill level differences will become even more important in the future in attracting economic growth.[7]

But will educational and skill improvements be enough to raise the productivity and standard of living of North Carolina workers in the twenty-first century? In the past the answer has been "yes," but is the past no longer a prologue to the future? Will the nature of work and the quantity of work be dramatically different in the twenty-first century than in previous eras?

An End to Work?

In the twenty-first century the traditional categories of jobs—white collar, blue collar, manufacturing, service—have increasingly become obsolete. Instead, what a worker can do—that is, the tasks a worker can perform—is now the preferred measure for worker classification.

Researchers today think of jobs categorized into three broad groupings of tasks.[8] *Abstract analytical and managerial tasks*—renamed "problem-solving tasks"—require creativity, judgment and evaluation, and problem-solving skills. *Routine cognitive and manual tasks*—termed "routine tasks"—are done in a logical and repetitive process needing little thinking. *Nonroutine manual tasks*—called "nonroutine tasks"—require flexibility and adaptation to observed situations that are different enough to not be routine and repetitive.

Problem-solving tasks are those requiring the highest levels of educational training. They have benefited most from the technological and digital revolution and the increase in societal demand for individuals working in scientific fields and complex organizations. Routine tasks have been those most susceptible to performance by technology and machinery, and thus individuals performing these tasks have been significantly adversely affected from technological unemployment. Nonroutine tasks have grown with the expansion of the personal service economy, but their formal training requirements—and thus their compensation—have tended to be low.

Recent changes in the distribution of employment among the three task categories are shown for both North Carolina and the nation in fig. 4.2.[9] Several trends are clear. Problem-solving task employment rose substantially in both the state and the nation in the late twentieth and early twenty-first centuries, increasing their share of all jobs by almost 50 percent to nearly one-third of the total in 2015. Nonroutine task jobs almost doubled their share to close to 20 percent in 2015 for North Carolina and

FIG. 4.2 Distribution of U.S. and North Carolina workforce among task job categories, 1980 and 2015 (workers 16 years and older).

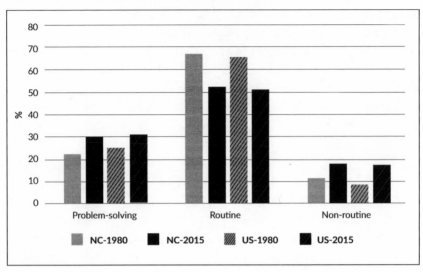

SOURCE: U.S. Census Bureau.

the nation. The relative gains in these two task categories came at the expense of routine task employment, whose share declined by approximately 15 percentage points for the state and the nation during the three-and-a-half-decade period.[10]

Certainly the relative decline of routine task jobs, whether cognitive or manual, has been a result of advances in labor-replacing technology and machinery, whereas these substitutions have been more difficult to make in problem-solving and nonroutine task jobs. This point is reinforced by noting that measures of labor productivity gains have been far greater for routine task jobs than for the other task categories.[11]

The questions are whether these trends will continue for routine task jobs and if they could be extended to the two other task categories, especially with significant advances in artificial intelligence.[12] Carl Frey and Michael Osborne performed an intensive analysis of the U.S. labor market that assigned a probability of an occupation's replacement by computerization (their term for technological unemployment). Their probability rates were based on detailed analysis of more than seven hundred occupations and an assessment of the likelihood of each occupation's tasks eventually being accomplished by either programming or machine technology. The researchers' conclusion was that 47 percent of U.S. employment in 2010 could eventually be replaced by technology in upcoming decades.[13] Both Jerry Kaplan and Michael

Chui, James Manyika, and Mehdi Miremadi arrived at similar rates, but Melanie Arntz, Terry Gregory, and Ulrich Zierahn estimated a much lower loss of jobs due to technology, at 9 percent for the United States.[14] Of course, the U.S. labor market has always been dynamic, continually creating new occupations while downsizing others. Yet Frey and Osborne's conclusion suggests an acceleration of recent occupational reorganization.[15] Some research predicts that the rate of occupational change will double in the decades ahead.[16]

Frey and Osborne's methodology was applied to North Carolina's occupational structure in 2013 (to match the year of Frey and Osborne's probabilities), and the results are given in table 4.1.[17] Using the same categorizations as Frey and Osborne, just under half of the occupations (44 percent) and employees (48 percent) face a high probability (over 70 percent) of replacement by technology. Another approximately 20 percent of occupations and employees have a moderate (31 percent to 70 percent) chance of technology replacement, and almost a third of occupations and employees have a low (0 percent to 30 percent) likelihood of replacement by technology.

There is a trend in the salaries of the three groups with an inverse relation between the probability of technology replacement and median salary. The median salary of the lowest probability group is almost double that of the highest probability group. The same inverse relation can be seen between the probability of replacement and the highest occupational salary of the group. Again, the highest salary of the lowest probability group is almost double the highest salary of the highest probability group.

North Carolina occupations with ten thousand or more employees in each of the three technology replacement categories, arrayed from lowest to highest probability of technology replacement, are listed in tables 4.2, 4.3, and 4.4. Each group, of course, contains a variety of occupations, but there definitely are patterns in both the tasks and the earnings of the occupations. Most of the occupations with a low probability for technology replacement (table 4.2) involve problem-solving tasks in the supervisory, health care, technology, legal, and protective and personal services industries.[18] Almost half of the occupations have earnings over $55,000, while only 14 percent pay under $30,000 (table 4.2). The occupations with a moderate likelihood of replacement by technology (table 4.3) include several nonroutine occupations in construction, food production, delivery, and personal services—occupations that could be replaced by technology if sufficient advances are made in artificial intelligence to allow performance of nonroutine tasks. Four times as many of the occupations have earnings under $30,000 as have earnings over

TABLE 4.1 Projected Occupational Changes in North Carolina from Technology Replacement

Probability of Replacement by Technology	Number of Occupations (% of Total)	Number of Employees (% of Total)	Median Salary	Low Salary/ High Salary	For 10,000 or More Employees, % of Occupations Paying over $55,000	For 10,000 or More Employees, % of Occupations Paying under $30,000
0%–30%	262 (37%)	1,245,150 (32%)	$57,370	$19,910/ $215,780	48%	14%
31%–70%	133 (19%)	775,700 (20%)	$39,940	$19,410/ $107,580	11%	44%
71%–100%	307 (44%)	1,882,190 (48%)	$33,110	$17,830/ $122,020	8%	63%

SOURCE: author's calculations using Frey and Osborne's methodology applied to North Carolina 2013 occupational data from the North Carolina Office of Employment Security. Carl Benedikt Frey and Michael A. Osborne, "The Future of Employment: How Susceptible Are Jobs to Computerisation?," Working Paper (Oxford University, September 2013).

$55,000. Occupations with the highest chance of technological replacement (table 4.4) are overwhelmingly composed of routine task jobs prominently in the food service, retail, hospitality, sales, and financial sectors.[19] Almost two-thirds of the occupations have earnings under $30,000, while less than 10 percent have earnings over $50,000.

It is a mistake, however, to think that only counties with a largely lower-skilled, lower-educated workforce will be affected by technological unemployment. An analysis of all the occupations with more than a 70 percent chance of replacement by technology showed that even counties in North Carolina with a high average level of educational attainment, such as Wake, Mecklenburg, and Forsyth, could face employment reductions of one-third from technological displacement (map 4.1).[20] This is because those high-skilled counties have a complementary low-skilled labor force in services (particularly food services), retailing, and sales—all tasks that are consistent with a takeover by technology.

A conclusion of this analysis is that a large number of lower- and middle-paying occupations face the potential of significant downsizing from technology, while many—but certainly not all—higher-paying occupations are much safer from technological encroachment.[21] Some analysts have documented an acceleration of technological unemployment after the Great

TABLE 4.2 North Carolina Occupations with Greater than 10,000 Employees and a
0 Percent to 30 Percent Probability of Replacement by Technology (Ranked from Lower to
Higher Probability of Replacement)

Occupation	Number of Employees	Annual Earnings
Supervisors of mechanics, installer, repairers	15,340	$59,610
Physicians and surgeons	17,880	$200,000
Elementary school teachers	40,430	$42,870
Computer systems analysts	16,210	$84,760
Preschool teachers	11,300	$25,530
High school teachers	24,190	$43,510
Registered nurses	88,350	$59,290
Supervisors of offices	38,070	$49,910
Supervisors of production facilities	21,370	$55,430
Nursing assistants	50,990	$22,860
College teachers	50,800	$75,000
Lawyers	11,820	$114,840
Computer systems managers	11,440	$129,280
Software developers	20,190	$92,410
Emergency medical technicians	10,430	$31,980
Licensed practical nurses	15,550	$41,570
Financial managers	15,210	$127,320
Supervisors of non-retail sales workers	10,370	$90,870
Childcare workers	22,500	$19,910
Law enforcement officers	19,630	$40,940
Management analysts	11,230	$84,330
Electricians	12,960	$39,890
General and operation managers	52,080	$125,240
Firefighters	12,800	$32,720
Supervisors of construction	18,200	$54,410
Middle school teachers	17,470	$42,160
Web and network developers	31,720	$60,000
Business operations specialists	28,240	$69,170
Supervisors of retail sales workers	42,890	$40,930
Medical assistants	13,890	$29,390

SOURCE: author's calculations using Frey and Osborne's methodology applied to North Carolina
2013 occupational data from the North Carolina Office of Employment Security. Carl Benedikt Frey
and Michael A. Osborne, "The Future of Employment: How Susceptible Are Jobs to Computerisation?," Working Paper (Oxford University, September 2013).

Recession and offer it as a reason for the slow job recovery.[22] The question
then becomes, where will those workers displaced by technology go? Will new
similar-paying occupations be developed? Or will these workers need to substantially upgrade or alter their human capital in order to obtain employment
in expanding occupations?

TABLE 4.3 North Carolina Occupations with Greater than 10,000 Employees and a 31 Percent to 70 Percent Probability of Replacement by Technology (Ranked from Lower to Higher Probability of Replacement)

Occupation	Number of Employees	Annual Earnings
Human resource specialists	12,430	$58,580
Packers	27,460	$21,360
Home health aides	47,860	$19,410
Customer service representatives	83,650	$31,550
Teacher assistants	33,070	$22,640
Auto service technicians	20,980	$39,130
Correctional officers	17,150	$31,890
Meat packers	10,180	$24,250
Market research analysts	12,130	$67,050
Supervisors of food preparation	33,160	$31,840
Maintenance and repair workers	39,810	$37,240
Stock clerks	47,310	$23,700
Machinists	11,530	$37,550
Heating and air conditioning installers	10,800	$39,690
Production worker helpers	17,280	$23,850
Janitors and cleaners	53,940	$21,730
Delivery service drivers	22,410	$32,550
Maids	28,820	$19,530

SOURCE: author's calculations using Frey and Osborne's methodology applied to North Carolina 2013 occupational data from the North Carolina Office of Employment Security. Carl Benedikt Frey and Michael A. Osborne, "The Future of Employment: How Susceptible Are Jobs to Computerisation?," Working Paper (Oxford University, September 2013).

Dueling Forecasts

A first step in answering these questions is to attempt to forecast the number and kinds of jobs in the future North Carolina. Projecting occupational and employment trends decades in advance is obviously a heroic undertaking. It is wise, therefore, to use alternative approaches in order to see the degree of consistency and range in the estimates. Two methods are used. The first applies the detailed occupational forecasts of the U.S. Department of Labor (DOL) to North Carolina's occupational structure in 2013 to develop forecasts for 2024 (the last year in the DOL forecast). The forecasts are then extended to 2050 using the implied trend between 2013 and 2024.[23] The second method applies the technology replacement rates from Frey and Osborne to occupations and then augments the results by the forecasted growth rates in the occupation's industry from the DOL forecasts and by the rate at which employment changes with changes in economic output.[24] So, for example, if Frey and Osborne

TABLE 4.4 North Carolina Occupations with Greater than 10,000 Employees and a 71 Percent to 100 Percent Probability of Replacement by Technology (Ranked from Lower to Higher Probability of Replacement)

Occupation	Number of Employees	Annual Earnings
Amusement and recreation attendants	10,520	$18,520
Personal care aides	13,740	$19,430
Bartenders	10,170	$20,810
Dishwashers	12,550	$17,980
Heavy truck drivers	48,370	$38,480
Medical secretaries	10,780	$30,200
Security guards	26,380	$24,880
Moving laborers	73,580	$25,280
Sales personnel in wholesaling and manufacturing	43,270	$60,070
Executive secretaries	25,060	$46,530
Food preparation workers	20,430	$20,290
Construction laborers	16,470	$25,920
School bus drivers	16,890	$24,850
Pharmacy technicians	11,680	$28,090
Retail salespersons	139,330	$24,430
Fast food restaurant workers	134,960	$17,830
Industrial truck drivers	19,250	$29,880
Accountants	29,000	$68,970
Waiters and waitresses	76,860	$18,890
Bill collectors	11,840	$32,490
Landscaping workers	27,360	$23,740
Receptionists	28,340	$26,220
Office clerks	68,750	$27,220
Cafeteria and coffee shop attendants	11,880	$18,160
Secretaries, except medical, legal, and executive	63,020	$32,790
Restaurant cooks	32,640	$21,340
Bill clerks	15,740	$33,610
Team assemblers	38,530	$28,040
Cashiers	106,010	$18,950
Counter and rental clerks	11,570	$24,860
Restaurant hosts and hostesses	12,430	$17,950
Inspectors and testers	18,870	$34,030
Bookkeeping clerks	43,900	$35,150
Driver/sales workers	14,390	$27,770
Shipping and receiving clerks	20,980	$30,280
Packaging machine operators	14,070	$30,320
Tellers	12,480	$27,690
Loan officers	10,400	$71,870
Other sales representatives	18,980	$63,170

SOURCE: author's calculations using Frey and Osborne's methodology applied to North Carolina 2013 occupational data from the North Carolina Office of Employment Security. Carl Benedikt Frey and Michael A. Osborne, "The Future of Employment: How Susceptible Are Jobs to Computerisation?," Working Paper (Oxford University, September 2013).

MAP 4.1 Projected Job Losses from Occupations Having a 70 Percent or Greater Likelihood of Being Replaced by Technology, by North Carolina County (% of Total Employment in 2013).

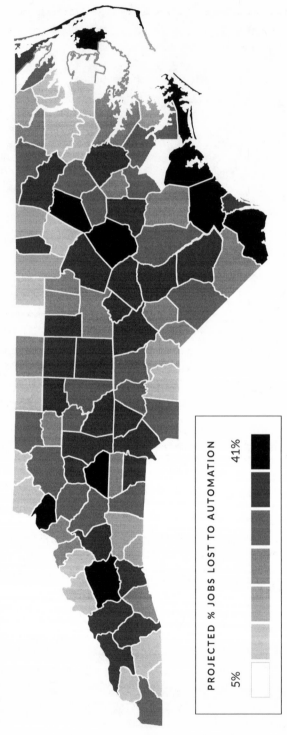

PROJECTED % JOBS LOST TO AUTOMATION

5%   41%

SOURCE: North Carolina State University Institute for Emerging Issues.

TABLE 4.5 Alternative North Carolina Employment Forecasts from 2013 to 2050

	U.S. Department of Labor	Frey/Osborne
Total jobs, % change, 2013–50	42%	–32%
Problem-solving share % point change	+8 % points	+26 % points
Routine share % point change	–9 % points	–17 % points
Nonroutine share % point change	+1 % point	–9 % points
Change in problem-solving task jobs	+1,044,810	+288,439
Change in routine task jobs	+327,532	–1,125,263
Change in nonroutine task jobs	+366,880	–460,723

SOURCE: U.S. Department of Labor, Bureau of Labor Statistics, "Employment Projections to 2024"; Carl Benedikt Frey and Michael A. Osborne, "The Future of Employment: How Susceptible Are Jobs to Computerisation?," Working Paper (Oxford University, September 2013). ; calculations by the author.

indicated that fast-food workers faced a 92 percent probability of replacement by technology, yet the fast-food industry was expected to expand by 50 percent with a 1 percent growth in employment for every 2 percent growth in output, then the forecasted number of fast-food workers would be found by reducing today's number by 92 percent and then increasing the result by 25 percent (50 percent × ½).

The results are presented in two ways: first showing the percentage point change in the three task-defined employment categories, and second showing the change in the number of jobs in the three task-defined employment categories.

The DOL forecasts are fairly optimistic (table 4.5). The 42 percent increase in the number of jobs is well above the estimated 36 percent increase in total population and 30 percent increase in working age (twenty-five to sixty-four years of age) population.[25] The Department of Labor also sees a continued expansion in the proportion of problem-solving task jobs, a contraction in the share of routine jobs, and little change in the proportion of nonroutine jobs.

The forecasts are much less optimistic using Frey and Osborne's expectations for technology replacement. Rather than increasing, total jobs decline by almost a third. The shifts between the three task-based job classifications are similar to the DOL forecasts, but they are much more pronounced. The share of problem-solving task jobs increases by 26 percentage points, to almost 60 percent of all jobs, while routine task jobs drop by 17 percentage points. Rather than rising modestly as in the DOL projections, nonroutine task job lose 9 percentage points in their total job share.

The two forecasts agree that the total number of problem-solving task jobs will increase; however, DOL forecasts the increase as three times more than Frey and Osborne. But the forecasts disagree in both the direction and the size of change in the other two task categories. Routine task jobs increase by more than 300,000 in the DOL projections but decline by more than 1 million using the Frey and Osborne methodology. Likewise, nonroutine task jobs increase by approximately 360,000 using DOL but decrease by more than 460,000 by Frey and Osborne.

These forecasts are both interesting and troubling. The interest comes from the continuing dynamism of the economy and the relative speed at which job options can shift. If accurate, both forecasts suggest that the North Carolina labor market will have moved from an economy based primarily on manual skills to one based on cognitive skills within the span of a century. And if recent trends continue, the faster growth in problem-solving task jobs also means that higher-paying jobs will be the most rapidly expanding category.

But the forecasts clearly raise worries. Both indicate a shift from routine and nonroutine task occupations to problem-solving task occupations, but to different degrees. The trends in the three task classifications of occupations following the two forecasts and the implications for the education system are shown in fig. 4.3. Even though a bigger percentage of jobs using the Frey and Osborne forecasts would be in the high-paying, problem-solving occupations, the number of such jobs would still be substantially lower than with the DOL forecasts.[26]

Yet the biggest concern is the 1.3 million total job loss predicted by the Frey and Osborne methodology. Even though the working-age population in North Carolina will increase more slowly than in the past, it will still expand, implying a rising unemployment rate for those who want to work. What will these workers do? Will new industries and occupations absorb them? What changes in public policy might be needed to address this employment dislocation?

Underclass or New Class?

The answers to these questions follow along the lines staked out by the pessimists and optimists of the economic future. Pessimists see a future world that requires fewer workers as machines, technology, and productivity increasingly control the marketplace.[27] They see the development of a new and expanded underclass of "precariats" who lack job security and depend on crime, charity, or governmental assistance to survive.[28] In 2015, more than 260,000 males of prime working age in North Carolina were already outside the labor force (not

FIG. 4.3 Alternative North Carolina workforce forecasts (percentage of total jobs).

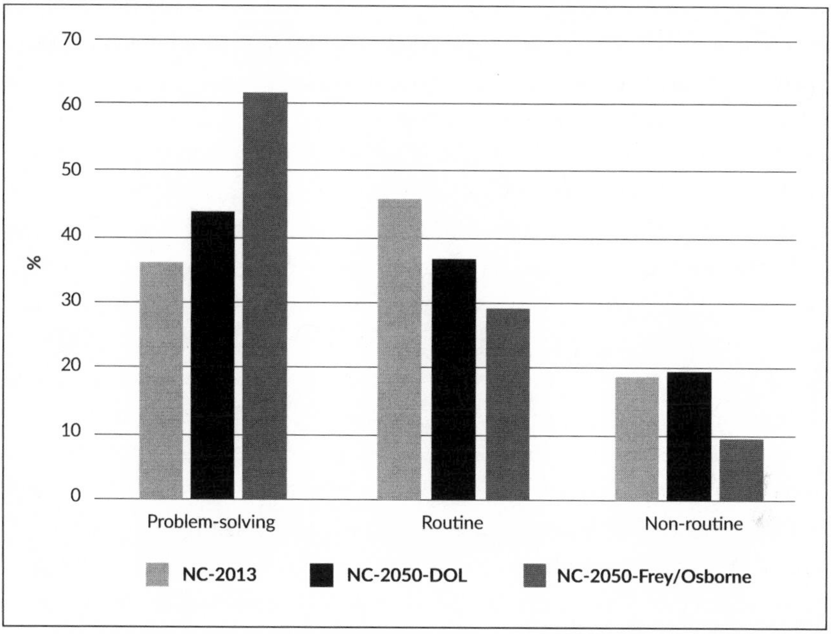

SOURCE: table 4.5.

working and not looking for a job).[29] Government make-work jobs, financed by public revenues paid from the increased concentration of income among those performing problem-solving tasks, would be needed to give the precariats purpose and to divert them from engaging in unproductive actions.[30] Pessimists therefore see the future labor market being composed of well-paid, highly trained cognitive workers engaged in problem-solving tasks, a much smaller and likely decreasing number of cognitive nonroutine task support workers, very few routine task workers, and a large and growing number of precariats who perform token tasks and are primarily supported by the public sector.[31]

The optimists see a brighter future ahead for the labor market future, based mainly on history. Citing two major transformations of North Carolina's labor market in just the twentieth century—from farm to factory, and from factory to services—the optimists say that another transformation will certainly happen. Even if income is increasingly concentrated in an educated elite, the optimists argue that the income will be spent and the spending will create economic opportunities and labor demand. Furthermore, optimists see the increased productivity resulting from technological advancement reducing prices and boosting real (inflation-adjusted) incomes, thereby creating more spending and more jobs.[32]

I see eight contenders for significant creation of new occupations, all developing from trends in the economy of the next four decades: household management, repair and maintenance of new technology, global interaction, logistics and data management and analysis, aged assistance, education and retraining, social interaction, and artisanship.

Household management. As the income-earning opportunities of households benefiting from the future economy (mainly those with problem-solving occupations) expand, their time becomes more valuable. These households will increasingly look for ways to reduce their time use in nonearning tasks by purchasing assistance for these chores. Shopping, meal preparation, cleaning, childcare, personal care, home maintenance, and household organization are all tasks open for paid performance. While some of these tasks can be—or will be able to be—accomplished by technology, the cognitive and on the spot decision-making requirement for many of them may be high enough to be best accomplished by human direction. Although a *Downton Abbey*–style situation of live-in servants is unlikely, paid assistants visiting residences on a regular basis to perform work is certainly possible. Some call this the "concierge economy," where workers will be summoned via phone apps.[33] The workers will be highly trained, screened for security and reliability, and professional in all aspects of their work. Hence, decent salaries in the mid- to high five figures (2015 dollars) could be expected.

Repair and maintenance of new technology. As technology becomes more pervasive in the economy, the need for its upkeep increases. While some of the repair and maintenance of technology can be done by other technology, much of the troubleshooting and analysis will—at least initially—be performed by humans who can react to specific and unusual situations. This set of occupations will be fast-changing and will require continuous retraining of personnel as technology evolves. New occupations will focus on emerging technologies in virtual reality, robots, advanced telecommunications and materials, 3-D manufacturing, and the "internet of everything."[34]

Global interaction. As world trade and interactions increase, occupations to facilitate these interrelations will develop.[35] Technology will certainly continue to enhance the ability of individuals to communicate across the world, but there are some personal interactions for which cybercommunications are not good substitutes. Occupations specializing in understanding foreign markets, dealing with foreign customs, recognizing foreign laws, navigating political obstacles for trade, and attracting and servicing foreign tourists are good examples. Language requirements for these occupations will be moderated with advances in translation technologies.

Logistics and data management and analysis. The plethora of data that will be collected in the emerging economy will be used for analysis to improve the efficiency and logistical operations of businesses—and even of households and government. A set of occupations will develop around these components that will become increasingly essential and high profile for almost every industry and economic sector to achieve and compete successfully.[36] In the early twenty-first century financial occupations were the stars; in the mid-twenty-first century it will be "logo (logistics) people"!

Aged assistance. The most dominant demographic trend of the next several decades is the relative growth of the elderly population, generally measured by the proportion of the population aged sixty-five and over. This trend clearly has implications for the health care industry. But a large number of the elderly will continue to be healthy and relatively active. They will not need hospitalization or institutionalized living, but they will need modest assistance to continue independent living. This will create occupations similar to those in the household management field, but with the focus on the special characteristics and requirements of the elderly.

Education and retraining. The next economy will be marked by fast changes in businesses and rapid turnover of occupations. Not only will individuals work for several employers over their career, but they will also work at several occupations. Education, training, and retraining opportunities will have to be focused on current trends, rapid, and affordable. New educational institutions will be required, which will also create new educational and training occupations.

Social interaction. Business writer Geoff Colvin argues that the relevant question is *not* "What will technology do next?" but instead "What *won't* technology do next?"[37] He sees little limit to the ability of technology to take over any job that can't be logically determined and analyzed, even those requiring cognitive decision-making at a high level. He cites examples of machines writing novels and technology analyzing legal precedents to formulate courtroom arguments. But what technology and machines will struggle to imitate, in Colvin's view, are the subtleties of human social interactions, such as perceiving an individual's mood from facial expressions and demeanor, developing innovative ideas through collective discussion and interaction, understanding differences in actions and reactions based on culture, and diagnosing illnesses and injuries from the verbal and physical actions of patients. He sees training in the humanities and the fine arts as providing the skills for these talents.[38] Indeed, some research has documented the growing importance of social skills in the workplace.[39]

Artisanship. Some see a revival of artisans and artisanship almost as a rebellion against low-cost, mass-made products that will likely dominate the twenty-first century.[40] The increased demand for specialty, hand-crafted products—particularly by upper-income households—could spark a boom for traditional artisans, such as carpenters, stone layers, and clothing and jewelry makers.

Despair and Hope in the Labor Market

The potential negative impacts of advancing technology on jobs, privacy, happiness, and control over our lives have led some to recommend regulation of new technology. This regulation would involve a determination and comparison of the broad costs and benefits to society—including work—of technological innovations. If they happened, such discussions would be national in scope, but North Carolina would be affected.[41]

Yet not everyone sees robots and technology pushing humans out of the workforce. Although advances have been made and trends can be projected, much work still needs to be done to improve the capability of robots beyond simple, routine acts.[42] So the massive technological unemployment that has been forecasted may be multiple decades away, at the earliest. Also, if workers are given more opportunities to invest in labor-saving technologies or in the companies employing these technologies, then that may be a method for workers to hedge against potential losses to their own labor earnings.[43]

There is also an argument that technology's substitution for labor could help revive industries in the United States that have left in search of lower-cost foreign labor.[44] Manufacturing is a prime example of such an industry. An expansion of manufacturing in North Carolina, even with relatively few workers in the factories, could still stimulate employment in other sectors through supply-chain and consumer spending.

But even if we accept these potential positive counterpoints to technological unemployment, North Carolina's workers will face other challenges in the twenty-first century. Some predict that permanent employment with firms will give way to a gig labor market, in which firms use workers on a temporary basis for short-term projects. Motivation would come from reducing business costs on employee benefits, as well as from fast-paced change in the economy, making permanent employees who are locked in to specific tasks a liability.[45] Furthermore, if technology allows firms to better supervise and monitor contingent employees, then one of the original reasons for the development of the modern firm with permanent employees is weakened.[46] The rise of the gig economy and contingent employment would open a debate about the role of government in mandating or financially supporting employee benefits. One side argues that such mandates and supports would be needed.[47] Another side maintains that employee fringe benefits—while seemingly funded by the firm—actually come at the expense of lower wages and salaries to employees.[48]

A labor issue that has emerged in recent decades centers on whether workers are receiving their fair share of production in their compensation. Historically, gains in worker compensation (the value of wages, salaries, and benefits) have tracked gains in worker productivity. However, beginning in the twenty-first century, some analysis suggests that this relationship has broken down, with worker productivity rising much faster than worker compensation, including in North Carolina.[49] Critics of current corporate practices say that the reason is reduced worker power, particularly with weakened unions.[50] An alternative explanation is that machinery and technology are responsible for more of the productivity improvements than in the past, and hence the economic returns and share to nonlabor inputs have increased.[51] Not all economists, however, accepted the apparent disconnect between worker compensation and worker productivity. Different adjustments for inflation, data sets, and equipment and technology depreciation rates can erase the divergence between compensation and productivity.[52]

Concerns about widening income inequality and a declining middle class will likely continue and may intensify, and recent studies show that some regions in North Carolina are unfortunate leaders in these trends.[53] The analysis presented above shows that technological unemployment will have the least effect on problem-solving occupations—which generally have the highest earnings—and more impact on routine and nonroutine occupations where earnings are lower. Technological unemployment may thus expand income inequality and narrow the steps in the income ladder from low to high earnings. Conversely, technology could increase the ability of workers to train for better-paying jobs in the future economy, thereby potentially expanding the middle class and shrinking income inequality.[54]

An issue related to work and income is family time management. With the majority of children now being raised in households with single parents (usually mothers) or two working parents, time allocated to child-rearing and childcare is being squeezed and is creating increasing stress on parents.[55] Many businesses are reluctant to offer more generous family leave time because such policies are viewed as reducing worker productivity and putting the business at a competitive disadvantage. One solution is government mandates applied to all businesses for increased family leave. Debates over such mandates have already been intense, and disagreements over the proper policy response would be expected to continue.[56] However, future technology allowing better telecommuting and home-work coordination could be an alternative solution.[57]

Last is a potential labor market issue related to one of the major trends of the century: aging. As individuals live longer, society faces the challenge of funding more years for retirees. However, Social Security already faces fiscal issues, and private pension plans and individual savings may be inadequate.[58] This means that there may be pressure for older individuals to remain in the labor market longer. Indeed, this has already been happening.[59] Yet if technology eliminates a significant number of jobs that are not replaced, the increase in the elderly's work participation will collide with unemployed younger individuals who are also looking for work. Aging plus technological unemployment will be a combustible combination!

North Carolina's labor market will be the most challenging aspect of the state's economy in the twenty-first century. For some it will be an exciting time, as new products and services, industries, and occupations are developed. In 2050, we will look back in surprise at what had changed. But for others it will be a trying time. Occupations and livelihoods will be destroyed, leaving many workers adrift with no obvious means of support.

Retraining, reskilling, and repurposing workers will be crucial elements in addressing this reality. The state's educational and training system, from prekindergarten to college, will need to respond to the new realities of the labor market in a timely and proactive manner that facilitates efficient and rapid transitions from outdated skills to in-demand competences. How this might be accomplished is the focus of chapter 5, "Resetting Education."

5. RESETTING EDUCATION

Reviewing Where We Are

If North Carolina is to create new occupations and jobs to replace those expected to be lost to technology, many pieces will have to fall in place. Perhaps the most important is the education and training system. Educational institutions and techniques will have to be revamped to accommodate the increasingly dynamic labor force continually remade during the twenty-first century. Educational change will have to occur at the pre-K–12 and post-12 levels.[1]

Progress in K–12 education in North Carolina has been mixed in the late twentieth and early twenty-first centuries. The National Assessment of Education Performance, the definitive measure of K–12 educational performance, shows general improvement over time in the state, but with slowing gains in recent years (fig. 5.1).[2] Although high school dropout numbers have continually declined, little progress has been made in reducing the number of prison incarcerations (fig. 5.2).[3] Wide geographic disparities in educational attainment persist in the state: several rural counties have very low proportions of adults with a college degree and relatively high proportions without a high school degree (map 5.1).[4] This is significant because substantial research shows a strong correlation between local educational attainment and economic improvement.[5] For example, if the number of high school dropouts and the number of incarcerated individuals in 2014 were working during that year at the average earnings of a high school graduate in the case of dropouts or the average earnings indicated by their education in the case of incarcerated individuals, then aggregate income in the state would have increased by a billion dollars.[6]

Complicating matters more, a large body of research over many decades shows that family and neighborhood factors often exceed school inputs in affecting the educational outcomes of students.[7] Lack of supportive parents and family members and the presence of crime and other social disruptions can offset the teacher and school inputs that students receive at educational institutions.

FIG. 5.1 Trends in NAEP test scores in North Carolina.

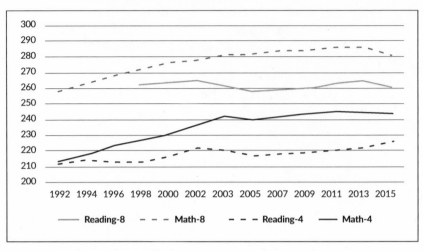

SOURCE: National Center for Educational Statistics; Institute of Education Services.

Some argue that such situations create a cycle of trapped children who never succeed academically, with the cycle being perpetuated over multiple decades.[8] There is also evidence suggesting that children from challenging environmental circumstances who are able to perform academically suffer social ostracism from their peers.[9] Economic mobility is obviously impinged by these conditions. Indeed, research findings suggest that the lack of economic mobility is among the highest in the nation in some North Carolina metropolitan regions.[10]

As indicated in chapter 4, North Carolina has closed—but not yet eliminated—the gap in higher educational attainment between the state and the nation. But even though the U.S. higher educational system, including institutions in North Carolina, is ranked the top in the world, several cracks expose three serious issues.

The first issue is student performance. National studies show a precipitous decline in student hours used studying, reading course materials, and attending class.[11] In North Carolina, still more than one-third of students at campuses of the UNC system have not graduated by six years, and the nongraduation rate is almost double for the state's community colleges.[12] Surveys show that a large proportion of these students will never receive a degree.[13] Still, national data suggest an earnings premium for workers who attended—but did not graduate—from college.[14]

The second issue is the relevance of higher education. While certainly the advanced training that college can provide is essential for many majors, there is also evidence that employers in many fields use a college degree only as a screen, or signal, indicating a level of competence. These employers assume that a college degree means a higher level of skills and a greater ability to learn

FIG. 5.2 Trends in high school dropouts and prison incarcerations in North Carolina.

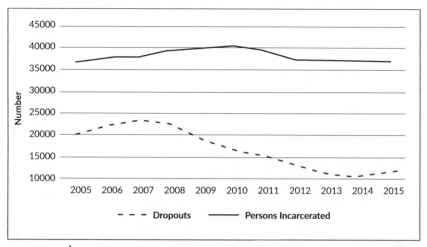

SOURCE: State Board of Education and State Department of Public Instruction, *Report to the Joint Legislative Education Oversight Committee, Consolidated Data Report, 2016* (Raleigh, 2016); North Carolina State Data Center.

and perform for the holder compared to individuals without a college degree.[15] For such employers, the field of study is not important because significant on-the-job training will be provided.[16] Such an attitude obviously calls into question the market value of college instruction as well as the time and money spent by students acquiring a degree.[17]

The third issue is cost. Trends in two costs—gross annual tuition and fees (so-called sticker price) for postsecondary public institutions in North Carolina, and those same tuition and fee averages after subtracting state-provided student grants and nongrants—are shown in fig. 5.3.[18] All dollar values are expressed in inflation-adjusted 2015 dollars. There has been a clear upward trend in student tuition and fees in the early twenty-first century in North Carolina, even after accounting for state assistance.[19] Using annual tuition and fees after subtracting all state aid as the basis of comparison, between 2004 and 2010 the increase was 9 percent; between 2010 and 2015, however, the increase was 55 percent.[20] Over the latter time period (2010–15), the average Federal Pell Grant per student recipient fell 12 percent.[21]

The recent jump in tuition coincides with a reduction in the relative public support in North Carolina for higher education. The percent of state GDP devoted to state appropriations to public higher education fell from 0.85 percent in 2008 to 0.72 percent in 2015. Over the same period the percentage of state GDP spent on tuition and fees rose from 0.28 percent to 0.37 percent.[22]

MAP 5.1 North Carolina Counties (Shaded) with Less than 15 Percent of the Adult Population Having a College Degree and More than 8 Percent of the Adult Population without a High School Degree

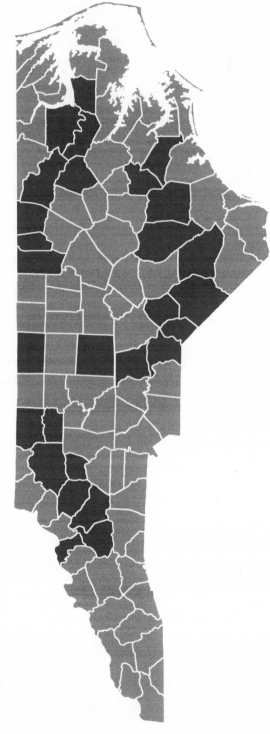

SOURCE: U.S. Census Bureau

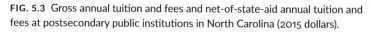

FIG. 5.3 Gross annual tuition and fees and net-of-state-aid annual tuition and fees at postsecondary public institutions in North Carolina (2015 dollars).

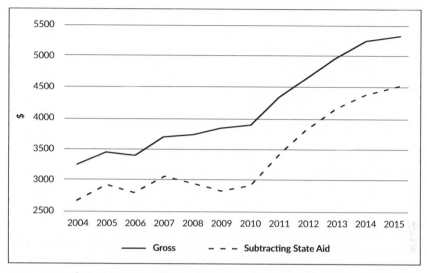

NOTE: costs are for in-state undergraduate students only and are weighted between two-year and four-year institutions by the relative total tuition costs of each (tuition and fees multiplied by number of students).

SOURCE: U.S. Department of Education, "Digest of Education Statistics"; National Association of State Student Grant and Aid Programs.

Numerous other explanations for why college costs have risen have been offered, including growth of administrative costs, inefficient use of teaching resources and an unwillingness to use less costly teaching methods, the increased relative value of a college degree, the need to keep talented faculty from moving to lucrative private-sector positions, the expansion of higher education to pursuits beyond the traditional teaching mission, and the increase in public subsidies for higher education, which—critics claim—have made users (students, parents) less sensitive to price (tuition and fee) increases.[23]

This review of education trends in North Carolina raises many questions. At the K–12 level, how can educational performance be improved from its recent stall? For students performing at very low levels or dropping out, what changes can lead them to educational success, particularly in light of the dominant impact of the students' family and neighborhood backgrounds? At the college level, how can student motivation be improved, how can college work be made more relevant to employers, and how can costs be contained—particularly if public support is reduced? These questions would always be important, but they will become even more urgent as the labor market undergoes a dramatic reshaping in the twenty-first century.

Monitoring Occupational Change

Education has been remade several times since World War II. The Soviets' launch of Sputnik in 1957 prompted the U.S. educational system to increase math and science training. The Civil Rights movement of the 1960s motivated added attention to funding disparities at the K–12 level and access disparities at the postsecondary level. Open classrooms, pre-K education, and the use of technology are other changes that have been implemented—at least partially—by educational systems.

In the twenty-first century, education will have to be reformulated again in order to accomplish the many goals expected of the system—including improving the educational attainment of those individuals who have been academically left behind, rapidly responding to changing career and workplace needs as the economy is continually remade, retraining workers needing to reskill their capabilities, equipping students with the capabilities and knowledge required by the workplace in a way that competencies can be easily perceived and measured by employers, and using new teaching technologies and methods to make education more accessible, relevant, interesting, and cost-effective. Plus, these objectives need to be pursued without overlooking a broader goal of education—to educate individuals to be better informed citizens and cognizant of the opportunities and joys of learning outside of a career—in history, philosophy, and the arts. Together, these aspirations are a tall order for the educational system.

Resetting education in the twenty-first century will first require more information about skills and occupations being downsized and skills and occupations being expanded. These data will keep educational institutions continually informed about how to use their resources to address the changing workplace. As such, the state should develop a process I term a "workplace skills and occupational monitoring system," where employers provide to the state—on a continuing basis—descriptions of jobs created and jobs depleted.[24] Firms' identities would be kept confidential to allay business concerns about such information being used by competitors. However, firms should perceive the value of such information in helping them maintain access to a qualified labor force.

Taking Pre-K through 12 to the Next Level

At the pre-K–12 level, there are two questions to address: What are the most effective teaching techniques to improve educational attainment, and what content should be taught? The early research on teaching techniques compared educational performance measures (such as test scores) at a single point in

TABLE 5.1 Rates of Return from Teaching Techniques

Technique	Study[A]	Annual Rate of Return
Increase per-pupil spending	Jackson, Johnson, and Persico	8.9%[B]
Pre-K schooling	Deming	7.9%
Reduce class size	Fredriksson, Ockert, and Oosterbeek	18%
Boarding schools	Curto and Fryer	5.7%[C]
Improve teacher quality	Chetty, Friedman, and Rockoff	4% to 10%[D]

A: See note 24 for full references.

B: Rate of return is for students from low-income households.

C: Does not include benefits from potential reduction in public costs, such as lower crime and public health expenditures.

D: Rate of return varies by salary increase needed to boost teacher quality; range is based on an annual salary increase of between $10,000 and $15,000 per teacher.

time for schools with different educational inputs (class size, teacher training, spending per student) and usually found little impact on performance from these inputs.[25] Current research has used a more intensive methodology by tracking a variety of both educational and career performance measures over time for students exposed to different levels of educational inputs. The goal is to link educational inputs to adult outcomes.

Recent examples of this research are summarized in table 5.1.[26] The annual rate of return is the ultimate improvement in annual labor earnings of the student as a percentage of the amount invested in the teaching technique. All of the rates of return are positive, ranging from 4 percent to 18 percent, suggesting gains in eventual labor earnings for students from investment in the technique.[27] Boarding schools are a unique approach where students live at the school during the week. They are designed to counter potential adverse impacts on learning from a student's challenging family or neighborhood environment. Although the per pupil costs are estimated to be twice those for traditional public schools, their benefits are estimated to still exceed their costs.[28] Investments in technology are a relatively new technique used to improve student outcomes. To date, however, the evidence is mixed on their effectiveness.[29]

North Carolina's investments in reducing classroom size, increasing per pupil spending, and improving teacher salaries decreased in the early twenty-first century, after being augmented in the late twentieth century (fig. 5.4). The state's pupil-teacher ratio dropped 20 percent from the early 1990s to the mid-2000s, but then reversed and rose. Per pupil spending

FIG. 5.4 Trends in teacher salary and per-pupil spending (left scale) and in class size (right scale) in North Carolina K–12 public schools (salaries and spending in 2015 dollars).

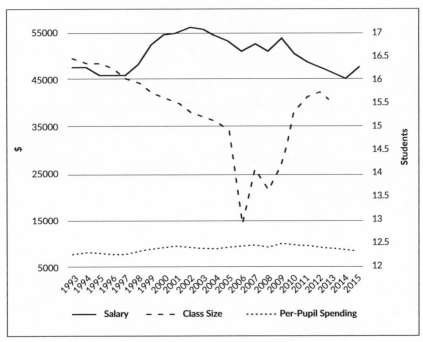

SOURCE: U.S. Department of Education, "Digest of Education Statistics"; North Carolina Department of Public Instruction.

(current expenditures) peaked in 2009 and then fell by 18 percent over the next six years. Average teacher salary has been linked by some to teacher quality.[30] It plunged 20 percent between 2002 and 2014 before modestly rising.[31]

There is also an emerging debate over the relative importance of improving student skills in subject matter material (such as math, science, and composition)—termed "cognitive skills"—versus developing noncognitive skills such as self-control, perseverance, agreeableness, and the willingness to delay gratification. While both types of skills are obviously important, some research suggests that instilling noncognitive skills, especially in early grades, may be vital to success for students acquiring cognitive skills.[32] Then the question becomes one of the process and techniques for achieving noncognitive skill development. Researchers have suggested interventions both by teachers and schools and by parents.[33] However, proper training in behaviors of both teachers and parents for nurturing noncognitive traits are imperative.

North Carolina will have to implement methods to improve K–12 educational performance to meet the labor market challenges of the twenty-first century.[34]

The economic returns to doing so, however, are potentially very large. One analysis estimates that if youths (aged sixteen to twenty-four) in North Carolina who are currently not participating in the labor force were equipped to be productive workers, then the state would realize a gain of $132 billion in additional earnings and reduced public service costs over the lifetime of the individuals.[35] Another study estimates that the real (inflation-adjusted) aggregate earnings of workers could be 72 percent higher in 2050 if achievable improvements in skill levels were attained.[36] Reducing class sizes and increasing per pupil expenditures appear to give the highest rates of return among the educational investments (table 5.1). However, these are average returns that likely vary over time and by circumstance. For example, boarding schools may be the best approach for students coming from household and neighborhood environments that are unsupportive for sustained learning. Therefore, a variety of teaching techniques should be implemented and monitored over time for their effectiveness.[37]

With the cognitive skill demands of workers increasing in the late twentieth and early twenty-first centuries, more high school graduates are attending college. In 1992, 50 percent of North Carolina high school graduates went on to college; by 2010, this rate had risen to 64 percent.[38] One consequence of this change has been a shift in high school curriculum content to college preparatory courses and away from vocational and technical courses that train students in skills and knowledge related to a particular occupation.[39] The percentage of high school credit hours in vocational and technical ("votech") courses dropped 16 percent between 1990 and 2009.[40]

There is a three-point argument that the pendulum has moved too far away from high school courses that provide specific job skills. Supporters of more high school votech courses say that too many high school graduates with little interest in college careers are being pushed to attend college. They use as evidence the one-third of entering college freshman who fail to obtain a degree within six years.[41] Votech promoters also argue that more such courses would address the perceived "male problem" in the economy of men with "physical intelligence" finding no training for those skills in high school.[42] Without an outlet for their interests, the concern is these students can become disinterested and disruptive.[43] Last is the point that the educational system is currently ignoring the careers resulting from votech training, and as a result, shortages of qualified workers in those occupations are already being seen.[44]

There have been moves to reintroduce votech programs in high schools. North Carolina has programs aligning high school courses and community college courses, sometimes resulting in college credit for high school courses.[45]

TABLE 5.2 Alternative Forecasts of Job Availability in Selected Technical Occupations in North Carolina, 2013–2050

Occupation	Using BLS Forecasts			Using Frey/Osborne Forecasts	
	Jobs in 2013	BLS 2050	Annual % Change	Frey/Osborne 2050	Annual % Change
Auto mechanic	20,980	60,419	2.9	32,620	1.2
Barber/hairstylist	7,780	24,074	3.1	21,613	2.8
Brick/cement mason	6,670	23,819	3.5	7,732	0.4
Carpenter	13,480	43,235	3.2	18,779	0.9
Computer programmer	7,200	27,615	3.7	14,447	1.9
Construction equipment operator	8,660	29,839	3.4	9,324	0.2
Electrician	12,960	43,084	3.3	36,004	2.8
HVAC equipment operator	10,800	44,484	3.9	18,065	1.4
Health technician	9,250	24,788	2.7	20,693	2.2
Health support aide	13,890	57,211	3.9	38,588	2.8
Machinist	11,530	32,031	2.8	16,662	1.0
Medical equipment repairer	1,180	6,455	4.7	4,066	3.4
Painter	4,130	12,329	3.0	5,546	0.8
Plumber	8,240	23,730	2.9	16,534	1.9

SOURCE: U.S. Department of Labor, Bureau of Labor Statistics (BLS); Carl Benedikt Frey and Michael A. Osborne, "The Future of Employment: How Susceptible Are Jobs to Computerisation?," Working Paper (Oxford University, September 2013); calculations by the author.

Wake County Public Schools, the state's largest system, opened a stand-alone technical high school in 2014.[46] There have also been calls for the state to expand apprenticeship programs with businesses, similar to what South Carolina has done with its auto manufacturing factories.[47]

Behind the proposals to ramp up votech courses in high schools is the assumption that the economy is lacking in qualified workers for a growing number of jobs in technical occupations. Two forecasts of job availability for a variety of technical occupations in North Carolina are contrasted in table 5.2. Job availability accounts for both job growth and replacement positions due to retirements. The U.S. Bureau of Labor Statistics forecasts are robust, with several occupations having annual availability openings growing above 3 percent annually (the average for all occupations). However, when the technological unemployment predicted by Frey and Osborne is taken into account, the annual growth rates become more modest for many occupations. The annual openings for brick and cement masons would only rise by about one thousand in 2050 compared to 2013, and the number of new carpenters needed to account for growth and retirements would be only five thousand higher in 2050 than in 2013.[48] The fastest growth is predicted for technical occupations in health care (health technician and aides and equipment repairers), personal services (barbers and hairstylists), and—as one holdover from the past—electricians.

The message is that technical fields that could be part of a high school vo-tech program are subject to the same rapid changes taking place in the general job market. Technological advances and applications will continue to affect both the types and numbers of votech occupations in the economy and therefore suitable for high school programs.

Shakeup in Higher Education

Just as in the nation, the college student population has exploded in North Carolina, rising 62 percent from 1990 to 2014.[49] But also like the nation, rising costs, a two-thirds six-year graduation rate, and questions about the quality and relevance of a college education have been raised in the state. These issues will have to be addressed for North Carolina to be competitive in the twenty-first century, particularly with the predicted rapid changes in labor force demands.

The fundamental questions facing higher education are what programs to provide and how to provide them. One issue is between generalization and specialization. Several factors argue for a general college education. First, many surveys of employers indicate that they value soft skills and the intangible benefits from a college education over narrow task skills.[50] In addition, 27 percent of college graduates indicate that they work in a field outside their college major.[51] Last is the realization that a large proportion of today's occupations will be significantly downsized—or perhaps cease to exist—in the future, and economists and others have little ability to predict emerging occupations accurately.

At the same time, occupations are increasingly being fragmented into specific tasks, and employers are often reluctant to provide detailed on-the-job training, especially for skills that can be taken to competitive firms if the employee leaves. In this case, if provision is left to private firms there would be an undersupply of specific skills, therefore providing an argument for acquisition of those skills through the public education system. Then the question becomes the degree to which educational costs are paid by the trainee (student) or by the public sector.

The primary method by which college professors instruct students has changed little since the Middle Ages, with professors lecturing and students listening and taking notes. New learning technology is changing teaching methods, however, and some theorists predict that the lecture format—and perhaps even colleges as educational institutions—may become obsolete.[52] Educational futurists predict that advances in artificial technology will allow for greater customized instruction and interaction with students through technological learning techniques. Some experts forecast that future teaching technology, by continually collecting data on an individual student's learning and comparing that information to extensive data banks of learning information, will be able to quickly and constantly access a student's learning capabilities and problems and develop customized teaching strategies at a speed and effectiveness superior to human instructors.[53]

The recommended twenty-first-century model of the educational system in North Carolina is illustrated in figure 5.5. High schools continue to provide basic skills to students, but with two tracks, one to college (renamed "analytical college") and the second to employment. Training for the employment track would be coordinated with the local community college (renamed "technical college"), where some courses are provided at the high school while others are at the technical college. Some technical programs could be completed at high school, but most will be finished at the technical college. Technical colleges will no longer teach basic skills like writing, reading, and basic math. These will now be mastered at the high school level.[54] Technical colleges will offer only the additional training in these areas needed for a specific technical skill. Also, technical colleges will not be used as stepping stones to analytical colleges, where students with poor high school grades who cannot qualify for today's four-year colleges take basic courses (English, math, and so on) to improve their grades and then transfer to the four-year programs. Technical colleges will focus on technical skills tied to specific occupations.[55]

Traditional four-year colleges and universities ("analytical colleges") will have two components: core and advanced. The core component will teach basic knowledge in broad fields, such as business, social sciences, mathematics, physical sciences, literature, and fine arts. Opportunities for interdisciplinary studies across broad fields would be available. The core component would give students the knowledge and skills in general fields that are long-lasting and not tied to particular occupations or tasks. Teaching of core courses would likely evolve over time as advanced teaching technology supplemented and then replaced some traditional teaching methods. Without the need for coursework preparing the student for a specific occupation and with the expectation that advanced

FIG. 5.5 A twenty-first-century education system.

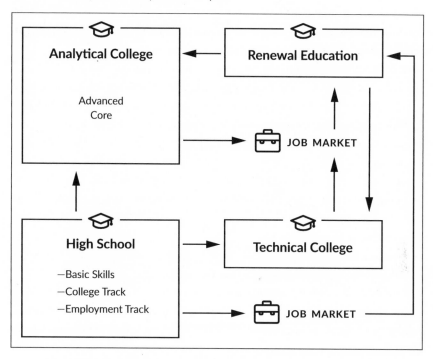

teaching technology would facilitate more rapid student learning, the core component could be completed in a shorter time than today, such as three years.[56]

The second part of the analytical college—the advanced component—will then provide additional training for specific occupations within a broad field. For example, core business majors will train for a specialty in international finance or in risk management, and core science majors would receive advanced training in genetics or in microbiology. The notion is that the advanced training will slot the student for a specific occupation available in the labor market. However, if in the future that occupation becomes obsolete, then the individual will still have the core training that will permit advanced training in other specific occupations. The time required by students in the advanced component will depend on the particular field, with the span likely being between one year and several (five to six for medical specialties) years. Although a mix of teaching methods (traditional and technological) will also be used at the advanced level, mentoring and teaching by in-person professors will likely be more important for the more complex, advanced studies. Technology will be used to increase access of advanced students to national and international teaching experts in their subject field.

All higher education institutions will not necessarily offer both core and advanced training in the future; in fact, there will likely be specialization in core and advanced training. Those institutions focusing on core training will develop expertise in teaching students in basic fields. Little or no research will be done at these institutions. Institutions specializing in advanced training will have a mix of teaching, research, and interaction with private firms. Advanced training institutions could also specialize within advanced fields, with some institutions offering only advanced scientific fields, others offering advanced business fields, and so on.

The ability of individuals already in the job market to seamlessly alter their training and skill set for a different occupation is a key feature of the twenty-first-century education system. This element is represented by the label "renewal education" in fig. 5.5. All workers in the job market—those with terminal high school degrees, terminal technical college degrees, and even graduates with analytical college degrees—face a significant possibility that their chosen occupation may be downsized or even eliminated during their work career. A big reason, as discussed earlier, is advances in technology. The education system of the twenty-first century must accept this reality and accommodate it. The arrows from the job markets to renewal education in fig. 5.5 represent high school, technical college, and analytical college graduates who find that they need to renew their education sometime during their work career. The arrows in fig. 5.5 then show those individuals returning to technical and analytical colleges for retraining. The educational system should strive to allow individuals to renew their training in a time-efficient manner.

Although the discussion of fig. 5.5 has been in the context of publicly supported higher education institutions, private for-profit companies providing higher educational learning will likely expand and compete with publicly supported institutions in the future. Some of these could be completely cyber-institutions providing digital degrees.[57] With minimal staff and no infrastructure, tuition costs would be very low. The private institutions would likely focus on instruction in core fields and topics.

Indeed, cybereducation and private educational companies could expand to such a degree as to cause a massive contraction of publicly supported colleges and universities.[58] These colleges and universities could transform into what one futurist terms "educational colonies."[59] Here, the concentration would be on the advanced educational training required by private companies. The private companies would share in the funding for research, infrastructure, and staffing with the public sector. North Carolina State University's Centennial Campus can be viewed as an early version of such an educational colony.[60]

These possible changes in the traditional structure of higher education will be massive and controversial, amounting to what some have dubbed the "disruption" of the modern higher education system.[61] In addition, with so much churning expected in the future labor market, a challenge for the twenty-first-century educational system will be altering occupationally focused fields of study. The system will need to have the ability—and exercise that ability—to rapidly delete some fields while adding other fields. This will not be easy. Structures, bureaucracies, personnel, and even equipment are developed around fields of study. Strong leaders will be required, particularly at the college levels, to reallocate resources as conditions require.

The value and relevance of college degrees, particularly for analytical colleges, can be enhanced by implementing competency tests for major fields of study.[62] Similar to state bar exams and national CPA tests, nationally consistent competency tests for each major and degree would ensure for employers a level of knowledge by graduates. Students would know that they ultimately faced a standard test taken by all their peers, and this realization should work to improve student focus and study habits. The tests would also work to level the playing field among educational institutions as well as among learning methods. That is, a student attending a college with a modest or unknown reputation who passed the competency test with high scores could presumably be considered just as valuable to an employer as a graduate from a well-known, high-reputation school. Likewise, a student who chose to obtain a degree through a low-cost method like distance education or app learning and who passed the competency test with flying colors would logically also be rewarded in the labor market. Competency tests would be best implemented nationally, but North Carolina could be a leader in implementing a state version.

To address college costs, experimentation with all forms of alternative learning methods should be encouraged and evaluated. This includes online classes, distance learning, learning via apps and videos, and traditional methods. There should also be efforts to speed the acquisition of degrees and competencies, with the expectation that more individuals will be returning to college for training in new careers. As technology replaces some buildings and faculty, the cost curve for postsecondary education could be bent downward.[63]

The University of North Carolina system has already made two changes in tuition policy designed to increase the speed of degree completion. Beginning in 2010, undergraduate students taking more than four years to complete their degree pay a substantial tuition surcharge (first 25 percent, later increased to 50 percent) for additional years of study.[64] Also in 2016, the state passed legislation freezing the tuition levels for entering freshman for four years of study at public university campuses.[65] Students taking longer than four years to achieve their degree would pay the current tuition rate prevailing in those years plus the tuition surcharge. These two rules provide powerful financial incentives for students to finish their degrees on time. Statistics following the 2010 change already showed an improvement in the efficiency rate at which students completed degrees.[66]

Last, innovative financing methods could be tested. Purdue University has implemented a loan—some call it income sharing—program in which students repay tuition loans once they are working based on a set period, interest rate, and proportion of salary. A unique element is that the loan terms vary by the student's major.[67] Another plan repays student college loans through the appreciation of assets eventually purchased by the graduate.[68] As formal education beyond high school becomes more necessary, the financial sector will likely develop a range of lending options.

A Rapid-Response Education System

The education system of the future will be both more rigid and more flexible than today's system. It will be more rigid in having a clearer demarcation of responsibilities for each component (pre-K–12, technical college, core analytical college, advanced analytical college) and clearer expectations for performance (mastery of basic skills at high school, college degree competency exams). But it will be more flexible in accommodating alternative learning methods, allowing for individualized speeds in acquiring education and training, and facilitating seamless reentry into the educational system as job skills required by the market change.

In describing the dynamics of the twentieth-century U.S. job market as a "race between education and technology," Claudia Goldin and Lawrence Katz meant that as technological developments destroyed some jobs, greater amounts of education had to be acquired to obtain a good job.[69] This race will continue in the twenty-first century, but with a twist. In the past, higher levels of education (meaning college education) usually guaranteed a job for a lifetime. This will not be the case in the twenty-first century. Technology increasingly will compete with human labor at all levels of education, including college training. So, the race might be better termed as being "between *newly created occupations* and technology." Education, training, and skills will constantly have to morph, adapt, and restructure to remain relevant to the new occupations generated in the economy. Many workers will go through a revolving door of changing their skill set over their work career. A rapid-response education system will be needed to accommodate this reality.

The decisions made in revamping education for the twenty-first century may be the most important facing public decision-makers in North Carolina. These decisions will literally make or break the state's adjustment to the new work environment, and the decisions will go a long way in determining the standard of living achieved by many of North Carolina's residents.

Certainly human skills and competencies are vital factors that affect economic growth. But so, too, are resources like water and energy. With the state's population expected to continue expanding in the century, will resources—or, more specifically, the lack of resources—put a severe limit on economic growth and the lifestyles most enjoy? The next chapter focuses on these important issues.

6. REQUIEM FOR RESOURCES?

Is Time Running Out?

North Carolina is known for its uncommon beauty and natural resources. The state's coast, forests and national parks, rivers and lakes, mountains, and world-class golf courses nestled in valleys and the flat Piedmont plateau are major attractions and contribute enormously to the quality of life enjoyed by its inhabitants. These natural resources are important for luring tourists as well as for attracting new permanent residents.

Yet these resources may be at risk in coming decades from several sources. Concern about climate change is ongoing, and two dangers are prominent. One is from heating of the planet, potentially resulting in rising coastal water levels, with obvious implications for tourism and the coastal economy. The second is what an upward trend in atmospheric temperatures might mean for the economy of North Carolina, particularly in agriculture and agribusiness.

A related worry is population growth. If North Carolina does add more than three million new people by 2050, their dwellings will need to be heated and cooled, appliances and electronic devices powered, and vehicles fueled. Moreover, the added households will require water for living, irrigation, and recreation. These uses will increase demands for electricity and water for homes and businesses and for fuels for heating and transportation. Where will these resources come from, and what will their provision and use do to the state's air and water quality and environmental attractiveness?

Will the twenty-first century be a time when North Carolina's natural resources and environment deteriorate beyond the point of no return, thereby eliminating one of the biggest advantages of living and working in the Tar Heel State? Or will time, technology, and a change in habits be enough to avert the calamity and preserve—as many think—what really makes North Carolina home?

Rising Levels?

If the predictions of some come true, the physical geography of North Carolina could be very different in the mid-twenty-first century. Global warming could cause two important measures to rise: sea levels and temperature levels. Higher sea levels would disrupt the coastal economy of North Carolina by moving the coastline inward and destroying a significant amount of property values and income-earning opportunities. Higher temperatures would most directly affect the agricultural economy of the state and could also have broader effects on energy usage, water use, and living patterns.

Predicting changes in sea levels and temperatures is both difficult and contentious. In the public discourse over these issues, competing positions have been hardened to the point that consensus among alternative viewpoints has been difficult to achieve.[1] The analysis presented here does not attempt to reconcile the ideas of those who argue that global warming is occurring with those who claim it is not. Instead, a "what if" approach is used. Assuming that there is a nontrivial chance that global warming is happening, what might be the impacts on North Carolina's coastal economy, agricultural economy, and overall economy? This way, state leaders and citizens can gauge how important global warming might be—if it is occurring.

Sea Invasion

North Carolina has one of the most expansive and alluring coastlines of any state. Spanning three hundred miles, it is interspersed with a series of barrier islands that have become prime playgrounds for coastal tourists—the economic livelihood of the region—and the home to thousands of households. In 2013, the seven coastal counties of the state had an annual GDP of $29 billion, employment of 384,000, a population of 697,000, and real property values of $96 billion. These values make significant contributions to the aggregate state economy, accounting for 6 percent of GDP, 9 percent of employment, 7 percent of population, and 12 percent of property values.[2]

Rising sea levels would threaten these numbers—literally—by moving the coastline inland (to the west) and making significant amounts of land, infrastructure (highways and utilities), residences, and businesses unusable. Even though buildings and infrastructure could be replaced, the economy still suffers by having the monies spent on replacement displaced from spending in other sectors.[3]

Since the potential existence and extent of global warming has been vociferously debated, it should not be surprising that there are several forecasts of possible sea level increases at North Carolina's coastline, with the difference exceeding 100 percent.[4] However, there is some consistency among the forecasts. Most of the barrier islands would be affected. On the mainland, counties in the north and central parts of the state's coast would be highly vulnerable, and Wilmington would be affected under the most severe forecasts.

The potential economic losses to the coastal North Carolina economy from rising sea levels are significant. Using a midrange sea level rise projection, academic researchers calibrated a cumulative $7.8 billion (2015 dollars) total residential and nonresidential property value loss and a cumulative $4.5 billion (2015 dollars) income loss to the tourism and fishing industries from the sea level rise through 2080.[5] The property value loss is 8 percent of total regional property values.

Such losses would be crippling for the coastal economy, similar to a slowly unfolding and continuous recession. A key question for North Carolina would be the availability of external funding—mainly from the federal government—for recovery of the losses and rebuilding. However, an issue with reliance on federal government assistance is that, if sea levels indeed rise, they would do so along all coasts and potentially generate multiple trillions of dollars of aggregate damages. This would strain even the resources of the federal government to compensate for those losses.

Still, unlike a hurricane, the adverse economic effects of a rising sea level would occur slowly over decades, thereby allowing both the private and public sectors time to react and possibly relocate economic activities. The economic losses would still occur, but with the losses spread over a long time frame, they would be easier to address. Continued monitoring of coastal sea levels will thus be essential for detecting trends and developing plans for addressing costs.

Suffering or Shifting Agriculture?

If global warming is occurring—and continues to occur—the effects on North Carolina's agriculture will be complex. Higher temperatures reduce yields for some crops and increase expenses for others to maintain yields. Countering these negative effects are a longer growing season and the potential for increased carbon dioxide that actually aids the production of many crops. Animals are also stressed by higher temperatures, but this stress can be controlled for the livestock raised in North Carolina (predominantly poultry and swine) by keeping the animals in climate-controlled enclosures.[6] Farmers and agricultural scientists have also shown a great ability to develop techniques that allow agriculture to adapt to changing climate conditions over time. Thus, if climate change transpires gradually over several decades, ways may be found to mitigate its adverse effects.[7]

North Carolina's agriculture has shifted from crop production to livestock production during the past several decades. In 1950, cash receipts from crops were 80 percent of total farm receipts; in 1980, they were still almost 60 percent of total receipts; but in 2012, livestock cash receipts had taken over and were 63 percent of total farm receipts.[8] Among North Carolina's crops, corn, soybeans, cotton, and tobacco account for almost 60 percent of receipts.[9] Research shows that corn and soybean yields are more adversely affected by temperature increases than are cotton and tobacco.[10] So one long-run impact of global warming on North Carolina agriculture might be two shifts. One would be a further move from crop production to livestock production, which would reinforce the long-run trend experienced in the state and complement the anticipated future expansion of livestock farming resulting from global dietary changes. The second shift would be within crop production, with a movement away from corn and soybeans to cotton and tobacco as well as some specialty crops (fruits, nuts, vegetables).[11]

With so much uncertainty surrounding the varied effects of global warming, it should not be surprising that numeric estimates of the phenomenon's total impact on agriculture are quite varied. Researchers have found negative effects ranging from a 4 percent to 80 percent drop in yields, yet some studies have concluded that agricultural production would actually benefit from higher temperatures and greater levels of carbon dioxide.[12]

The losses to the North Carolina economy for a range of reductions in agricultural production are shown in table 6.1. Two sets of losses are displayed: losses confined to the farming level, and losses including the farming level and the associated food-processing industry in the state. Both sets include the direct losses to the agricultural industry plus the corresponding losses to suppliers. The loss calculations do not, however, include mitigating effects from possible shifts in agricultural production away from those farm industries most sensitive to global warming to the least sensitive farm industries. Hence, for each output loss percentage, the losses should be considered as the worst-case scenario outcome.

The losses (all in 2015 dollars) reach serious levels—especially when the processing level is included—for farm output reductions of 10 percent or greater. Hence, if the most damaging of the global warming predictions occur, the economic impact on North Carolina could be very large. Or, optimistically, the dramatic advances achieved in agricultural productivity will continue and counteract any potential losses from global warming.[13]

TABLE 6.1 Potential Total Annual Losses to the North Carolina Economy from Global Warming's Negative Impact on Farming and Affiliated Industries (Using a 2015 GDP Baseline)

Output loss	Farm Level Loss ($ Billions)	Farm Level Loss (Jobs)	Farm and Processing Levels Loss ($ Billions)	Farm and Processing Levels Loss (Jobs)
2%	0.14	880	1.4	2,730
4%	0.29	1,760	2.8	5,460
10%	0.71	4,400	7.0	13,650
20%	1.43	8,800	14.0	27,300
30%	2.15	13,200	21.0	40,950

SOURCE: U.S. Department of Commerce; IMPLAN for North Carolina; author's calculations. Total North Carolina GDP in 2015 was $499 billion and total North Carolina payroll employment in 2015 was 4.2 million. All dollar values are in 2013 purchasing-power dollars.

Too Many People, Too Little Water?

North Carolina's natural resources, particularly water resources, will face increased usage in the twenty-first century as a result of the state's continued population growth. As indicated in chapter 1, the state's population is projected to increase by 3.8 million—a 40 percent increase—between 2010 and 2050. Using a total water consumption rate of 1,464 gallons per person per day, this means 5.6 billion *additional* gallons of daily water usage in the state in 2050 compared to 2010.[14] Plus, there could be greater usage of water by farmers to counter increased moisture evaporation from soil caused by global warming.

Compounding these increased demands is the possibility that weather changes in the twenty-first century may make water supplies more unstable. Some scientists claim that one result of global warming is more periods of heavy rainfall followed by stretches of drought.[15] This creates a feast or famine situation of rain, runoff, and flooding during some years and drought, parched soil, and low reservoirs in other years. Uncertain water supplies will adversely affect heavy water users like agriculture and population centers.

There are two ways of dealing with this situation—one on the supply side and the other on the demand side—and North Carolina will have to consider both in the twenty-first century. The size of the state's water capacity (supply) could be increased through the construction of new reservoirs or the expansion of existing reservoirs. Or the growth in usage (demand) could be moderated by improvements in the efficiency of water use (gallons used per person) or by implementing innovative pricing techniques.

North Carolina has several major water reservoirs, mainly in the highly populated Piedmont (central) region and in the western mountains. The permeable sandy soil of the coastal plain makes it difficult to construct reservoirs. Only two major reservoirs have been built in North Carolina since 1987. One reason is cost. To supply the additional 5.6 billion gallons of daily water usage for North Carolina's expected growth between 2010 and 2050 could require reservoir capacity construction costing between $24 billion and $59 billion (2015 dollars).[16] Another reason is potential negative side effects of reservoirs on downstream communities. Reservoirs built by blocking river flows (the typical case) reduce the water availability to communities farther downriver (toward the river's terminus) from the reservoir. Thus, although reservoirs may benefit the communities they serve, the structures may impede water usage in other communities. This has become more of an issue as North Carolina has experienced population growth.[17]

Lakes Kerr and Gaston are large reservoirs north of the growing Triangle market and straddling the North Carolina and Virginia border. Lake Gaston supplies the city of Virginia Beach (part of the Hampton Roads metropolitan area) and is largely off-limits to North Carolina. During the severe drought of 2007–8 there was discussion of reconsidering the building of a fifty-mile-long pipeline connecting Kerr Lake and the Triangle metropolitan area (mainly Raleigh).[18] Such an endeavor, however, would require agreements between both states and several communities.

Therefore, considering both the difficulty and the cost of developing more water capacity, North Carolina will have to increase reliance on demand-side strategies of improved efficiencies in water usage and alternative water pricing techniques. The challenge faced by the state in improving water usage efficiency is shown in fig. 6.1. Two measures of water efficiency are shown: daily usage (gallons) per person, and daily usage per dollar of North Carolina GDP (in 2015 dollars). Both measures improved (fell) in the decade 1985–1995 decade; per person consumption then rose in the next decade, 1995–2005, before leveling off in 2005–10. Consumption per GDP has shown little fluctuation since the mid-1990s.

One way to improve water efficiency is through greater water recycling. Technologies exist to treat household wastewater (gray water) at the individual residential unit. Alternatively, household wastewater can be piped upstream to a treatment plant, treated, and then released for reuse in the community. Studies suggest that implementation of water recycling methods can significantly reduce usage rates, by as much as 27 percent to 38 percent depending on the residential structure.[19]

FIG. 6.1 North Carolina water usage efficiency.

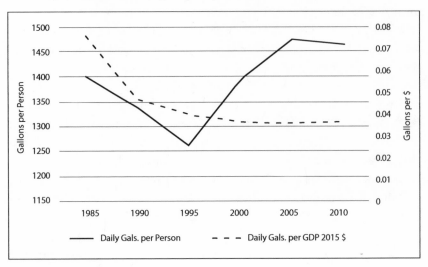

NOTE: N.C. GDP in 1985 is estimated from personal income.
SOURCE: North Carolina State Data Center; U.S. Department of Commerce.

Tiered pricing of water use is another way to achieve conservation. Rather than a rate charged per used gallon that is the same for all amounts of water consumption, users pay progressively higher rates per gallon for greater quantities of water used. For example, consider the Jones and Smith households. Jones uses 1,500 gallons per month while Smith uses 3,000 gallons per month. A flat water rate would mean both Jones and Smith pay the same price per gallon—say, one cent per gallon. An example of a tiered system would be one cent for each of the first thousand gallons, two cents per gallon for each of the next thousand gallons (gallons 1,001–2,000), and three cents per gallon for any additional gallons.[20] So Jones pays one cent per gallon for gallons 1–1,000 and two cents per gallon for gallons 1,001–1,500. But Smith pays one cent per gallon for gallons 1–1,000, two cents per gallon for gallons 1,001–2,000, and three cents per gallon for gallons 2,001–3,000. Smith, especially, faces a financial incentive to reduce water consumption.

Research has shown that tiered pricing can be a powerful way to reduce water consumption voluntarily. Estimates range from a 10 percent to 30 percent reduction in consumption rates, with the most careful study showing a 17 percent drop in water consumed per day.[21] Raleigh introduced tiered water pricing in 2010 and experienced a 10 percent reduction in per capita consumption during the following three years.[22] Furthermore, such reductions can be achieved with only modest increases in average rates paid.[23] Almost half

(47 percent) of residential water customers in North Carolina already pay some form of tiered rates.[24]

North Carolina would have to reduce its per capita water consumption by 28 percent between 2010 and 2050 to avoid constructing new reservoirs to service the increased state population over that period. This is a doable goal that could be achieved through a variety of combinations of expanding tiered rates and increasing water use efficiency. For example, applying tiered rates to 75 percent of water users and implementing wastewater recycling for 72 percent of users would achieve the reduction. Alternatively, applying tiered rates to 100 percent of water uses and using wastewater recycling for 60 percent of users would also reduce the consumption rate by 28 percent.[25]

Water is the source of life. Considered plentiful and free when our population was smaller and the economy simpler, water is increasingly scarce, and pricing is therefore necessary to minimize waste and maximize efficient use. Expanding the use of tiered pricing first will motivate the private sector to respond with the technology for reuse of wastewater. By midcentury, most North Carolinians could consider these techniques the norm. Both local and state policy makers will find water issues a top priority in order to satisfy household use and attract new and expanding businesses.

How Will We Be Powered?

How North Carolina's economy will be powered in the future will be determined by two factors: the efficiency of energy consumed and the type of energy used. Dramatic changes are expected for both elements as the state moves to midcentury.

There has been very good news on energy efficiency. Like the nation as a whole, North Carolina has been using fewer units of energy to produce each dollar of economic output as well as to sustain each person (fig. 6.2). Between 2010 and 2014, total energy consumption in the state actually dropped.[26] This is even though the state's economy is using more energy-powered products in everyday life than in previous decades. The best example of the gains in energy efficiency is in transportation. Average miles per gallon (mpg) for drivers rose 22 percent between 2000 and 2014.[27]

The gains in energy efficiency have been achieved through a combination of private incentives and government regulation. The price of energy rose over 50 percent faster than other prices between 1980 and 2007.[28] The created a natural motivation for energy consumers to reduce consumption and favor products that used energy more frugally. Supporting this trend, government

FIG. 6.2 Energy consumption in North Carolina and the United States.

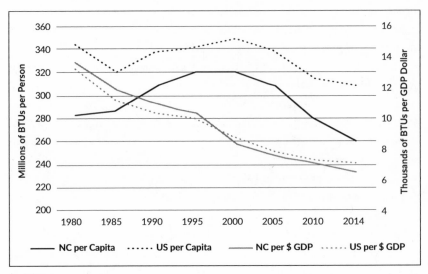

NOTE: GDP is in 2015 dollars.
SOURCE: U.S. Department of Energy, Energy Information Agency.

(primarily the federal government) began mandating improvements in energy efficiency, especially in transportation, in 1975. The required miles per gallon for passenger cars was increased 67 percent (from 18 mpg to 30 mpg) from 1978 to 2011.[29]

Some futurists predict that energy efficiency will continue to improve in the twenty-first century—maybe even at accelerated rates.[30] There are two reasons for this optimism. One is advancements in the capability of technology to monitor and alter energy use. Homes and businesses of the future will be equipped to minimize energy losses, detect energy waste, and move many energy uses to off-peak times, thereby reducing the need to build more peak-time capacity.[31] The other is the continuing introduction of more energy-efficient products and machinery, from vehicles to dishwaters to stoves. With electricity rates, in particular, anticipated to continue to rise and government mandates for improved energy efficiency continuing to be enforced, it is expected that the economic incentive for greater energy efficiency will be maintained.[32]

With no change in energy efficiency, total energy consumption in North Carolina would increase 133 percent between 2014 and 2050.[33] If the improvement in state energy efficiency between 1980 and 2014 continued until 2050, then total energy consumption in the state would increase by only 13 percent between 2014 and 2050. However, if the state's annual improvement in energy efficiency could be increased 15 percent (from 1.3 percent to 1.5 percent), then the state's larger economy in 2050 could be fueled by the same amount of total energy used in 2014. Clearly, gains in energy efficiency are the key to minimizing North Carolina's need to construct new energy capacity.

The second major question about energy in North Carolina—what sources will provide it—is also expected to see big changes. North Carolina has traditionally relied more on coal and nuclear sources for its power and less on natural gas and oil. For example, in 2014, coal supplied 19.6 percent of the state's power compared to 18.3 percent for the nation overall, and nuclear power accounted for 16.8 percent of the state's power versus 8.5 percent for the nation. In contrast, the state used natural gas for 18 percent of its power compared to 27.9 percent for the nation, and oil was the source of 31.3 percent of the state's power versus 35.6 percent in the nation.[34]

Coal and nuclear will likely have their shares significantly reduced in future decades. Coal's usage will drop due to tighter pollution standards favored by the Environmental Protection Agency.[35] Duke Energy, the largest producer of electricity in the state, closed nine coal-fueled power plants in North Carolina between 2011 and 2013 and has plans to close more.[36] After announcing plans to expand the Shearon Harris Nuclear Power Plant in central North Carolina in 2008, Duke Energy canceled the plans in 2013, citing a lack of need.[37] Cost and issues with storage of spent nuclear fuel were also likely reasons.[38]

Natural gas will be the main replacement for coal and nuclear power in meeting the state's future energy consumption. Although approval for the exploration of natural gas within the state was granted in 2015, the consensus opinion is that only modest supplies would be recovered even if the exploration was deemed profitable.[39] Instead, the state's natural gas will increasingly come from the large production fields in Ohio and Pennsylvania. A new natural gas pipeline running the eastern length of the state will accommodate the supplies and should also improve economic development opportunities in eastern rural regions.[40] The new pipeline would match an existing line in the western part of the state.

Renewable energy sources—mainly solar, wind, and biomass—will also experience usage growth in the early to mid-twenty-first century, but the question is how much. Cost and storage continue to be the two big issues. North Carolina has the capacity for solar power, with an average of 2,651 hours of sun annually, the twenty-fourth most among the states.[41] However, for plants entering service in 2020, solar power is still estimated to be 67 percent more expansive than natural gas and 32 percent costlier than conventional coal and nuclear power.[42]

Still, the cost disadvantage of solar power has been falling, and some analysis suggests that it will be cost competitive with other sources as soon as 2020, even if government subsidies are discontinued.[43] Yet if this occurs, for solar power to be truly competitive, significant improvements in storage capacity will have to be advanced. Only then will solar power permit reductions in peak capacities carried by traditional sources.[44]

There is currently only one commercial wind power facility planned in North Carolina.[45] Wind power is possible in the state, but only at coastal and mountain counties where wind speeds are strong and consistent enough to generate adequate power.[46] Offshore wind power is still more expensive than other power sources, but—like other technologies—costs could fall as usage increased.[47] Use of wind power in other states has exposed environmental and wildlife concerns, so proper siting to minimize these impacts is important.[48] Storage of the intermittent power and construction of the infrastructure to deliver the power to users are also considerations for wind power.

Biomass power is energy generated from organic materials, such as wood. Production of power from biomass sources is sixteen times greater as solar power production in North Carolina. Biomass power also contributes a higher percentage of the state's total power (5.7 percent) than it does for the nation overall (4.7 percent).[49] Biomass power in North Carolina is mainly from wood waste. It is currently less expensive than solar and wind power, approximately comparable in cost to conventional coal power, but 25 percent costlier than power generated from natural gas.[50] There are also potential environmental concerns with biomass power.[51]

The most challenging issue for generating power from biomass sources is space. The biomass source (wood, crops) needs room to grow. To meet 10 percent of North Carolina's annual energy needs requires approximately one million acres of growing space, from a total of thirty-two million acres in the state.[52] Competing uses for North Carolina's land therefore limits the amount of energy generated from biomass sources.

The U.S. Department of Energy has provided national forecasts of the uses of major energy sources in future decades.[53] These forecasts were applied to North Carolina's existing energy source profile in 2014 to derive the state's expected power sources in 2050 (table 6.2).

The shifts in power sources observed in North Carolina in recent decades are expected to continue. Reliance on coal and nuclear will decline, while usage of natural gas, oil, and renewable sources will increase. The increased use of oil and natural gas will be driven by enhanced supplies, while the growth of renewable sources—mainly solar—will reflect improved price competitiveness.[54] Hydropower—a minor source of power provision statewide but very

TABLE 6.2 North Carolina Power Sources in 2014 and 2050

Power source	2014^	2050
Coal	19.6%	15.7%
Nuclear	16.8%	12.6%
Oil	31.3%	34.6%
Natural gas	18.0%	24.3%
Hydropower	1.8%	1.5%
Renewable	6.1%	11.3%

SOURCE: U.S. Department of Energy, Energy Information Agency; calculations by the author.
A: Percentages do not add to 100 due to exclusion of net interstate flows of energy to the state.

important in western counties—will decline in relative importance because new projects are not expected to be constructed.

Cleaning up Our Mess

Environmental awareness awoke in the late twentieth century, and since then considerable progress has been made in reducing the levels of pollutants released into the environment. In North Carolina between 2000 and 2013, annual emissions of the major air pollutant carbon dioxide dropped 17.8 percent on a total tonnage basis and even more (33 percent) on a tonnage per capita basis. Both reductions were greater than those at the national level. Reductions were also achieved in lowering carbon dioxide used per energy unit (btu) and per economic output (GDP) in the state, and these improvements also exceeded national gains.[55] In 2000, the American Lung Association gave twenty-six of thirty-one North Carolina counties surveyed a grade of F on the number of unhealthy high ozone days. In 2014, they assigned a grade of F to only four of forty-five counties surveyed on the same criteria. All four counties were part of the state's largest and fast-growing metropolitan region of Charlotte (Lincoln, Mecklenburg, and Rowan) or the Triad metropolitan area (Forsyth).[56]

The air quality issue in the state's large metropolitan regions is driven by auto emissions.[57] Even though pollutant emissions per vehicle have been significantly reduced, the number of vehicles in large urban areas continues to increase.[58] There are likely three paths for addressing the issue. One is based on technology—specifically in replacing oil-based gasoline-powered vehicles with either electric or natural gas–powered vehicles. Both alternative vehicles are technically possible, but both have a variety of challenges, including cost, performance, and fueling infrastructure.[59] Electric vehicles currently seem to have the edge in cost and performance, and the vehicles can be fueled at users' residences.[60] Some futurists even see rental driverless vehicles potentially reducing the total number of vehicles needed by 80 percent to 90 percent, with a corresponding improvement in air quality.[61]

The second path is to use economic theory's standard approach to pollution. This is to apply a fee to the pollutant and thereby motivate creators to reduce pollution levels voluntarily.[62] For gasoline-powered vehicles, the fee would typically be added to the price of gasoline with the expectation that drivers would respond by driving less, increasing ride-sharing, living closer to their place of work, making greater use of available mass transit, or purchasing alternatively powered vehicles. Indeed, revenues from the emissions tax would best be used to financially support these mobility options. Results from metropolitan areas that have instituted such emissions fees indicate that they can achieve a decline in pollutants and an improvement in air quality. However, the studies show that the per gallon fee would need to be substantial in order to obtain significant pollution reductions.[63]

The third path to reducing vehicle pollution is to encourage a shift from individual vehicles to mass transit for moving people. The energy used to transport individuals a given distance is considerably less for mass transit—buses and trains—than for vehicles.[64] Hence, with less energy used per trip for mass transit, emissions are reduced.[65] However, construction costs for systems such as light rail are significantly higher—maybe three times so—per mile than for a comparable highway.[66] Balancing these costs are not only the reduction in energy use and pollution but also lessened traffic congestion and the potential for increased property values along the transit lines.[67] One way to offset both the higher construction and operating costs of mass transit is to apply revenues collected from the pollution fee on individual vehicles. Another funding source is taxation of the increased property values near the mass transit operation.[68] With increased urbanization expected in North Carolina and with a continuing issue with air quality in large urban areas, mass transit will increasingly look better over time as a transportation option.

Although significant gains have been made in water quality for human use in the state, concerns remain about the quality of the state's surface waters for aquatic life and fish consumption.[69] Many of these apprehensions are directly related to an industry that has grown to be big business in North Carolina, especially in rural areas: the hog industry. Waste from large hog farms has presented a continuing problem for water pollution.

As already discussed, North Carolina agriculture has undergone nothing short of a total makeover in the past half century. The state's farming moved from being dominated by crops—particularly tobacco—to being led by livestock—mainly poultry and hogs. This shift helped rural areas cope with the decline in domestic tobacco usage and allowed them to benefit from the increase in domestic and international meat consumption. The shift literally saved North Carolina agriculture from being an insignificant and irrelevant economic sector.

A central challenge from the expansion of meat farming is the disposal of waste. Chicken production grew 65 percent between 1992 and 2014, and there's been a corresponding increase in chicken waste.[70] Chicken litter is often spread on fields as fertilizer; however, this litter can release nitrogen (a water pollutant) into the groundwater and waterways. Even more challenging is the increase in hog waste from the 334 percent jump in hog production between 1992 and 2014.[71] Liquid hog waste is stored in large lagoons, many of which were damaged during Hurricane Floyd in 1999 and spilled their contents over large areas of eastern North Carolina.[72] When the lagoons are kept intact, their contents become fertilizer and are sprayed over crop fields. Although the resulting nutrients provided to crops are beneficial, those same nutrients can also enter the groundwater and waterways as pollutants that promote algae growth and kill wildlife.[73]

The number of hog farms in the state was capped in 1997, in part to allow time for scientists to find a technical solution to the disposal of hog waste.[74] As of 2015, no waste disposal technologies had been found that would not increase costs, reduce herd sizes, and reduce profits to hog farmers.[75] Hence, the state's hog industry is in limbo. As discussed in chapter 3, there will be increased foreign opportunities for meat sales that would allow for expansion of meat production in the state and income gains in mainly rural counties. Yet much of this cannot happen until the environmental issues with hog waste are solved.

Technology and Economics to the Rescue?

The natural beauty and environmental quality of North Carolina is something that cannot be created. Once damaged, it is hard—perhaps impossible—to reclaim. Population growth, climate change, and expanding production will put increased pressure on our air, water, and land in the twenty-first century.

Perhaps ironically, two factors that some blame for stress on the environment—technology and the capitalist system—could be used to rescue our environment. The hope is that technology can be used to reduce consumption rates of natural resources, and prices (the heart of the capitalist system) can be appropriately applied to motivate households and businesses to be more frugal users of water and fuel.[76]

But can environmental issues, as well as other challenges like education, workforce training, and economic development, be addressed privately, or will public action be required? More broadly, what should be the role of government in our twenty-first-century economy and life? This is the important question addressed in the next chapter.

7. GOVERNMENT'S ROLE—LEAN IN OR BACK OFF?

Rethinking Government's Purpose

Government in North Carolina will have to change to successfully address the challenges beyond the Connected Age. Although it appears contradictory, government will have to do both more in some areas and less in others. The realignment of government functions will be difficult, and considerable political tension will ensue during the process. However, without it North Carolina may miss opportunities provided by the new economy and suffer more of the costs associated with the fast-moving transformation of economic sectors.

The needed reorientation of government will occur on both sides of the public ledger: revenues and expenditures. The future revenue structure will require several adjustments. It will have to be flexible enough to accommodate rapid changes in the composition of the economy. It will have to be sensitive to the new ways businesses and individuals earn income—therefore being formulated in such a way as to not inhibit new ventures and earnings methods. It will also need to be supportive of households in occupational transition—a situation that is expected to accelerate as the century proceeds.

On the spending side, the dominant tension will be generational: between programs committed to assisting the growing retirement segment of the population and programs helping those entering the workforce as well as those in transition within the workforce. The key to resolving this tension will be improved program efficiency, particularly in the delivery of educational programs and health care programs. Technology will be the major factor in enhancing results per dollar spent and allowing government to fulfill its multiple roles in the dynamic and—for many—challenging economy.

A central public question of the twenty-first century will be the role of government in economic development. To what degree can government, particularly at the state level, guide and promote business and job creation? The political motivation is to accommodate citizens who often want government to "do something" to improve their lives. However, is this role possible—and even productive—during a period of rapid, uncertain, and often unexpected change in the economic landscape?

A Twenty-First-Century Tax System

North Carolina's tax system has undergone several makeovers in the state's history. In the nineteenth-century agrarian economy, local government spending dominated state government spending and the tax on the major form of wealth—property—was the primary revenue generator. This system was logical in an economy dominated by farms, slow transportation and little communication, and small cities and towns.

The rise of manufacturing, urbanization, and faster forms of interaction in the early twentieth century created demands for more public services in education, utilities (water, sewer, electricity), and transportation (road building). North Carolina's shift of education and transportation spending from local governments to the state government combined with the institution of state-level income and sales taxes in the 1930s moved government power to the state and reduced the reliance on property taxes.[1]

The twentieth-century structure of state taxation remained largely intact in the twenty-first century with one exception. As the service economy grew and the manufacturing economy declined in relative size, the sales tax base contracted. This was because the original state sales tax constructed in the 1930s was applied to sales of manufactured products—the simple reason being that the service sector was largely nonexistent. As retail sales of services expanded, the sales tax was not altered to keep up with the change. Although some modest additions of service sales to the sales tax base were made in the 2013–15 sessions of the state general assembly, sales tax revenues as a percent of the North Carolina economy were still significantly lower in the early twenty-first century than in the twentieth century.[2]

North Carolina's tax structure is inadequate for the likely economic changes in the decades ahead. Consider the expected increase in 3-D manufacturing, which could allow households to create finished manufactured products within their home. Would the manufacture of these products be subject to the sales tax? What about the expansion of concierge services to households: how would the existing sales tax apply to them? What if business-employee arrangements evolve to include more employee ownership options, or cyberbuying becomes the norm? What complications might these situations present for the existing income tax?

These questions, combined with a fast-evolving economy with unpredictable outcomes, argue for a revenue-raising system with several characteristics. It should have a broad tax base that is expansive enough to capture the varying ways in which production, consumption, and earnings can occur. It should be simple and transparent so that citizens will readily understand and trust the calculations of their tax payments. It should be divorced from economic decision-making except in two circumstances: in situations where the taxpayer generates uncompensated benefits or unpaid costs that the tax system can help correct, or in situations where the tax system can more efficiently achieve a public goal compared to alternative methods for achieving the same goal.

Income is the broadest economic measure common to all households. Two tax systems meet the requirements stated above: a tax on income received (income tax), and a tax on income consumed (consumption tax). The difference between the two is the treatment of earnings that are invested. Investment is critical for developing productivity gains in the economy, and productivity improvement is the major factor in raising standards of living.[3] Investment can also be viewed as delayed consumption (the planting of seed corn is a famous analogy). So, if investment is considered an activity to be encouraged, then the tax would be applied to consumption (income minus funds invested). Taxation of invested funds would occur, but only when dividends from the investment are received and spent or when the original investment amount (principal) is sold and spent. The alternative system would simply tax all income, with no distinction between monies consumed (spent) and monies invested.

In essence, both the income tax and the consumption tax collapse North Carolina's two major revenue generators—the state sales tax and the state income tax—into one system. The current retail sales tax, with its complicated inflexible distinctions between spending that is taxed and that which is not taxed, is eliminated. With one exception explained below, deductions (including the standard deduction) are eliminated in the income tax. If an economic activity is deemed to have broad external benefits (renewable energy might be an example) or broad external costs (pollution) not reflected in the prices of the activities, then direct subsidies or direct penalties would be applied to the activities' prices. In this way the actions are visible and not hidden within the tax code.

The earned income tax credit (EITC) has been a successful method to efficiently provide additional resources to needy households.[4] The current federal EITC uses the income tax system to reduce taxes owed and possibly to provide additional funds when all income taxes are eliminated for working households with financial dependents. In the decades beyond the Connected Age, periods of reduced or completely lost earnings will become more common as the economy is transformed and remade. More households will suffer periods of financial destitution, and some of the periods may be very long. An expanded EITC program applied to all households—whether working or not and whether with financial dependents or not—will be an effective and efficient way of ensuring a basic standard of living.[5] However, the EITC would have to be carefully crafted to provide recipients a continuing incentive to increase their work earnings. This means reducing the EITC support at less than a dollar for every increased dollar of earnings.[6]

The new income or consumption tax would be shared by state and local governments. The revenue raised by the single applied rate would be apportioned to the state and local governments according to an agreed formula designed by the governments. Progressivity in the tax system—especially for low-income households—would be addressed by the expanded EITC program. One deduction would be allowed—that for spending on children, using the justification that children create positive broad benefits for the economy by their expected future contributions to the labor force. However, rather than an arbitrary value for the child spending deduction, the annual average cost of raising a child from the yearly U.S. Department of Agriculture report would be used. As with the current state income tax, monthly withholding amounts would be made to the governments to allow for continuous financing.

The new tax system will eliminate a separate corporate income tax. Corporations are a way of organizing economic activities and disbursing earnings. Earnings paid to owners and investors in North Carolina will be taxed as part of the income or consumption tax. Owners and investors living outside of North Carolina do not create costs for the state and thus would not have their earnings subject to North Carolina tax. The public costs imposed by business activities mainly relate to public protection (police and fire), infrastructure (water, sewer, highways), and land use. Because these costs are correlated with property size (primarily buildings and land), the property tax on the value of business property would be maintained for local governments, and a new state business property tax would be created to fund those same property-related functions performed by the state.[7] As with the income or consumption tax, the property tax would be applied together by state and local governments with different rates allocated for each. Property owned by households would also be subject to the aggregate property tax.

TABLE 7.1 Alternative Revenue-Neutral Income and Consumption Tax Systems, 2014

	Income-Based System	Consumption-Based System
1. Gross amount	$284 billion	$227 billion
2. Child spending deduction	$39 billion	$39 billion
3. State EITC	$12 billion	$12 billion
4. Net tax base (1–2)	$245 billion	$188 billion
5. Revenue required	$26 billion	$26 billion
6. Net tax rate (5/4)	10.6%	13.8%
7. Gross tax rate (5/1)	9.2%	11.5%
8. Local and state property tax revenue	$11 billion	$11 billion

SOURCE: U.S. Census; U.S. Department of Agriculture; U.S. Department of Commerce; North Carolina State Data Center; North Carolina Department of Revenue; calculations by the author.

Where direct usage of a government service occurs, user fees are the most efficient way of funding the service. Highway funding has traditionally followed this model, with highway construction and maintenance paid with a per gallon fuel (gasoline) tax. However, increased fuel efficiencies and increased use of alternative fuels have rendered this model inadequate. Highway funding of the future will use an alternative usage model—mainly based on mileage traveled—applied by funders of the roads, whether they be public or private entities.

The alternative income- and consumption-based tax systems designed to replace the existing taxes funding the state General Fund as well as nonproperty-based revenues of counties and municipalities are given in table 7.1. The "gross amount" for income is estimated total personal income in the state, excluding transfers. Similarly, the "gross amount" for consumption is estimated spending in the state by consumers.[8] The "child spending deduction" total is based on U.S. Department of Agriculture estimates of the annual cost of raising a child by age groups for a moderate standard of living and aggregated by the number of children by age in the state.[9] The "state EITC" support amount is for households under 80 percent of the household median annual earnings and assumes the same payment by the federal government.[10] The "net tax base" takes the gross amount of tax base and subtracts amounts for the child spending deduction. The "revenue required" is the existing combined state and local tax revenues from "own sources," found by excluding federal transfers, motor vehicle tax revenues, educational and hospital fees, and the existing local and new state property tax revenue, then adding the state EITC, and finally subtracting an amount needed to maintain the long-run average percentage of total state and local tax revenue to state GDP.[11] The "net tax rate" is then the required revenue divided by the net amount of tax base, and the "gross tax rate" is the required revenue divided by the gross tax base. "Local and state property tax revenue" is based on maintaining the average rate levied by local governments and adding a similar levy on commercial and industrial property for the state government.[12] These revenues would be used for government functions that benefit business property owners, such as public safety and education. Transportation would continue to be funded separately, preferably with types of user fees.

Both systems are simple and transparent. Both support children and limited-resource households. The generous child spending deduction and EITC support also make both systems progressive, despite the single tax rate. For example, households with two children earning under $34,000 annually pay no income tax or consumption tax, whereas the same households earning $100,000 pay a 7.5 percent income tax rate or a 4.5 percent consumption tax rate.[13] Tax rates can be easily changed to accommodate changing public priorities and responsibilities. But most important, the systems can accommodate changes in the way income is earned and spending occurs—factors that are likely to be very dynamic as the twenty-first century progresses.

Avoiding a Generational War

Although economists and public policy analysts disagree on many facets of the fiscal future, on one fiscal matter there is wide agreement: if current trends continue, public spending on programs targeted to the elderly, particularly in the health area, will take increasing amounts of public resources and will crowd out spending on other governmental functions.[14] One solution is to increase the relative size of public funding through higher state and local taxes. However, total state and local tax revenues in North Carolina as a percent of the state's GDP has averaged a relatively stable 7.9 percent for two decades (1992–2013), rising only during recessionary years when the tax base (GDP) falls.[15] Hence, unless public support in North Carolina for government receiving a larger share of the economy significantly increases, the reasonable expectation is that the relative size of public funding will remain constant and that potential reallocation of public resources between functions will take place.

The trends for North Carolina in public spending for three important state functions, education, transportation, and health care, are shown in fig. 7.1.[16] Between 1950 and 1980 relative spending (spending as a percentage of GDP)

FIG. 7.1 The coming generational squeeze: Could health care crowd out education?
(North Carolina public spending as a percent of GDP).

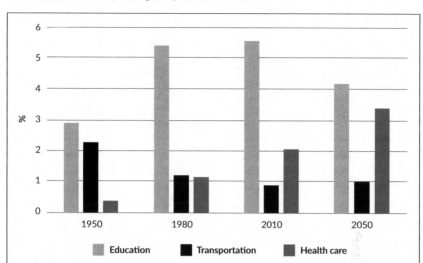

SOURCE: U.S. Census, "Statistical Abstract"; U.S. Department of Commerce; Congressional Budget
Office; author's calculations.

on education in the state almost doubled, but between 1980 and 2010 there was
only a modest increase. Relative transportation spending was cut by 60 percent
from 1950 and 2010. However, relative spending on health care tripled from
1950 to 1980 and almost doubled again between 1980 and 2010.

The last entries in fig. 7.1 (bars on far right) show how the three spending
categories might fare in 2050. Based on projections from the Congressional
Budget Office, relative public spending on health care will rise to 3.4 percent of
GDP at midcentury.[17] The main driving force is the aging of the population. If
we assume that the sum of the three relative shares remains the same in 2050
as in 2010 and that the relative share of transportation spending is maintained
at about 1 percent, then relative spending on health care can rise only if relative
spending on educations falls.

This scenario would thus set up a generational clash, between educational
spending mainly for the young versus health care spending primarily for the
old. The clash would pit the educational training necessary for worker productivity in the twenty-first century versus societal compassion for the elderly.

There are four possible solutions to this generational clash (fig. 7.2). The
"best" is in the first box, where efficiency gains in both private and public sectors allow residents to have more of everything: education, health care, food,
cars, electronics, and so on. So North Carolinians can spend relatively less in

FIG. 7.2   Possible outcomes from the impending generational clash.

	PUBLIC SECTOR Efficiency Gains	PUBLIC SECTOR Efficiency Stagnation
PRIVATE SECTOR Efficiency Gains	1. BEST Private and public efficiency gains allow more of everything	2. SECOND BEST Private sector improvements subsidze public sector expansion
PRIVATE SECTOR Efficiency Stagnation	3. SECOND BEST Public sector improvements subsidize private sector expansion	4. WORST Public (private) sector can only expand if private (public) sector contracts

education and health care but get better results because they are spending the resources more wisely and effectively. The "worst" outcome is in the fourth box, where the lack of efficiency gains in both private and public sectors means that one sector can expand only if the other contracts. So the state can spend relatively more on health care—while maintaining overall public spending—if less is spent on education. Or, to spend more on both health care and education requires less spending and thus less consumption of private goods and services. The other two outcomes are "second-best," or in-between, outcomes. In the second box, efficiency gains in the private sector allow society to spend more on public programs without reducing the consumption of private products, while in the third box, efficiency gains in the public sector—including health care—facilitate more health care consumption without added relative costs.

The economist William Baumol argued that past efficiency gains in the private sector have allowed higher costs in health care.[18] If these trends continue, the second box would thus be the most likely outcome. The generational clash would be avoided because efficiency gains in the private sector would allow more resources to be devoted to the public sector. Other analysts foresee that major technological improvements in health care will dramatically improve the sector's efficiency, making the first or third boxes the expected future result.[19]

Efficiency changes in both the private and public sectors will result primarily from national and international forces, not forces specific to North Carolina. However, because the state has significant technology, health care, and medical instruments sectors, North Carolina could be a leader in the development of technological applications designed to improve efficiency in health care. The state may thus be on the forefront of efforts to reduce the potential generational clash.

Another possible way to bend the cost curve in public health care expenditures is to change the way the state pays for health care support. Health care programs that cover approved procedures and services run the risk of having open-ended budgets, making it difficult for legislators to allocate a specific annual amount to spend. There is also the argument that such fee-for-service systems motivate more health care services, many of which may have low benefits relative to costs.[20]

An alternative is for states to budget a specific annual expenditure for health care support and to allocate this support on a per client basis. There are two ways to implement this system. One is for the state to provide the support directly to selected health care firms in return for the firms enrolling eligible households. The second way is for the state to provide the support directly to eligible households in the form of a health insurance voucher, which would then be used by the households to purchase health insurance policies from private providers. There is some evidence that such consumer-directed health plans act to moderate health care costs.[21]

In 2015, North Carolina enacted legislation to move away from fee-for-service in the Medicaid program and to adopt the system of making a fixed annual payment to providers.[22] The move has sparked controversy over the adequacy of the per client payments, the possible motivation for providers to reduce service in order to lower costs, and the fear that future providers may refuse the payment and service if profit rates are deemed inadequate.[23]

The decision of North Carolina to curtail micromanaging health care expenditures is the correct approach for the twenty-first century, a time when medical treatments and medical technology will be evolving rapidly. Providing financial support for health care, rather than controlling the type and amount of medical care, is consistent with a consumer-focused economy. But the state should go a step further and put the consumer in charge of health care decisions by implementing a financial support system of health care vouchers.

The concept of health care vouchers is simple.[24] Income eligible households would receive a financial voucher from the state to purchase a private-market health insurance policy necessary for the household to obtain some defined standard of care. Households with more severe medical conditions would receive a larger voucher than healthier households. Also, for households under the Medicaid income threshold, those with higher incomes would receive a smaller voucher; however, the tiered voucher amount would be structured so that a one-dollar gain in earnings would always result in much less than a one-dollar reduction in the voucher. Converting North Carolina's Medicaid expenditures in 2015 to a voucher system would have resulted in an average voucher of $6,698 per eligible person, more than the average price of private market insurance in the same year.[25]

Eligible households would use the health care vouchers to purchase health insurance policies from private companies. Households would face the typical insurance policy tradeoffs between premium costs, deductibles, copayments, and size of coverage. The state's role, in addition to identifying qualified households, would be twofold: sanctioning the policy options provided by insurers and educating households on how to evaluate the trade-offs in health insurance plans.

Complementary with a move to health insurance vouchers and the empowering of limited-resource households to purchase adequate care will be the need to ensure competition in the health care market. Competition will provide health care providers with a continuing incentive to improve efficiency and adopt cost-saving technology. North Carolina should therefore review and reconsider its certificate of need (CON) requirements. CON requires health care providers to demonstrate that major infrastructure (hospital space, equipment) expansions will not financially harm other providers. The idea is to prevent an oversupply of facilities, undesired competition among providers, and potential financial losses for providers who lose patients to those with better facilities and equipment. In 2014, North Carolina ranked fourth among the states and the District of Columbia in the number of CON laws.[26]

CON laws are a form of central planning of health care facilities, and there are three reasons for North Carolina to reevaluate them. One is the lack of consistent evidence that CON laws moderate health care costs; indeed, some studies suggest that the rules increase costs by limiting supply.[27] Second, the rapid technological changes expected in how health care is delivered and practiced will make it difficult—if not impossible—for central planners to foresee and judge the equipment and facility purchases that providers will be motivated to make in the dynamic health care market. Third, an adequately funded voucher system for limited-resource households requires a complementary competitive supplier side that is innovative, cost-efficient, and attentive to consumer needs. CON laws are contrary to this system. Indeed, if the state supports the consumer side of health care and allows private investors to support the provider side, the financial failure of some suppliers will be common and necessary.

Public Nudges for Learning, Commuting, and Public Safety

As discussed in chapter 5, how and who provides educational training in North Carolina will likely undergo dramatic changes in the twenty-first century. More focus will be put on preparation and learning at the pre-K through 12 level so that remedial education at the college level can ultimately be eliminated and college education can focus on career development. This means that a higher percentage of North Carolina's public education spending will be directed at the pre-K through 12 level.

Change is often slow in the public sector, resulting from the need to attain broad consensus for policy and program adjustments. Yet rapid change—including experimentation and advances achieved only through a combination of successes and failures—will be a defining feature of the twenty-first century. Ways to promote the application and evaluation of alternative teaching methods at the pre-K through 12 level should be encouraged. Specialized traditional schools, charter schools, cyberschools, home schools, boarding schools, and business- or privately sponsored schools will all be part of the mix of finding the best approach in learning for students. Also, it will be crucial to realize that the best approach will not be the same for all students.

With more public funds directed to the pre-K through 12 level, college institutions (technical, core, advanced) will elevate their interactions and funding with the private sector. Private firms will increasingly fund research, particularly at the advanced college level. Two forms of private-sector loan contracts for college students will become more common. In one a student receives funding from a private company in exchange for agreeing to work for that company for a specified period. In the other, a college student borrows funds from a private financial institution and repays the loan from a share of the salary increase made possible by his or her degree.[28]

As technology reshapes the economy at a faster pace, retraining and career changes will become more important to more individuals. The way the state assists the jobless requires revision. The current unemployment compensation system provides inadequate support and incentives for retraining. This system should be replaced with two elements. One has already been discussed: the expanded EITC system. On being unemployed, an individual would refile his or her income (or consumption) tax forms indicating loss of income. This would then prompt the institution of EITC payments sufficient to provide for a basic living standard for the individual. The second component would be a lump-sum jobless voucher payment to the individual permitting two options: residential relocation to a region where the individual's current skills are still in demand and where there is a high likelihood of employment, or a return to college (technical, core, or advanced) for retraining in new skills.[29] Jerry Kaplan has developed a private-sector version of the lump-sum jobless voucher in which the individual secures a private loan backed by agreement from a firm to hire the individual on completion of training. The job-training loan is then repaid from a share of the person's future earnings.[30]

Government will increasingly take a back seat in transportation development as the twenty-first century proceeds. The initial role of government in building and maintaining roads was based on the premise that highways were a public good: once highways were built, users were impossible or highly costly to restrict. Toll booths and gates initially allowed private developers to recoup their costs, but as roads become more prevalent and complex, drivers making frequent stops at toll booths and gates became impractical. Government stepped in, built and operated the roads, and paid for them primarily with forms of a user fee, such as a tax per gallon of gasoline purchased, a sales tax on the purchase of a vehicle, and a tax on vehicle licenses.

Technology has now largely removed the "public good" label from roads. Sensors can easily be embedded in road entry and exit points to record identifications from drivers and to charge a fee based on miles driven. Privatized transportation infrastructure will be more common at midcentury as the technology for monitoring road usage becomes easier. Private commuter shuttle service, customized to where people live and work, will also be substitutes for public bus systems.[31] A corollary to this shift will be the construction of more planned communities in which the developer designs and constructs all the elements of living, including residences, infrastructure, retail stores, work sites, schools, community facilities, and infrastructure like roads. It is also possible that technological changes such as driverless vehicles, drone deliveries, and 3-D manufacturing could reduce the level of needed highway construction.[32]

Although incarceration costs per inmate and recidivism rates have decreased in North Carolina in the early twenty-first century, imprisonment remains costly, averaging more than $30,000 per inmate annually in 2015.[33] If incarcerated individuals even earned 10 percent of the state median annual income, they would increase total household earnings by $230 million and release $1.1 billion of public funds for other uses in North Carolina.[34]

FIG. 7.3 North Carolina state budget allocations (percent) in 2015 and 2050 (shares of state general fund and transportation funds combined).

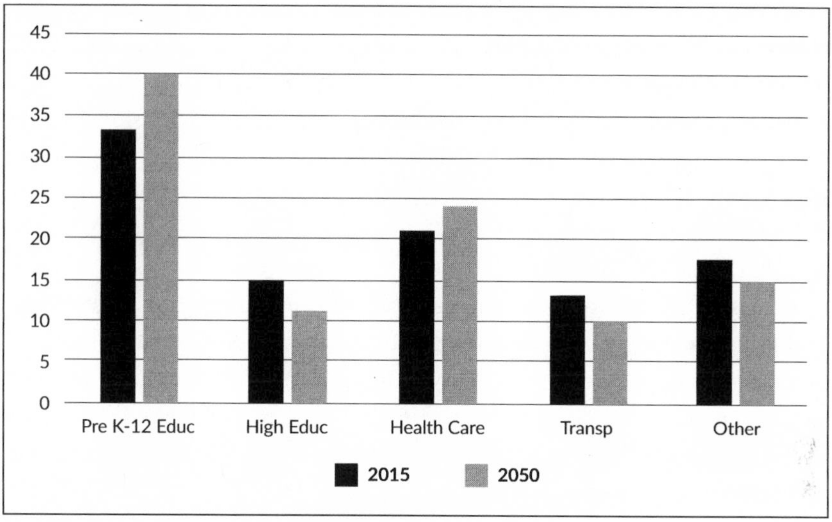

SOURCE: North Carolina Fiscal Research Division; author's calculations.

There is thus economic logic to moving inmates out of prison and into productive work and earnings.[35] Public programs for accomplishing this goal have long existed. But some European countries have been using private firms motivated by private financial incentives to do the same thing. In the United Kingdom, for example, firms are paid a fee if they are able to turn individuals headed toward public dependency or crime into productive earners, thereby creating the dual benefits of increased private productivity and reduced public expenditures. Although the initiative is still at a modest scale, there have been encouraging results.[36]

Savings in state health care expenditures and incarceration spending combined with substantial privatization of transportation programs and infusion of new private support into higher education would release funds for additional spending on pre-K through 12 education and worker retraining, both areas requiring increased public focus in the twenty-first century. How the allocation of state funds might change between the early twenty-first century and 2050 is shown in fig. 7.3. The share of state spending on pre-K–12 would increase by 7 percentage points, from 33 percent to 40 percent of state-funded public spending. State funding for health care—mainly Medicaid—would also rise from 21 percent to 24 percent of the budget, largely because of the aging population.[37] Budget shares to the other functions would fall.

Another point needs to be made about state programs. As state spending changes in the twenty-first century, and especially as new programs are introduced and tried, evaluating programs to determine how effectively they achieve objectives will be more important. North Carolina already has an office doing this work: the Program Evaluation Division of the North Carolina General Assembly. State leaders would be advised to devote additional resources to this office for the timely assessment of a broader range of programs.[38]

State Economic Development Policy: From Conductor to Observer?

Most states have active economic development programs. These include supporting business planning and promotion, providing funding for nonprofit organizations such as business incubators and rural development centers, making grants to businesses, constructing infrastructure (such as access roads) for specific businesses, and enacting provisions in the tax code that reduce business taxes.

From 2006 to 2012, state funding for these economic development activities averaged $1.4 billion (2015 dollars) annually.[39] By far the largest category was business tax reductions (also called tax expenditures), which accounted for over 80 percent of funding. Trimming of sales tax payments by businesses made up the biggest part (over 50 percent) of business tax reductions.[40]

State involvement in guiding economic development—especially using the incentive of tax reductions to attract businesses—has long been debated. Supporters offer numerous defenses: other states have similar programs, so elimination of the programs in a state would be "unilateral disarmament"; the public sector is willing to take more risk in directly or indirectly funding some economic development projects because the state has broader social goals (bringing jobs to high-unemployment areas) not considered by the private sector; and the programs can be a more efficient use of public funds if they achieve private-sector spending that reduces public-sector social support spending.[41]

Opponents are quick to disparage public economic development efforts on the basis of both logic and results. Logically they say that it is impossible for government to pick private companies that will succeed in the marketplace with any reasonable degree of success. For this to be achieved, private rewards—the profit motive—must be on the line. Only private entrepreneurs with private money to win or lose will expend the needed due diligence to explore and evaluate business ventures. Opponents back up their logical argument with studies questioning the success of government guiding the private economy. For example, an analysis of data from the North Carolina

Department of Commerce showed that the majority of jobs promised from incentive projects announced between 2009 and 2014 had failed to occur by 2015.[42] Opponents therefore recommend a passive approach to government's role in economic development, focusing on education and training of the workforce and adequate availability of both natural (water, energy) and physical (infrastructure) resources necessary for economic growth.

The debate over the degree of state government involvement in economic development will continue in the twenty-first century, but the expectation is that several trends will push North Carolina toward passive involvement. With more rapid changes in the economy and uncertainty about where and when earnings and occupational opportunities will occur, it will become increasingly difficult for government to pick presumed winners and meet job goals.[43] For example, auto assembly plants, considered to be a megaprize for business recruiters, will likely continue to replace workers with machinery and technology. Hence, an auto plant promising a thousand direct jobs today may have only a handful of employees by midcentury.

Likewise, if North Carolina moves toward either the income or consumption taxes outlined in an earlier section, there will be no business sales taxes to reduce. Sales (termed consumption in the new tax system) taxes will be levied only on final buyers of products and services. Businesses that purchase inputs to be used in the production of a product or service will not pay a sales tax on those input purchases.

Plugging Pension Problems

North Carolina's pension fund for teachers and state employees is ranked as one of the most secure in the nation. The Center for Retirement Research at Boston College put the North Carolina system tenth among 150 public pension plans in the ratio of assets to liabilities in 2014.[44] Indeed throughout the twenty-first century North Carolina's public pension system has been placed among the best.[45]

Still, there are some questions about the state's pension system. One is a technical—yet very important—issue about converting the dollar value of future pension payments to a current (present) value to be used in comparison to current investment totals. Pension plans (including North Carolina's) have continued to use interest rates for this conversion that are much higher than the low interest rates that have prevailed in the early twenty-first century.[46] The use of these higher interest rates makes the future pension payment obligations lower in value today than if a more modest interest rate had been used. Some estimates suggest that if more reasonable interest rates are used, then North Carolina faces a deficit in its pension funding that would require a 9.5 percent increase in tax revenues to close.[47]

This interest rate issue is directly related to a second issue, which is the large management fees public pension plans pay in an attempt to achieve higher investment earnings. In 2012, North Carolina's public pension system paid over $300 million in investment fees.[48] Some of these fees were paid to hedge fund managers and other investment companies. Of course, the expectation is that purchasing professional investment services will yield higher investment returns, even after subtracting the fees.

Research shows, however, that the management fees for state public pension plans do not pay for themselves.[49] This suggests one win-win strategy for addressing potential pension shortfalls. The pension funds could be invested in a set of diverse, low-fee mutual funds designed to replicate the options in the investment world. Little or no attempt would be made to adjust the portfolio allocation over the business cycle, following the notion that beating the market is impossible on a consistent basis.[50] Some research shows that this strategy would pay off over time by increasing after-fee investment returns and decreasing the necessary future tax increases necessary to eliminate pension shortfalls. For example, the analysis shows that the low-fee, diversified mutual fund strategy would reduce the needed tax increases in North Carolina from 9.5 percent to 7.3 percent.[51]

Even with this change in investment strategy, North Carolina may have to consider other options for plugging a possible looming pension shortfall. One may be to move some or all employees from the current defined benefit plan—in which the state guarantees a pension amount based on the worker's salary history and years of service—to a defined contribution plan—where pension amounts are not guaranteed but are based on contributions as well as the investment returns earned. A state study commission recommended that defined contribution plans be offered as an option to both new and current employees.[52] Another alternative is to offer employees a higher current salary in exchange for no or a reduced state pension. Some research suggests that public employees value pension promises far less than their monetary amount. Hence, states could lower lifetime costs associated with employees by reducing promised future benefits by more than the corresponding increase in today's salaries.[53]

Government in the Twenty-First Century

So, what will government in North Carolina look like in 2050? Government's role will continue to be important, but in a different way. Clearly, government will not be the director of the economy. The economy has always been too dynamic and unpredictable for government to play this role, and this will be even more evident in the twenty-first century with massive economic changes occurring within years, rather than decades. Government can certainly try to understand ongoing trends and calibrate impacts of the trends, but attempting to control the trends is impossible.

Instead, the major role of twenty-first-century government will be *facilitating adjustment to change*. In this task, two areas will receive priority: pre-K through 12 education and reskilling of workers displaced by economic change. Increased public resources should be allocated to both tasks. Higher education will expand by relying more on private resources, and transportation functions currently performed by government will be increasingly privatized. Innovative approaches using private incentives will be applied to the prison population to move inmates back into productive positions in society. Simplified investment approaches combined with shared public-private ownership will ensure the solvency of North Carolina's public pensions. State health care expenditures will be contained through a combination of cost-saving technology and consumer-driven control via health insurance vouchers.

An unpredictable economy with changes in the way products are made and individuals work, earn, and spend will necessitate adjustments in the tax system. Tax bases will be broad-based with minimal distortions from deductions and credits. Single rates will be used to avoid disincentives from income increases upping tax rates. Supporting children and limited-resource households—through an enhanced negative income tax—will be the only adjustments to this simple, transparent system. The logical tax bases for this approach are income or consumption.

Last, the fast-changing economic future will make it difficult and often counterproductive for government to use incentives and tax breaks to select business winners. If, according to futurist George Gilder, "creativity is always a surprise," then the increasingly creative twenty-first century argues for a passive role of government in economic development—again, mainly in education and retraining.[54]

Of course, the political composition and context of the state's electorate will be important in determining the public policy responses to the challenges confronting North Carolina. Three potential flashpoints may impede consensus for developing policy approaches. One is ideological. In the early twenty-first century North Carolina emerged as a "purple" state, virtually divided equally between Democrats and Republicans. Differing perspectives and fierce competition between the two major parties could result in policy stalemates and an inability to design appropriate public responses to the rapid economic transformation in the state.

A second flashpoint is the urban-rural divide. As discussed in chapter 2, the state's geographic differences have been expanding and are expected to widen even further in coming decades, with one-third of the counties losing population by midcentury. Representatives of these counties will be motivated to lobby for public resources to fight against these changes. However, if the changes are the result of broad socioeconomic forces sweeping through the state—forces that are beyond the state's (and nation's) control—then resources used to impede the forces are resources that might be better used to adapt to the changes.

The final potential political flashpoint is generational, where there is a strong likelihood of increased public spending for the elderly (age sixty-five and older) population coming at the expense of educational spending for the young. In this battle between the two ends of the demographic spectrum—pitting the larger numbers of millennials and postmillennials (also known as the homeland generation) against the declining size of the baby boom generation— the more reliable political participation of the boomers could mean they are the expected winner, at least in the early third of the twenty-first century. However, the political views of the millennials are still evolving. Although they express support for helping those with limited resources, they also oppose higher tax rates. They question conventional wisdom and are more likely to embrace changes created by new technology and alternative forms of organizing economic relationships, such as the gig economy.[55] Therefore, as they eventually become the dominant force in both the economy and politics in the state, the millennials and their successors could be expected to push for the kind of creative and outside-the-box public policies that will likely be needed to address the upcoming economic turbulence in North Carolina.

North Carolina has a tradition of developing consensus when public actions are needed to tackle economic and social change. Citizens and leaders of the state will be challenged to continue this tradition as North Carolina moves beyond the Connected Age.

8. IS THE FUTURE IN OUR HANDS?

Big changes are coming to North Carolina's economy in the twenty-first century—changes that will affect how we live, where we will live, what we will do in our jobs, how much we will earn, how we are educated and trained, how we are assisted and supported, how we will move around, and what fuels we will use to transport us, heat and cool us, and power our industries.

Most of these changes will be part of big global trends in demography, technology, international linkages, and the environment. Draconian measures could be used to control the changes—measures like limiting the application of new technology and imposing controls on where households live—but such controls are inconsistent with the principles of choice in an open economy.

Does this mean we are powerless to affect our future? Before answering, it is helpful to realize that we do not live in the first era of significant change. Demographically, the world has undergone periods of population decline, population explosion, and, recently, moderating population growth. There have also been eras of great migrations, both among and within countries. Technologically, it can be argued that the application of the tractor and other machinery to the farm—which prompted millions of people in the country and in North Carolina to move from rural to urban areas and to change the economy from agrarian-based to manufacturing-based—was more disruptive to everyday lives than anything seen in recent decades. And although the international connections developed since World War II have been significant, they are rivaled by similar linkages built at the turn of the nineteenth to twentieth centuries and, of course, by the European settlement of the New World in the sixteenth and seventeenth centuries.

What is common with all these changes is that there was a response. Feeding the growing population of the planet has been met by productivity gains in farming. Migrating populations have been assimilated into new cultures and become part of growing countries and economies. High school education was expanded to give displaced farmers the reading and writing skills necessary to be successful in an urban environment, and in the past three decades college education has been broadened to train more workers for the expanding service and professional jobs.

Even though the forces pushing the trends that shape our lives likely cannot be controlled, our responses to them can. If the forces create disruption, then our response should be adaptation. Therefore, as recounted in this book, North Carolina must prepare for a new set of adaptations to address a new set of changes. Most of these adaptations will be done through private decision-making, but the state will have a supporting—but not dominating— role in facilitating these adjustments and providing assistance to households who must make major changes in their lives.

The coming period of change and adjustment will be different than past periods in two ways. One is in its speed. Modern technology has increased the pace of everything, such as sending and receiving information, moving resources, and evaluating opportunities. It is expected that the big technological innovations of the future in areas like artificial intelligence, virtualization, nanotechnology, and the internet of everything will move the altering forces of technology even faster. Both our recognition of change and our response and adjustment to that change will also have to be faster.

The second distinguishing feature of the current dynamic period may be in jobs—or more specifically—in the lack of jobs. New developments in technology will continue to do wonderful things for us, particularly in stretching our limited natural resources to accommodate a larger population, reducing environmental degradation, and improving efficiency and outcomes in education and health care. Yet economists have long recognized that technological change eliminates some jobs even as it creates new ones, usually in different industries. This process has been beautifully summarized in Joseph Schumpeter's phase "creative destruction," meaning that the destruction of some economic sectors releases the resources necessary to build new industries.[1] Thus, the release of farmworkers provided the labor base for manufacturing's growth, and likewise the downsizing of labor inputs in manufacturing have made workers available for today's expanding service and information sectors.

The worry is it may not happen this way in the future. Technology is becoming so sophisticated and wide-ranging in its applications to an ever broader range of tasks that some see a world in which human inputs are superfluous and unneeded. Literally, some see an end to human work. Thus, what humans do in a world increasingly dominated by technology may be the greatest challenge of the twenty-first century.

It is a cliché to say that change happens. An easy prediction is that North Carolina will be a very different state, with different people, industries, jobs, and issues, in 2050 than today. Such a forecast is not very helpful. But even though we may not know exactly the types and characteristics of these differences, we can look at the trends in today's changes, and we can elicit the ideas and predictions of those who have been thinking about and trying to predict the future for some educated ideas about what the future may bring. These objectives have been the main goals of this book—to give North Carolinians a heads-up of what might be down the road and how we can prepare for our travel down that road.

Should we be optimistic or pessimistic about North Carolina in 2050? Applying Nehru's observation, we likely have little control over the economic hand—the forces, trends, and inventions—that we will be dealt in coming decades. But we do have control over how we play that hand—that is, how we adapt and adjust by redesigning public programs like education and skills training and constructing a tax system that provides needed resources without stifling inevitable public and private transformations.

Fortunately, North Carolina has a reputation as a doer state, continually making changes to adapt to new and challenging times. Following the devastation of the Civil War, the state worked to attract and expand the growing manufacturing sector in such industries as textiles, furniture, and tobacco. During the Great Depression, North Carolina revamped its tax system to save public schools and support higher education. As transportation moved from rails to roads following World War II, the state embarked on a massive road construction project to link farms, factories, and cities. And as part of its economic overhaul in the late twentieth century, North Carolina was one of the first states to recognize the emerging technology sector by creating the path-breaking Research Triangle Park in 1959.

The Tar Heel State now faces new challenges. Once again the economy is being redefined, and the redefinition will not be without stress. The economic forces shaping our destiny will enable some people, industries, and regions to gain while causing others to lose. Technology is changing the nature of work and life in ways that both expand and constrict the human experience. This book has strived to identify where and how these gains and losses could occur and the options available for addressing them.

Building on its history and experience, North Carolina can once again successfully confront the challenges ahead and adapt to the new realities for the betterment of the state's people. In 2050, North Carolina will be different in many ways that we cannot imagine today. Yet imagination is exactly what the state needs to consider its future and how that future can be formed.

ACKNOWLEDGMENTS

Thanks to the people, businesses, and places of North Carolina who have inspired me to learn about our state and try to forecast its future. Special thanks are also extended to Lucas Church, Jessica Newman, Jay Mazzocchi, and Laura Jones Dooley at the University of North Carolina Press for taking the raw manuscript and turning it into a wonderful book.

NOTES

Abbreviations

N&O   *News and Observer* (Raleigh, N.C.)
NYT   *New York Times*
WSJ   *Wall Street Journal*

Preface

1. For a description of the structural changes in North Carolina's economy in the latter twentieth century, see Michael L. Walden, *North Carolina in the Connected Age: Challenges and Opportunities in a Globalizing Economy* (Chapel Hill: University of North Carolina Press, 2008).

2. U.S. Census Bureau, *Census of 1970, Population* (Washington, D.C.: Government Printing Office, 1971); U.S. Census Bureau, *Census of 2010, Population* (Washington, D.C.: Government Printing Office, 2011).

3. U.S. Department of Commerce, Bureau of Labor Statistics, "State and Metro Area Employment, Hours and Earnings," https://www.bls.gov/sae/#data. 16 April 2015.

4. Ibid.

5. For a collection of alternative forecasts for the future, see Robert M. Whaples, Christopher J. Coyne, and Michael C. Munger, eds., *Future: Economic Peril or Prosperity?* (Oakland, Calif.: Independent Institute, 2016).

6. For details on the "revolutions," see Desmond Lachman, "Have the Limits to Economic Growth Really Been Reached?," *The American* (blog), *American Enterprise Institute*, April 26, 2014, https://www.aei.org/publication/have-the-limits-to-economic-growth-really-been-reached. There is no agreement on the number of distinct industrial or technological revolutions. For example, Carlota Perez, *Technological Revolutions and Financial Capital: The Dynamics of Bubbles and Golden Ages* (Cheltenham, U.K.: Edward Elgar, 2002), identifies five technological revolutions: the first beginning with the cotton mill in the late eighteenth century; the second featuring steam and railways in the mid-nineteenth century; the third with the development of steel, electricity, and heavy engineering in the late nineteenth century; the fourth based on oil, the automobile, and mass production in the early twentieth century; and the fifth built on information and telecommunications beginning in the last fourth of the twentieth century.

7. Richard Florida, *The Great Reset: How the Post-Crash Economy Will Change the Way We Live and Work* (New York: HarperCollins, 2010).

8. Robert Bryce, *Smaller Faster Lighter Denser Cheaper: How Innovation Keeps Proving the Catastrophists Wrong* (New York: Public Affairs, 2014); James Manyika et al., *Disruptive Technologies: Advances That Will Transform Life, Business, and the Global Economy* (Washington, D.C.: McKinsey Global Institute, May 2013); Joel Mokyr, "Is Technological Progress a Thing of the Past?," *Vox: CEPR's Policy Portal* (blog), September 8, 2013, http://voxeu.org/article/technological-progress-thing-past.

9. Barry Eichengreen, "Secular Stagnation: The Long View," NBER Working Paper 20836 (Boston: National Bureau of Economic Research, January 2015). Some say that the recent decline in productivity measures are due to measurement issues, particularly in incorporating the benefits of technology to consumer decision-making. Timothy Aeppel, "U.S. Productivity: Missing or in Hiding?," *WSJ*, July 17, 2015. Others argue that measurement error is not a factor and instead say that productivity took a one-time boost during 1995–2004 with the spread of information technology innovations. David M. Byrne, John G. Fernald, and Marshall B. Reinsdorf, "Does the U.S. Have a Productivity Slowdown or a Measurement Problem?" *Brookings Papers on Economic Activity* (Spring 2016): 109–57; Chad Syverson, "Challenges to Mismeasurement Explanations for the U.S. Productivity Slowdown," NBER Working Paper 21974 (Boston: National Bureau of Economic Research, February 2016). Some say that the efficiency benefits of technology may have been countered by the frivolous use of the same technology for such nonproductivity-enhancing activities as gaming, texting, and video-watching while at work. James Gottschalk, "Bringing U.S. Productivity Out of the Shadows," letter to the editor, *WSJ*, July 25–26, 2015.

10. Arguments for this optimistic future are presented by Joel Kurtzman, *Unleashing the Second American Century: Four Forces for Economic Dominance* (New York: Public Affairs, 2014); Josef Joffe, *The Myth of America's Decline: Politics, Economics, and a Half Century of False Prophecies* (New York: W. W. Norton, 2014); and Susan Lund et al., *Game Changers: Five Opportunities for U.S. Growth and Renewal* (Washington, D.C.: McKinsey Global Institute, July 2013).

11. Susan Helper, Timothy Krueger, and Howard Wial, *Why Does Manufacturing Matter? Which Manufacturing Matters? A Policy Framework* (Washington, D.C.: Brookings Institute, February 2012).

12. Stefan Heck and Matt Rogers, *Resource Revolution: How to Capture the Biggest Business Opportunity in a Century* (New York: Houghton Mifflin Harcourt, 2012).

13. For an optimistic view of the impact of technological change on jobs, see James Bessen, *Learning by Doing: The Real Connection between Innovation, Wages, and Wealth* (New Haven, Conn.: Yale University Press, 2015). Optimists especially see future job gains in STEM (science, technology, engineering, and mathematics) occupations. Jonathan Rothwell, *Still Searching: Job Vacancies and STEM Skills* (Washington, D.C.: Brookings Institute, July 2014).

14. Joel Kotkin, *The Next Hundred Million: America in 2050* (New York: Penguin, 2010).

15. Born between 1980 and 2000, the millennial generation includes eighty-six million individuals, the largest generation in numbers in the early twenty-first century. Chuck Jaffe, "Will Millennials Save Us?," *WSJ*, April 4, 2016.

16. Richard Dobbs et al., *Urban World: Cities and the Rise of the Consuming Class* (Washington, D.C.: McKinsey Global Institute, June 2012).

17. Pedro Bento, "Competition as a Discovery Procedure: Schumpeter Meets Hayek in a Model of Innovation," *American Economic Journal: Macroeconomics* 6, no. 3 (July 2014): 124–52; Marina Gorbis, *The Nature of the Future: Dispatches from the Socialstructed World* (New York: Free Press, 2013); Jeremy Rifkin, *The Zero Marginal Cost Society: The Internet of Things, the Collaborative Commons, and the Eclipse of Capitalism* (New York: St. Martin's, 2011); Peter Diamandis and Steven Kotler, *Bold: How to Go Big, Create Wealth, and Impact the World* (New York: Simon and Schuster, 2015). Martin Baily and Barry Bosworth see reason for optimism about innovation based on the observation that the rate of issuance of patents to U.S. residents has increased substantially since 1970. Martin Baily and Barry Bosworth, "U.S. Manufacturing: Understanding Its Past and Its Potential Future," *Journal of Economic Perspectives* 28, no. 1 (Winter 2014): 3–26.

18. Lawrence H. Summers, "The Age of Secular Stagnation: What It Is and What to Do about It," *Foreign Affairs* (March–April 2016): 2–9. Marc Levinson argues that a major reason for the growth slowdown is that U.S. economic growth in the three decades following World War II was unusually high, based on the U.S. economy being the only major economy to escape devastation during the war, and hence being the only available economy to supply both domestic and international demand. Marc Levinson, *An Extraordinary Time: The End of the Postwar Boom and the Return of the Ordinary Economy* (New York: Basic Books, 2016).

19. Robert J. Gordon, "Is U.S. Economic Growth Over? Faltering Innovation Confronts the Six Headwinds," NBER Working Paper 18315 (Boston: National Bureau of Economic Research, August 2012); Robert J. Gordon, "The Demise of U.S. Economic Growth: Restatement, Rebuttal, and Reflections," NBER Working Paper 19895 (Boston: National Bureau of Economic Research, February 2014); Robert J. Gordon, *The Rise and Fall of American Growth: The U.S. Standard of Living since the Civil War* (Princeton, N.J.: Princeton University Press, 2016).

20. There is also the concern that Moore's Law—based on the notion that computer power doubles every two years with no additional cost—may have run its course and is no longer occurring. "Double, Double, Toil and Trouble," *Economist*, March 12, 2016, 1–14. In contrast to this dismal view, Pagan Kennedy believes that inventions will occur as long as there are problems to solve but that the process of creating new ideas, techniques, and products cannot be planned and directed. Pagan Kennedy, *Inventology: How We Dream Up Things That Change the World* (Boston: Houghton Mifflin Harcourt, 2016).

21. Gordon C. Bjork, *The Way It Worked and Why It Won't: Structural Change and the Slowdown of U.S. Economic Growth* (Westport, Conn.: Praeger, 1999). Indeed, Jorgen Randers forecasts a continued increase in the standard of living in coming decades, even assuming slowing or eventually negative population growth. Jorgen Randers, *2052: A Global Forecast for the Next Forty Years* (White River Junction, Vt.: Chelsea Green, 2012).

22. John G. Fernald and Charles I. Jones, "The Future of U.S. Economic Growth," *American Economic Review: Papers and Proceedings* 104, no. 5 (May 2014): 44–49; Canyon Bosler et al., "The Outlook for U.S. Labor-Quality Growth" (Paper presented at

NBER/CRIW Conference on Education, Skills, and Technical Change: Implications for Future U.S. GDP Growth, Atlanta, Ga., July 11, 2016); Jacques Bughin, James Manyika, and Jonathan Woetzel, *Diminishing Returns: Why Investors May Need to Lower their Expectations* (Washington, D.C.: McKinsey Global Institute, May 2016).

23. They say that the play-it-safe bureaucratic mentality of large modern corporations is adverse to the risk-taking necessary for innovations. Fredrik Erixon and Björn Weigel, *The Innovation Illusion: How So Little Is Created by So Many Working So Hard* (New Haven, Conn.: Yale University Press, 2016).

24. Paul Taylor, *The Next America: Boomers, Millennials, and the Looming Generational Showdown* (New York: Public Affairs, 2014).

25. Nicole Maestas, Kathleen Mullen, and David Powell, "The Effect of Population Aging on Economic Growth, the Labor Force and Productivity," NBER Working Paper 22452 (Boston: National Bureau of Economic Research, July 2016); Etienne Gagnon, Benjamin K. Johannsen, and David Lopez-Salido, "Understanding the New Normal: The Role of Demographics," Finance and Economics Discussion Series 2016-080 (Washington, D.C.: Board of Governors of the Federal Reserve System, 2016). The American economist Alvin Hansen anticipated this argument decades ago when he said that an aging population would lead to reduced investment and a slowdown in economic growth. Alvin H. Hansen, *Full Recovery or Stagnation?* (New York: W. W. Norton, 1938).

26. Harry S. Dent Jr., *The Demographic Cliff: How to Survive and Prosper during the Great Deflation of 2014–2019* (New York: Portfolio/Penguin, 2014).

27. For an excellent discussion of the possible linkages between government programs and the birth rate, see Isaac Ehrlich and Jinyoung Kim, "Social Security, Demographic Trends, and Economic Growth: Theory and Evidence from the International Experience," NBER Working Paper 11121 (Boston: National Bureau of Economic Research, February 2005).

28. Jan Vijg, *The American Technological Challenge: Stagnation and Decline in the Twenty-First Century* (New York: Algora, 2011).

29. James Pethokoukis, "Is There Too Little 'Creative Destruction' in the U.S. Economy?," *AEIdeas* (blog), May 12, 2014, https://www.aei.org/publication/is-there-simply-too-little-creative-destruction-in-the-us-economy/. Ryan Decker et al., "The Role of Entrepreneurship in U.S. Job Creation and Economic Dynamism," *Journal of Economic Perspectives* 28, no. 3 (Summer 2014): 3–24. However, Matthew Yglesias explains the recent decline in entrepreneurship by noting that the most common age for starting new companies is in midlife (forties). In recent decades the proportion of the population in midlife has declined. Yglesias speculates that once Generations X and Y reach midlife, the rate of entrepreneurship will rise. Matthew Yglesias, "Entrepreneurship Is on the Decline in America—But It Will Turn Around Soon," *Vox*, August 5, 2014, http://www.vox.com/2014/8/5/5968783/entrepreneurial-decline-litan. A related concern is the recent observed slowdown in the rate improvement of computing power. John Markoff, "Smaller, Faster, Cheaper, Over," *NYT*, September 27, 2015.

30. Tyler Cowen, *The Great Stagnation: How America Ate All the Low-Hanging Fruit of Modern History, Got Sick, and Will (Eventually) Feel Better* (New York: Dutton, 2011). Many economists point to the 1920s and 1930s as a period when several

game-changing innovations affected everyday life. For a comprehensive description, see David Kyvig, *Daily Life in the United States, 1920–1940* (Chicago: Ivan R. Dee, 2002).

31. Charles Murray, *Coming Apart: The State of White America, 1960–2010* (New York: Crown Forum, 2012); Müge Adalet McGowan and Dan Andrews, "Labour Market Mismatch and Labour Productivity: Evidence from PIAAC Data," OECD Economics Working Papers 1029 (Paris: Organisation for Economic Co-operation and Development, 2015). McGowan and Andrews estimate that 20 percent of U.S. workers in 2012 had skills not matching their occupation and that eliminating this mismatch could boost productivity by 2 percent. For a complementary discussion, see also June Carbone and Naomi Cahn, *Marriage Markets: How Inequality Is Remaking the American Family* (New York: Oxford University Press, 2014).

32. Tyler Cowen, *Average Is Over: Powering America beyond the Age of the Great Stagnation* (New York: Dutton, 2013).

33. Joseph E. Stiglitz, *The Price of Inequality: How Today's Divided Society Endangers Our Future* (New York: W. W. Norton, 2013). There is a debate about the extent to which income inequality has increased based on different measures of the concept. For example, Richard Burkhauser, Jeff Larrimore, and Kosali Simon find reductions in income inequality from 1989 to 2000 when taxes, income transfers, and changes in household size are taken into account. Richard Burkhauser, Jeff Larrimore, and Kosali Simon, "A 'Second Opinion' on the Economic Health of the American Middle Class," NBER Working Paper 17164 (Boston: National Bureau of Economic Research, June 2011).

34. David Madland, *Hollowed Out: Why the Economy Doesn't Work without a Strong Middle Class* (Berkeley: University of California Press, 2016); Standard & Poor's, "How Increasing Income Inequality Is Dampening U.S. Economic Growth, and Possible Ways to Change the Tide," *RatingsDirect*, August 5, 2014, 3–27. Politically, Francis Fukuyama worries about the increase in income inequality and the resulting middle-class decline undermining democracy. Francis Fukuyama, *Political Order and Political Decay: From the Industrial Revolution to the Globalization of Democracy* (New York: Farrar, Straus and Giroux, 2014).

35. Nir Jaimovich and Henry Siu, "The Trend Is the Cycle: Job Polarization and Jobless Recoveries," NBER Working Paper 18334 (Boston: National Bureau of Economic Research, August 2013); David Autor, David Dorn, and Gordon Hanson, "The Geography of Trade and Technology Shocks in the United States," *American Economic Review: Papers and Proceedings*, 103, no. 3 (May 2013): 220–25; Gregory Clark, *A Farewell to Alms: A Brief Economic History of the World* (Princeton, N.J.: Princeton University Press, 2009); Enrico Moretti, *The New Geography of Jobs* (New York: Houghton Mifflin Harcourt, 2012); Pol Antràs, Alonso de Gortari, and Oleg Itskhoki, "Globalization, Inequality, and Welfare," NBER Working Paper 22676 (Boston: National Bureau of Economic Research, September 2016). The authors emphasize the role of globalization as a factor behind increasing income inequality.

36. William Nordhaus, *The Climate Casino: Risk, Uncertainty, and Economics for a Warming World* (New Haven, Conn.: Yale University Press, 2013).

37. John Maynard Keynes, "Economic Possibilities for Our Grandchildren," in *Essays in Persuasion* (New York: W. W. Norton, 1963), 358–73.

38. Jeffrey Sachs and Laurence Kotlikoff, "Smart Machines and Long-Term Misery," NBER Working Paper 18629 (Boston: National Bureau of Economic Research, December 2012); Erik Brynjolfsson and Andrew McAfee, *The Second Machine Age: Work, Progress, and Prosperity in a Time of Brilliant Technologies* (New York: W. W. Norton, 2014).

39. Oliver Coibion, Yuriy Gorodnichenko, and Dmitri Koustas, "Amerisclerosis? The Puzzle of Rising U.S. Unemployment Persistence," *Brookings Papers on Economic Activity* (Fall 2013): 193–241; Martin Ford, *Rise of the Robots: Technology and the Threat of a Jobless Future* (New York: Basic Books, 2015).

40. Carl Benedikt Frey and Michael A. Osborne, "The Future of Employment: How Susceptible Are Jobs to Computerisation?," Working Paper (Oxford University, September 17, 2013).

41. Paul Beaudry, David Green, and Benjamin Sand, "The Great Reversal in the Demand for Skill and Cognitive Tasks," NBER Working Paper 18901(Boston: National Bureau of Economic Research, March 2013); Andrew Weaver and Paul Osterman, "Skill Demands and Mismatch in U.S. Manufacturing: Evidence and Implications," Working Paper (Boston: MIT Sloan School of Management, November 2013).

42. Daniel Alpert, *The Age of Oversupply: Overcoming the Greatest Challenge to the Global Economy* (New York: Portfolio/Penguin, 2013).

43. Joel Mokyr, Chris Vickers, and Nicolas Ziebarth, "The History of Technological Anxiety and the Future of Economic Growth: Is This Time Different?" *Journal of Economic Perspectives* 29, no. 3 (Summer 2015): 31–50; Martin Ford, *The Lights in the Tunnel: Automation, Accelerating Technology and the Economy of the Future* (New York: Acculant, 2009). Ford recommends a guaranteed income for all households, especially those displaced by technology.

44. Claudia Goldin and Lawrence F. Katz, *The Race between Education and Technology* (Cambridge, Mass.: Harvard University Press, 2008). See also Lawrence F. Katz and Robert A. Margo, "Technical Change and the Relative Demand for Skilled Labor: The U.S. in Historical Perspective," NBER Working Paper 18752 (Boston: National Bureau of Economic Research, February 2013).

45. More specifically, private goods are those in which the benefits of consumption of the goods occur only to the user. Public goods are those where the benefits of consumption are broadly and equally enjoyed by large numbers of individuals; that is, once public goods are available, the benefits are widely available. Private goods therefore are amenable to private provision and private payment by the user. Public goods are logically provided by government and financed through public taxes or fees.

46. Jawaharlal Nehru quoted in *Saturday Review*, vol. 50, 1967.

Chapter 1

1. The 1920s ended the out-migration of North Carolinians—many African American—to northern factories following the conclusion of World War I and also included the return of soldiers to their homes. During the depression years of the 1930s, a significant reverse migration occurred of northern families moving to their birthplaces in the South.

2. For more discussion, see Michael L. Walden, *North Carolina in the Connected Age: Challenges and Opportunities in a Globalizing Economy* (Chapel Hill: University of North Carolina Press, 2008), chap. 2.

3. The net in-migration rate is net migration divided by total population. U.S. Census, "Geographical Mobility/Migration, State-to-State Migration Flow," www.census.gov/data/tables/time-series/demo/geographic-mobility/state-to-state-migration.html.

4. Ibid.

5. Rebecca Tippett, "Why Do People Move to North Carolina?," *Carolina Demography*, January 28, 2014, UNC Carolina Population Center, http://demography.cpc.unc.edu/2014/01/28/why-do-people-move-to-north-carolina/.

6. The statistics for socioeconomic characteristics of movers are based on an analysis of a national sample of households. David K. Ihrke, Carol S. Faber, and William K. Koerber, *Geographical Mobility: 2008 to 2009*, U.S. Census, P20-565 (Washington, D.C.: Government Printing Office, November 2011). The reference to movers having higher incomes than nonmovers is from an analysis specifically of North Carolina households during the period 1993–2011. Michael Mazerov, *State Taxes Have a Negligible Impact on Americans' Interstate Moves* (Washington, D.C.: Center on Budget and Policy Priorities, May 9, 2014).

7. Maggie Foley and Fiorentina Angjellari-Dajci, "Net Migration Determinants," *Journal of Regional Analysis and Policy* 45, no. 1 (2015): 30–35.

8. The forecasted population numbers for the nation for 2030 and 2050 are from the U.S. Census, https://www.census.gov/population/projections/data/national/2014.html. The forecasted population numbers for North Carolina for 2030 are also from the U.S. Census; https://www.census.gov/population/projections/data/state/projectionsagesex.html. The following steps were followed to develop the total population forecast for North Carolina for 2050. First, the forecasted North Carolina population in 2035 was taken from the North Carolina Office of Budget and Management, www.osbm.nc.gov/demog/county-projections. Next, the forecasted North Carolina population change from the U.S. Census for 2030 to 2035 was extrapolated to 2040. Then the decadal percentage point differences in total population growth between North Carolina and the nation were averaged for the decades from 2010 to 2040. This average difference (2.37 percentage points) was added to the forecasted percentage point increase in the U.S. total population between 2040 and 2050 and used to derive the forecasted North Carolina total population forecast in 2050. A form of the cohort component method was then used to divide the North Carolina total 2050 population into the age brackets.

9. U.S. Bureau of the Census, "American Community Survey," https://www.census.gov/programs-surveys/acs/; Jack Martin and Stanley Fogel, *Projecting the U.S. Population to 2050: Four Immigration Scenarios* (Washington, D.C.: Federation for American Immigration Reform, March 2006). Hispanic refers to persons from a Cuban, Mexican, Puerto Rican, South American, Central American, or other Spanish culture or background regardless of race. For an analysis of the growing economic influence of the Hispanic population in North Carolina, see James H. Johnson Jr. and Stephen J. Appold, *Demographic and Economic Impacts of International Migration to North Carolina* (Chapel Hill, N.C.: University of North Carolina, Kenan-Flagler Business School, April 2014).

10. In addition, North Carolina has ranked either fifth or sixth among U.S. states in total factor productivity, a measure of the efficiency of production in a state that combines both labor and nonlabor inputs. Roberto Cardarelli and Lusine Lusinyan, "U.S. Total Factor Productivity Slowdown: Evidence from the States," Working Paper 15/116 (Washington, D.C.: International Monetary Fund, May 2015).

11. United Nations, Department of Economic and Social Affairs, Population Division, *World Population Prospects: The 2012 Revision* (New York: United Nations, 2013).

12. In 2050, the share of the world population age nineteen and under is projected to be 28 percent, compared to 21.5 percent and 19.5 percent, respectively, for the nation and North Carolina for the share age eighteen and under. United Nations, Department of Economic and Social Affairs, Population Division, *World Population Prospects: The 2012 Revision*.

13. Paul S. Davies, Michael J. Greenwood, and Haizheng Li, "A Conditional Logit Approach to U.S. State-to-State Migration," *Journal of Regional Science* 41, no. 2 (May 2001): 337–60; Stuart A. Gabriel, Joe P. Mattey, and William L. Wascher, "The Demise of California Reconsidered: Interstate Migration over the Economic Cycle," *Economic Review, Federal Reserve Bank of San Francisco*, no. 2 (1995): 30–45; Alicia Sasser, "Voting with Their Feet? Local Economic Conditions and Migration Patterns in New England," Working Paper 09-1 (Boston: New England Public Policy Center at the Federal Reserve Bank of Boston, 2009).

14. The time span analyzed for payroll employment is 1990 to 2016, showing gains of 38 percent for North Carolina versus 31 percent for the nation. U.S. Department of Labor, Bureau of Labor Statistics, https://www.bls.gov/sae. The time span analyzed for home prices is 1991 to 2016, showing a nominal increase in the price of a home with similar characteristics being 109 percent in North Carolina and 127 percent in the nation. Federal Housing Finance Agency, https://www.fhfa.gov.

15. Jon Bakija and Joel Slemrod, "Do the Rich Flee from High State Taxes? Evidence from Federal Estate Tax Returns," NBER Working Paper 10645 (Boston: National Bureau of Economic Research, July 2004).

16. Kenneth M. Johnson, Richelle Winkler, and Luke T. Rogers, *Age and Lifecycle Patterns Driving U.S. Migration Shifts*, Issue Brief 62 (Durham: University of New Hampshire, Carsey Institute, Spring 2013).

17. Indeed, internal migration within the country has been trending downward since the 1980s. Raven Molloy, Christopher L. Smith, and Abigail Wozniak, "Internal Migration in the United States," *Journal of Economic Perspectives* 25, no. 3 (Summer 2011): 173–96.

18. The Grace Kelly, "Minnesota Is the Most Livable State in Climate Change," *Daily Kos*, March 2, 2014, http://www.dailykos.com/story/2014/3/2/1281623/-Minnesota-is-the-Most-Livable-State-in-Climate-Change.

19. Martin and Fogel's analysis, in *Projecting the U.S. Population to 2050*, made alternative forecasts for North Carolina's 2050 population under four immigration scenarios: amnesty with worker visas, a high rate of immigration, the current rate of immigration, and no immigration. The range was a state population of 11.8 million with no immigration, 13.4 million with the current rate of immigration, 13.7 million with a high rate of immigration, and 15.2 million with amnesty and worker visas. The two midrange forecasts are similar to those projected earlier in the chapter.

20. See, e.g., Jonathan V. Last, *What to Expect When No One's Expecting: America's Coming Demographic Disaster* (New York: Encounter Books, 2013); and Philip Longman, *The Empty Cradle: How Falling Birthrates Threaten World Prosperity and What to Do about It* (New York: Basic Books, 2004).

21. Richard Florida, "The Great Growth Disconnect: Population Growth Does Not Equal Economic Growth," *Citylab*, September 30, 2013, http://www.citylab.com/2013/09/great-growth-disconnect-population-growth-does-not-equal-economic-growth/5860; John Seager and Lee S. Polansky, eds., *The Good Crisis: How Population Stabilization Can Foster a Healthy U.S. Economy* (Washington, D.C.: Population Connection, 2016).

22. Indeed, population growth is forecasted to continue in North Carolina, but with a gradually slowing growth rate.

23. U.S. Census Bureau, "Statistical Abstracts Series," http://www.census.gov/library/publications/time-series/statistical_abstracts.html.

Chapter 2

1. U.S. Census Bureau, *Statistical Abstract of the United States, 1970*, http://www.census.gov/library/publications/1970/compendia/statab/91ed.html.

2. U.S. Census Bureau, *Annual Estimates of the Population for Incorporated Places over 100,000* (Washington, D.C.: Government Printing Office, May 2013).

3. U.S. Census Bureau, *Statistical Abstract of the United States, 2010*, http://www.census.gov/library/publications/2009/compendia/statab/129ed.html.

4. U.S. Census Bureau, *Growth in Urban Population Outpaces Rest of Nation*, CB12-50 (Washington, D.C.: Government Printing Office, March 26, 2012); U.S. Department of Agriculture, *Rural America at a Glance*, EB-24 (Washington, D.C.: Government Printing Office, November 2013). Although the designations "rural" and "nonmetropolitan" are used interchangeably, there are definitional differences. The concept of "rural" is based on population density. One definition defines a rural county as one with fewer than five hundred people per square mile. U.S. Census Bureau, "2000 Urban and Rural Classification," https://www.census.gov/geo/reference/ua/urban-rural-2000.html. A nonmetropolitan county is one without an urbanized area of fifty thousand or more people or is a county that does not have substantial commuting to an adjacent county with an urbanized area of fifty thousand or more people. Department of Agriculture, *Rural America at a Glance*.

5. There is debate about the causes of lower levels of educational attainment in rural counties. Some argue that the reason is a lack of educational resources in rural school districts compared to urban school districts. Others place the reason on characteristics of rural students, who may be more likely to come from poverty and lower socioeconomic backgrounds. Studies tend to show a positive relation between educational attainment and the income levels of students' families. For an excellent review of this debate, see Soo-Young Byun, Judith Meece, and Matthew Irwin, "Rural-Non-Rural Differences in Postsecondary Educational Attainment Revisited," *American Educational Research Journal* 49, no. 3 (June 2012): 412–37.

6. North Carolina Commission on Workforce Development, *State of the North Carolina Workforce, 2011–2020* (Raleigh, June 2011), 37–49.

7. Claudia Goldin and Lawrence F. Katz, *The Race between Education and Technology* (Cambridge, Mass.: Harvard University Press, 2008).

8. Historically, urban regions have been centers of creativity. Scholars studying factors related to creative thinking conclude that cities offer several supportive benefits to innovation, including exposure to diverse people and opinions, greater observance of problems and challenges that can spark creative solutions, and even the chaos, tensions, and uncertainty of living in dense environments that can lead to thinking outside the box. Eric Weiner, *The Geography of Genius: A Search for the World's Most Creative Places from Ancient Athens to Silicon Valley* (New York: Simon and Schuster, 2016); Deirdre Nansen McCloskey, *Bourgeois Equality: How Ideas, Not Capital or Institutions, Enriched the World* (Chicago: University of Chicago Press, 2016); Tim Hanford, *Messy: The Power of Disorder to Transform Our Lives* (New York: Riverhead Books, 2016). Also, research examining the development of new industries in the early twenty-first century show that they have typically begun in cities with abundant numbers of college graduates. Thor Berger and Carl Benedikt Frey, "Industrial Renewal in the 21st Century: Evidence from U.S. Cities," *Regional Studies* (2015), DOI: 10.1080/00343404.2015.1100288; Antoine van Agtmael and Fred Bakker, *The Smartest Places on Earth: Why Rustbelts Are the Emerging Hotspots of Global Innovation* (New York: Public Affairs, 2016).

9. Edward Glaeser, *Triumph of the City: How Our Greatest Invention Makes Us Richer, Smarter, Greener, Healthier, and Happier* (New York: Penguin, 2011), 127–28.

10. Michael L. Walden, *North Carolina in the Connected Age: Challenges and Opportunities in a Globalizing Economy* (Chapel Hill: University of North Carolina, 2008), 41–82.

11. Gretchen Livingston and D'Vera Cohn, *U.S. Birth Rate Falls to Record Low: Decline Is Greatest among Immigrants*, Pew Social and Demographic Trends (Washington, D.C.: Pew Research Center, November 29, 2012).

12. U.S. Department of Energy, Energy Information Administration, "Prices and Trends," https://www.energy.gov/public-services/energy-economy/prices-trends.

13. Higher gas prices that increase the value of metropolitan locations will—by increasing the demand for such locations—also eventually increase the price (per square foot) of housing in metropolitan areas. The resulting higher cost of housing in metropolitan areas will reduce some of the advantage of urban residential locations. Thomas Blake, *Commuting Costs and Geographic Sorting in the Housing Market* (San Jose, Calif.: eBay Research Labs, March 21, 2016).

14. Leigh Gallagher, *The End of the Suburbs: Where the American Dream Is Moving* (New York: Penguin, 2013); Nielsen Reports, *Millennials: Breaking the Myths* (New York: Nielsen, January 27, 2014); Nielsen Reports, *Millennials Prefer Cities to Suburbs, Subways to Driveways* (New York: Nielsen, March 4, 2014); Rebecca Diamond, "The Determinants and Welfare Implications of U.S. Workers' Divergent Location Choices by Skill: 1980–2000," *American Economic Review* 106, no. 3 (March 2016): 479–524; Lena Edlund, Cecilia Machado, and Maria Micaela Sviatschi, "Bright Minds, Big Rent: Gentrification and the Rising Returns to Skill," NBER Working Paper 21729 (Boston: National Bureau of Economic Research, November 2015); Tanja Buch et al., "How to Woo the Smart Ones: Evaluating the Determinants That Particularly Attract Highly Qualified People to Cities," HWWI Research Paper 159 (Hamburg: Hamburg Institute of International Economics, December 2014). Edlund et al. show that young,

well-educated households working long hours have chosen centrally located, high-priced residences in order to reduce commuting time and preserve time for leisure activities. Buch and colleagues find that young, college-educated workers are attracted to cities with more days of sunlight, more restaurants, and greater cultural diversity.

15. Joel Kotkin, "The Geography of Aging: Why Millennials Are Headed to the Suburbs," forbes.com, December 9, 2013; Joel Kotkin, *The Human City: Urbanism for the Rest of Us* (Chicago: B2 Books, 2016). Kotkin's point is that household age largely determines residential location, and as millennials age, their locational preferences will change. He argues that older millennials have already begun choosing suburban locations, and recent data support his view. Diana Olick, "Your New Neighbor in the 'Burbs? A Millennial. Yes, Really," cnbc.com, March 9, 2016; Laura Kusisto, "Suburbs Outstrip Cities in Population Growth," *WSJ*, December 5, 2016.

16. Georgeanne Artz, "Rural Brain Drain: Is It a Reality?," *Choices* 18, no. 4 (2003): 11–15.

17. Mary Beth Watson Fritz, Sridhar Narasimhan, and Hyeun-Suk Rhee, "Connection and Coordination in the Virtual Office," *Journal of Management Information Systems* 14, no. 4 (1998): 7–28.

18. Glaeser, *Triumph of the City*, 11–12.

19. Table 2.1 is based on discussion in Edward Glaeser, "The Economic Approach to Cities," NBER Working Paper 13696 (Boston: National Bureau of Economic Research, December 2007).

20. In contrast, the prices of some consumer goods have been found to be cheaper in urban areas than in rural areas. Jessie Handbury and David Weinstein, "Goods Prices and Availability in Cities," *Review of Economic Studies* 82, no. 1 (January 2015): 258–96.

21. An example of a developing "live, work, play" planned community in North Carolina is Chatham Park in Chatham County, part of the Triangle metropolitan region.

22. For a discussion of the new possibilities of remote living, see Joel Kotkin, *The New Class Conflict* (Candor, N.Y.: Telos, 2014). Some have advocated the expansion of broadband internet connections to rural areas as a method to spur rural economic development. Current research has not found a link between the addition of broadband service and economic improvement of the local resident population, such as through enhanced local entrepreneurship. The economic improvement that does occur appears to be from the location of outside firms bringing an outside workforce to the local area. Jed Kolko, "Broadband and Local Growth," *Journal of Urban Economics* 71, no. 1 (January 2012): 100–113.

23. Laura Stevens, "E-Commerce Is a Boon for Rural America, but It Comes with a Price," *WSJ*, September 11, 2016.

24. Christopher Mims, "Advances in Driverless Cars Will Fuel Suburban Sprawl," *WSJ*, June 20, 2016.

25. Map 2.2 is based on county population forecasts through 2035 made by the state demographer of North Carolina and a continuation of the implied trends through 2050 calibrated by the author.

26. Richard Florida, "The Mega-Regions of North America," Martin Prosperity Insights, Rotman School of Management, University of Toronto, March 11, 2014, http://martinprosperity.org/content/the-mega-regions-of-north-america.

27. Ibid.

28. A new intercity transportation mode in the development stage is the "hyperloop," a system moving people in tubes reaching 700 mph. Promoters say the technology could be in prototype form by the 2020s. Josh Lipton, "Hyperloop Will Be Here and the Impact Will Be Huge," *CNBC*, March 7, 2016, http://www.cnbc.com/2016/03/07/hyperloop-will-be-here-in-2020-and-the-impact-will-be-huge.html.

29. John Pender and Faqir Bagi, "Attracting Retirees as a Wealth Creation Strategy," in *Rural Wealth Creation*, ed. John Pender et al. (London: Routledge, 2014), 232–47.

30. An example of this strategy is the community of River Landing in Duplin County. Allison Williams, "Hog Heaven," *Business North Carolina*, April 2016, 8–10.

31. Pender and Bagi, "Attracting Retirees as a Wealth Creation Strategy."

32. For a glimpse at this possible future, see Frederick Pilot, *Last Rush Hour: The Decentralization of Knowledge Work in the Twenty-First Century* (Portland, Ore.: Bookbaby, 2015).

Chapter 3

1. These manufacturing industries existed in North Carolina in the nineteenth century, but they experienced their greatest growth in the early twentieth century. Hugh Lefler and Albert Newsome, *The History of a Southern State: North Carolina* (Chapel Hill: University of North Carolina Press, 1954).

2. Historical research shows that the shift from farming to manufacturing began to occur as early as the first half of the nineteenth century, when farming could have accounted for as much as 70 percent of both GDP and employment. Robert Gallman and Thomas Weiss, "The Service Industries in the Nineteenth Century," in *Production and Productivity in the Service Industry*, ed. Victor Fuchs (New York: Columbia University, 1969), 287–352.

3. The GDP shares are after adjusting for price changes over time, so technically they are "real" GDP shares. The price adjustments were made using price indices specific to farming and manufacturing; www.census.gov/library/publications/1975/compendia/his_stats_colonial-1970.html, and www.bls.gov/ppi/; U.S. Department of Commerce, Bureau of Economic Analysis, "Price Indices for Gross Domestic Product," table 1.1.4, www.bea.gov/iTable/iTable.cfm?ReqID=9&step=1#reqid=9&step=3&isuri=1&903=4. Aggregate GDP values for North Carolina are from the U.S. Department of Commerce, Bureau of Economic Analysis, "Regional Economic Accounts," https://www.bea.gov/regional/, for years since 1970 and are estimated using a methodology created by Angus Maddison for years before 1970, www.worldeconomics.com. Production values (in dollar values) for farming are from various editions of the *Census of Agriculture* and for manufacturing from various editions of the *Census of Population and Housing*.

4. A major reason for the relative decline in manufacturing in North Carolina after 2000 was the entry of China into the World Trade Organization and the movement of non-durable manufacturing in the state—particularly textiles and apparel—to locations in Asia. Justine Pierce and Peter Schott, "The Surprisingly Swift Decline of U.S. Manufacturing," *American Economic Review* 106, no. 7 (July 2016): 1632–62. But again it is important to note that a falling GDP share does not necessarily imply falling production. Between 1977

and 2015 in North Carolina, the output of the state's factories rose 139 percent. Similarly, the output from the state's farms jumped 283 percent. U.S. Department of Commerce, Bureau of Economic Analysis, Regional Economic Accounts (hereafter cited as Regional Economic Accounts), "Quantity Indices for Real GDP," table 1.1.3, www.bea.gov/iTable/iTable.cfm?ReqID=9&step=1#reqid=9&step=3&isuri=1&903=3.

5. Expansion of state economy as measured by increase in real GDP.

6. U.S. Department of Commerce, Regional Economic Accounts, www.bea.gov/regional.index.htm; U.S. Department of Commerce, State and Local Employment, www.bls.gov/sae/. GDP share percentages for services are based on price-adjusted values for 1990 and after and price-unadjusted values for 1980 and earlier. Economic sectors other than farming, manufacturing, and services include construction, trade, transportation, communications, finance, and government.

7. Regional Economic Accounts.

8. The long-run average annual growth rate in GDP per capita for the nation from 1900 to 2015 has been only slightly higher, at 1.77 percent. The gains are adjusted for inflation.

9. For views on the future of retailing, see Ali Hortacsu and Chad Syverson, "The Ongoing Evolution of U.S. Retail: A Format Tug-of-War," *Journal of Economic Perspectives* 29, no. 4 (Fall 2015): 89–122.

10. The "relative productivity" and "location quotient" measures use data for 2012.

11. "High tech" textiles and apparel include acoustical materials, fire-resistant fabrics, and fabrics that can warm and cool the user.

12. United Nations, Department of Economic and Social Affairs, Population Division, *World Population Prospects: The 2012 Revision* (New York: United Nations, 2013).

13. "A Billion Shades of Grey," *Economist*, April 26, 2014.

14. In 2011, the location quotient for manufacturing equipment and supplies in North Carolina was 1.2, and its relative productivity measure was 1.8. U.S. Census Bureau, *Annual Survey of Manufacturers, 2011* (Washington, D.C.: Government Printing Office, 2013).

15. Some elderly households also make use of the Medicaid program—which is jointly funded by federal and state governments—but households over age sixty-five account for only 14 percent of Medicaid's costs. Center on Budget and Policy Priorities, "Policy Basics: Introduction to Medicaid" (Washington, D.C., August 16, 2016, www.cbpp.org/research/health/policy-basics-introduction-to-medicaid).

16. An example of an optimist is former AOL founder Steve Case. Steve Case. *The Third Wave: An Entrepreneur's Vision of the Future* (New York: Simon and Schuster, 2016).

17. The U.S. Chamber of Commerce ranked the Triangle region (combining the Raleigh-Cary and Durham–Chapel Hill metropolitan regions) fourth in the nation for innovation and entrepreneurship in the technology sector. Donna Harris and Patrick McAnaney, *Innovation That Matters* (Washington, D.C.: U.S. Chamber of Commerce Foundation, 2016). Richard Florida ranked the Raleigh-Cary metro area (one part of the Triangle region) sixth and the Durham–Chapel Hill metro area (the second part of the Triangle region) eighth in his high-tech index. Richard Florida, "America's Leading High-Tech Metros," *Atlantic CityLab*, June 28, 2012, http://www.citylab.com/tech/2012/06/

americas-leading-high-tech-metros/2244/. *Bizjournals* ranked Raleigh-Cary tenth among the nation's top 100 high-tech metro areas. Scott G. Thomas, "America's Top 100 High-Tech Centers," *Business Journals*, March 16, 2011, http://www.bizjournals.com/bizjournals/on-numbers/archive/americas-tech-centers.html. Among the top one hundred tech centers by the latter ranking, Charlotte was fifty-ninth and Greensboro was seventy-third. Perhaps more impressive, Raleigh-Cary created the second highest number of high-tech and STEM jobs in the country between 2001 and 2013. The leader was Austin. Joel Kotkin, "The Most Surprising Cities Creating the Most Tech Jobs," *Forbes*, January 20, 2013.

18. Research Triangle Partnership, "Clusters," 2014, www.researchtriangle.org.

19. The Carnegie Foundation created the Research I designation to indicate universities involved in significant research activities. Carnegie Foundation for the Advancement of Teaching, *Research I Universities* (Pittsburgh, Pa., 1994). In 1994, only fifty-nine universities were classified as Research I institutions. In 2000, the Carnegie Foundation redesigned its university and college designations and eliminated the category Research I, but the classification is still used.

20. The percentage of adults (age twenty-five and over) with a bachelor's degree or higher was 43 percent in the central North Carolina corridor counties of Mecklenburg (Charlotte), Forsyth (Winston-Salem), Guilford (Greensboro), Durham (Durham), Orange (Chapel Hill), and Wake (Raleigh), compared to 28 percent for the state and 30 percent for the nation. U.S. Census Bureau of the Census, "American Community Survey, 2013," https://www.census.gov/programs-surveys/acs/.

21. "Material Benefits," *Economist*, September 7, 2013; Rachel Pannett, "An End to Laundry? The Promise of Self-Cleaning Fabric," *WSJ*, April 26, 2016.

22. Tess Pennington, "It Ain't Just for Smoking: Known but Beneficial Uses for Tobacco," August 27, 2010, http://readynutrition.com/resources/it-aint-just-for-smoking-known-but-beneficial-uses-for-tobacco_27082010/.

23. For details on how the world has become interconnected, see Parag Khanna, *Connectography: Mapping the Future of Global Civilization* (New York: Random House, 2016). For an alternative viewpoint suggesting that international trade may not expand or may even recede, see Tyler Cowen, "Economic Development in an 'Average Is Over' World," Working Paper, April 8, 2016, https://www.gmu.edu/centers/publicchoice/faculty%20pages/Tyler/Manila.pdf.

24. "Developing Economies Increase Share of Global Output," *DATAblog*, World Bank, July 8, 2010, http://blogs.worldbank.org/opendata/developing-economies-increase-share-global-output. For detailed geographic forecasts of world economic growth, see Richard Dobbs et al., *Urban World: The Global Consumers to Watch* (Washington, D.C.: McKinsey Global Institute, April 2016).

25. The World Bank, "Global Economic Prospects, June 2014," http://pubdocs.worldbank.org/en/767961448980802634/Global-Economic-Prospects-June-2014-Shifting-priorities.pdf; Jacques Bughin et al., *Lions on the Move II: Realizing the Potential of Africa's Economies* (Washington, D.C.: McKinsey Global Institute, September 2016).

26. Alex Dixon, "RDU Considers 2nd Non-Stop International Flight," *Herald Sun* (Durham, N.C.), October 6, 2014.

27. Bruce Blonigen and Anca Cristea, "Airports and Urban Growth: Evidence from a Quasi-Natural Experiment," NBER Working Paper 19278 (Boston: National Bureau

of Economic Research, July 2012); Jan Bruecker, "Airline Traffic and Economic Development," *Urban Studies* 40, no. 8 (July 2003): 1455–69.

28. Michael L. Walden, *Economic Benefits of International Air Service to the Triangle Region*, Report Submitted to the RDU International Airport Authority (Raleigh: North Carolina State University, October 2014). In 2016, Delta began a new nonstop flight from RDU International Airport to Paris.

29. John D. Kasarda and Greg Lindsay, *Aerotropolis: The Way We'll Live Next* (New York: Farrar, Straus and Giroux, 2011).

30. Ibid., 169–73.

31. Michael Powell, "Runway Nation," *NYT Book Review*, March 6, 2011, 17.

32. Michael Chiulli, *The New Panama Canal and North Carolina: Potential Economic Impacts and Opportunities* (Durham, N.C.: Sanford School of Public Policy, Duke University, 2014).

33. Charles Mitchell, "Impact of the Expansion of the Panama Canal: An Engineering Analysis," Working Paper (University of Delaware, 2011); Jennifer Bratton, Dustin Burke, and Peter Ulrich, *Wide Open: How the Panama Canal Expansion Is Redrawing the Logistics Map* (Boston: Boston Consulting Group, June 2015).

34. Chiulli, *New Panama Canal and North Carolina*; AECOM, *North Carolina Maritime Strategy*, Report Prepared for the North Carolina Department of Transportation (Los Angeles, June 26, 2012).

35. Chiulli, *New Panama Canal and North Carolina*. By 2016, North Carolina had already seen some increased cargo traffic at its ports as a result of the expanded Panama Canal. Office of the Governor of North Carolina, "Governor McGrory Announces New Container Service Partnership with the North Carolina Ports Authority" (Press release, Raleigh, October 31, 2016).

36. Chiulli, *New Panama Canal and North Carolina*; AECOM, *North Carolina Maritime Strategy*. Six feasible sites have been identified for a new deepwater port in North Carolina, including three near Wilmington, one near Morehead City, and two in Pamlico County near Pamlico Sound.

37. John Murawski, "Deepwater Port Plans Put on Ice," *N&O*, July 22, 2010.

38. Cambridge Systematics, *NC I-95 Economic Assessment: Final Report*, Prepared for the North Carolina Department of Transportation (Cambridge, Mass., May 2013). Transshipment terminals at the intersections of major roads and rail lines, where incoming freight is sorted for final delivery, are another likely economic development opportunity resulting from increased international cargo traversing the state. For the potential economic impact from one such proposed terminal in North Carolina, see WSP/Parsons Brinckerhoff Engineering Services, *Project Scorpion: Evaluation of a Proposed Intermodal Terminal* (Raleigh, N.C., January 2016). The analysis calculates a four-to-one economic benefit–cost ratio for the project. A study by North Carolina State University estimated that an inland cargo transit hub servicing increased East Coast shipments could generate twenty-six thousand jobs and $2.8 billion of annual economic activity in the state by 2035 (forecasts are midrange estimates). David Kay et al., *Economic Impacts of a North Carolina Intermodal Facility* (Raleigh: North Carolina State University, Institute for Transportation Research and Education, April 2016). In 2016, CSX Transportation announced an intention to construct an inland cargo terminal in Edgecombe County

("CSX Finally Finds Home for Cargo Hub in Rocky Mount," July 19, 2016, www.wral
.com/CSX-to-build-massive-cargo-terminal-in-edgecombe-county/15861789/).

39. An example of a partnership between the state and a foreign firm is the I-77 expansion near Charlotte, jointly funded by the state of North Carolina and the Spanish firm Cintra. The funding split is 12 percent from North Carolina and 88 percent from Cintra. Steve Harrison, "Toll Road Firm Had Setbacks," *Charlotte Observer*, June 30, 2014.

40. Justin Ervin and Zachary A. Smith, *Globalization: A Reference Handbook* (Santa Barbara, Calif.: ABC-CLIO, 2008).

41. Janet Larsen, "Meat Consumption in China Now Double That in the U.S.," April 24, 2012, http://www.treehugger.com/sustainable-agriculture/meat.html.

42. Nikos Alexandratos and Jelle Bruinsma, *World Agriculture: Towards 2015/2030*, ESA Working Paper no. 12-13 (Rome: Food and Agricultural Organization of the United Nations, 2012 revision); www.fao.org/docrep/016/ap106e/ap106e.pdf. It is expected that the world will increase meal calories consumed per person by almost 25 percent between 2010 and 2050. "Factory Fresh," *Economist*, Technology Quarterly: The Future of Agriculture, June 11, 2015, 4.

43. The data are for 1948 to 2012. U.S. Department of Agriculture, Economic Research Service, *Agricultural Productivity in the U.S.* (Washington, D.C.: Government Printing Office, 2014).

44. C. Hurt and K. Zering, "Hog Production Booms in North Carolina: Why There, Why Now?," *Ohio Challenge* 7, no. 1 (October 1994): 15–17; Hiram M. Drache, *Creating Abundance: Visionary Entrepreneurs of Agriculture* (Danville, Ill.: Interstate, 2001), 187–210.

45. North Carolina Department of Agriculture and Consumer Services, *North Carolina Agricultural Statistics* (Raleigh, 2013); National Chicken Council, *Top Broiler Producing States* (Washington, D.C., 2010).

46. "Inside the World's Largest Pork Processing Plant," *ChemInfo*, June 16, 2010, www.cheminfo/videos/2010/06/inside-the-worlds-largest-pork-processing-plant.

47. North Carolina Department of Agriculture and Consumer Services, *North Carolina Agricultural Statistics*. Growth is measured in animal numbers.

48. Jay Price, "Demand for Pork Rises but Cap Stays," *N&O*, December 21, 2014.

49. Although ocean transport is generally the most inexpensive for exports, in the early twenty-first century some North Carolina meat exports (mainly to Japan) were trucked to West Coast ports rather than shipped via the Panama Canal. Even with the Panama Canal expansion, this method may continue to be used for specific meats. J. Andrew Curliss, "In the Chute or to Tokyo: From Pig to Global Market," *N&O*, December 16, 2014.

50. Trans-Pacific Partnership, "What Is the Trans-Pacific Partnership?," 2014, www
.transpacificpartnership.org. The U.S. withdrew from the treaty in 2017.

51. Jacob Bunge, "Sizzling Steaks Made in the Lab," *WSJ*, February 1, 2016; Mark Post, "Cultured Meat from Stem Cells: Challenges and Prospects," *Meat Science* 92, no. 3 (November 2012): 297–301. For a fascinating look at how science and technology are being used in innovative food production, see Jayson Lusk, *Unnaturally Delicious: How Science and Technology Are Serving Up Super Foods to Save the World* (New York: St. Martin's, 2016).

52. Michael L. Walden, "The Economic Potential from Developing North Carolina's On-Shore and Off-Shore Energy Resources," Working Paper (North Carolina State University, April 2013).

53. Timothy Considine, "Economic and Environmental Impacts of Oil and Gas Development Offshore the Delmarva, Carolinas, and Georgia," Working Paper (University of Wyoming, September 2014).

54. The percentages for all states include the direct effects of production and employment at the energy firms as well as the effects from supplier firms and retail firms from economic activity generated at the energy firms. U.S. Department of Commerce, Bureau of Economic Analysis, "State GDP," www.bea.gov/iTable/iTable .cfm?reqid=70&step=1&isuri=1&acrdn=2#reqid=70&step=1&isuri=1; W. Frank Barton, "Oil and Gas Multipliers," Working Paper (Wichita State University, 2012).

55. Forecasts suggest the new interstate pipeline could be built by late 2018 and double the quantity of natural gas flowing into North Carolina. John Murawski, "New Natural Gas Pipeline to N.C. Could Dampen Interest in Fracking," *Charlotte Observer*, June 13, 2014.

56. U.S. Department of Energy, "North Carolina Energy Profile," www.eia.gov/ state/?sid=NC#tab-4. Net electricity generation is the remainder after subtracting the energy usage at the electric power generation facility.

57. "Report: 20 Percent Solar in Reach," *Environment North Carolina*, November 20, 2014, http://www.environmentnorthcarolina.org/news/nce/report-20-percent-solar-reach.

58. "Power to the People: Storing Renewable Energy on the Grid," *Economist*, December 6, 2014.

59. John Downey, "Strata Solar Plans Massive Solar Farm," *Strata Solar*, April 13, 2012, http://www.stratasolar.com/2012/04/13/strata-solar-plans-massive-solar-farm/.

60. State of North Carolina, *Report of the Governor's Scientific Panel on Off-Shore Energy*, Report Submitted to Governor Perdue (Raleigh, September 30, 2011).

61. U.S. Department of Energy, State Profiles and Energy Estimates, www.eia.gov/ state/.

62. Derek Medlin, "Duke Suspends Plans for Shearon Harris," May 3, 2013, www .wral.com/duke-suspends-plans-for-shearon-harris-expansion/12408113/.

63. The value is for 2014. California Department of Food and Agriculture, "California Agricultural Production Statistics," https://www.cdfa.ca.gov/statistics. Steve Bock, "California vs. North Carolina: Farming and Drought," *Carolina Opinion*, May 17, 2015, www.carolinaopinion.com/politics-1/2015/5/17/california-vs-north-carolina-farming-drought. If North Carolina were able to supplant California as an East Coast supplier of fruits and vegetables, it would revive the role played by the state's truck farmers in the early twentieth century. Adrienne Monteith Petty, *Standing Their Ground: Small Farmers in North Carolina since the Civil War* (New York: Oxford University Press, 2013).

64. The technology and professional sector includes the information and professional/businesses services industries as defined by the Bureau of Economic Analysis (BEA). Also defined by BEA are durable manufacturing, including industries that produce long-lasting manufactured outputs; tourism, composed of the arts, entertainment, and accommodation industries; and agribusiness, including farming and farm-product processing.

65. However, future manufacturing will likely not be structured in the same way as manufacturing of the past. For forecasts of how manufacturing operations might change, see Michael Rüssman et al., *Industry 4.0: The Future of Productivity and Growth in Manufacturing Industries* (Boston: Boston Consulting Group, April 2015).

66. Research Triangle Park in the Triangle region of Raleigh, Durham, and Chapel Hill—one of the original technology parks—recently began a major expansion and "refreshing" ("Park Center—Re-Imagine What RTP Can Be," www.rtp.org/about-us/park-center/). The new version of technology and innovation research parks emphasize shopping, eating, and residential amenities for workers. Bruce Katz and Julie Wagner, *The Rise of Innovation Districts: A New Geography of Innovation in America*, Metropolitan Policy Program Report (Washington, D.C.: Brookings Institute, May 2014).

Chapter 4

1. See Claudia Goldin and Lawrence F. Katz, *The Race between Education and Technology* (Cambridge, Mass.: Harvard University Press, 2008), for an excellent discussion of the changing workplace roles of workers and technology and implications for educational training.

2. For a review of human capital's role in economic growth, see Joseph E. Stiglitz and Bruce C. Greenwald, *Creating a Learning Society: A New Approach to Growth, Development, and Social Progress* (New York: Columbia University Press, 2014).

3. One reason for North Carolina's better educational gains than the nation overall may be the state's greater support of higher education, which has been found to be positively related to larger education enrollments and better improvements in workforce educational attainment. John Kennan, "Spatial Variation in Higher Education Financing and the Supply of College Graduates," NBER Working Paper 21065 (Boston: National Bureau of Economic Research, April 2015).

4. The annual gains in the three levels of educational attainment varied somewhat for the last decade of the twentieth century and the first fifteen years of the twenty-first century. For North Carolina, the average annual percentage point gain for high school or greater attainment was 0.81 points between 1990 and 2000 compared to 0.6 points between 2000 and 2015; for a bachelor's degree or greater attainment, the average annual percentage point gain was 0.51 points between 1990 and 2000 compared to 0.49 points between 2000 and 2015. For the nation, the greatest difference was for high school or greater attainment, where the average annual percentage point gain was 0.52 points between 1990 and 2000 compared to 0.49 points between 2000 and 2015.

5. U.S. Department of Education, "National Assessment of Educational Progress," State Profiles: North Carolina, 2015, www.nces.ed.gov/nationsreportcard/states/.

6. See, e.g., P. Aghion, L. Boustan, and J. Vandenbussche, *The Causal Impact of Education on Economic Growth: Evidence from the United States*, Brookings Papers on Economic Activity (Washington, D.C.: Brookings Institute, Spring 2009).

7. Norbert Jorek, Johan Gott, and Michelle Battat, *The Shifting Geography of Offshoring* (Chicago: A. T. Kearney, 2009), https://www.atkearney.com/documents/10192/fda82529-b60a-4fae-8d92-22cfd69b95b3.

8. See Daron Acemoglu and David Autor, "Skills, Tasks, and Technologies: Implications for Employment and Earnings," in *Handbook of Labor Economics*, vol. 4b, ed. Orley Ashenfelter and David Card (Amsterdam: North Holland, 2011), 1043–72; Frank Levy and Richard J. Murnane, *The New Division of Labor: How Computers Are Creating the Next Job Market* (Princeton, N.J.: Princeton University Press, 2004); Lynn A. Karoly and Constantijn Panis, *The Twenty-First Century at Work: Forces Shaping the Future Workforce and Workplace in the United States* (Santa Monica, Calif.: Rand Corporation, 2004); and Gideon Rose, ed., *The Fourth Industrial Revolution: A Davos Reader* (New York: Foreign Affairs, 2016).

9. There are no official statistical counts of jobs using the task definitions. Following Acemoglu and Autor ("Skills, Tasks, and Technologies"), problem-solving task jobs are defined as managerial, professional, technical, and public administration occupations; routine task jobs are defined as clerical, administrative, and sales occupations (routine cognitive) and as transportation, production, and operative occupations (routine manual); and nonroutine task jobs are defined as remaining service occupations, mainly in the personal and business services. In *The Work of Nations: Preparing Ourselves for 21st-Century Capitalism* (New York: Vintage Books, 1992), former U.S. labor secretary Robert Reich refers to "problem-solving task" jobs as "symbolic-analytic service" jobs, to "routine task" jobs as "routine production services" jobs, and to "nonroutine task" jobs as "in-person services" jobs. He largely correctly anticipated the trends in each task category over the next quarter century.

10. During the period 2002–15, the median wage of occupations reducing employment exceeded the median wage of occupations adding employment by $1.50 per hour. Michael L. Walden, "Occupational Change in North Carolina: Implications for Coping with Technological Unemployment," Working Paper (North Carolina State University, Institute for Emerging Issues, May 2016).

11. Based on comparing labor productivity rates (real dollar GDP/employment) for sectors categorized by the three tasks for the nation and North Carolina for the years 1997 (earliest available) and 2015. Data from the U.S. Department of Commerce, Bureau of Economic Analysis, www.bea.gov/iTable/iTable.cfm?reqid=70&step=1&isuri=1&acrdn=2#reqid=70&step=10&isuri=1&7003=900&7035=-1&7004=naics&7005=-1&7006=37000&7036=-1&7001=1900&7002=1&7090=70&7007-=-1&7093=levels.

12. Martin Ford, *Rise of the Robots: Technology and the Threat of a Jobless Future* (New York: Basic Books, 2015); "The Return of the Machinery Question," *Economist*, June 25, 2016, 1–16.

13. Carl Benedikt Frey and Michael A. Osborne, "The Future of Employment: How Susceptible Are Jobs to Computerisation?," Working Paper (Oxford University, September 2013). Using Frey and Osborne's methodology, Frey, Osborne, and Craig Holmes find that some countries face much higher likelihoods of technological unemployment. Carl Benedikt Frey, Michael A. Osborne, and Craig Holmes, *Technology at Work v2.0: The Future Is Not What It Used to Be*, Citi GPS: Global Perspectives and Solutions (Oxford: Citi and Oxford University, January 2016).

14. Jerry Kaplan, *Humans Need Not Apply: A Guide to Wealth and Work in the Age of Artificial Intelligence* (New Haven, Conn.: Yale University Press, 2015), 152; Michael

Chui, James Manyika, and Mehdi Miremadi, "Four Fundamentals of Workplace Automation," *McKinsey Quarterly*, November 2015; Michael Chui, James Manyika, and Mehdi Miremadi, "Where Machines Could Replace Humans—and Where They Can't (Yet)," *McKinsey Quarterly*, July 2016. James Huntington also discusses the job displacement by modern technology. James B. Huntington, *Work's New Age: The End of Full Employment and What It Means to You* (Eldred, N.Y.: Royal Flush, 2012). World Economic Forum, *The Future of Jobs* (Zurich, January 2016), analyzes the impacts of technological development on world labor markets. Melanie Arntz, Terry Gregory, and Ulrich Zierahn arrive at a much lower rate of future technological employment by arguing that most occupations are a combination of tasks, some of which can be automated and others that cannot. Hence, they separate the tasks of an occupation between those that can be replaced by technology and those that cannot, and they continue employment in those parts of reconfigured occupations where human labor is still necessary. Melanie Arntz, Terry Gregory, and Ulrich Zierahn, *The Rise of Automation for Jobs in OECD Countries*, OECD Social, Employment and Migration Working Paper 189 (Paris: OECD, 2016). In contrast, Frey and Osborne, "Future of Employment," use the primary task of an occupation in defining its susceptibility to technological unemployment. As an example, if the major task of paralegals is case research, then Frey and Osborne eliminates this occupation if computer programs can perform the case research. But if a secondary task of paralegals is customizing the case research for a specific case—something which may not be easily performed by a computer program; in this case, Arntz, Gregory, and Zierahn would keep a reconstituted paralegal occupation with employment based on the customization of computer-based case research.

15. Ian Wyatt and David Hecker, "Occupational Changes during the 20th Century," *Monthly Labor Review* (March 2006): 35–57. The McKinsey Institute found that one third of U.S. jobs that existed in the early twenty-first century did not exist twenty-five years earlier. James Manyika et al., *Global Growth: Can Productivity Save the Day in an Aging World?* (London: McKinsey Global Institute, January 2015). Ford, *Rise of the Robots*, sees potential for a return of some jobs to the United States from foreign countries ("re-shoring") if technological unemployment reaches all countries, but he estimates that the gain would be small.

16. James Manyika et al., *Digital America: A Tale of the Haves and Have-Mores* (London: McKinsey Global Institute, December 2015).

17. Support for the Frey-Osborne index is found by a statistically significant inverse relation between higher levels of the index (meaning a greater likelihood of technological unemployment for an occupation) and the occupation's job growth rate between 2002 and 2015. Walden, "Occupational Change in North Carolina."

18. For an analysis of the impact of technological unemployment on professional occupations, see Richard Susskind and Daniel Susskind, *The Future of the Professions: How Technology Will Transform the Work of Human Experts* (Oxford: Oxford University Press, 2015).

19. A new wave of technology-driven mechanization is even coming to agriculture: robot-controlled fruit pickers are one example. Ilan Brat, "Goodbye Field Hand, Hello Fruit-Picking Robot," *WSJ*, April 24, 2015.

20. North Carolina State University, Institute for Emerging Issues, "Future-Work Disruption Index for North Carolina," February 1, 2016, https://iei.ncsu.edu/disruptionindex/.

21. An example of high-paid occupational layoffs from technology is the Cisco announcement in 2016 of 5,500 layoffs, including many software engineers, due to the replacement of machine-based computing and data storage with cloud-based computing and data storage. David Ranii, "Cisco Plans to Lay Off 5500 Employees," *N&O*, August 17, 2016.

22. Nir Jaimovich and Henry Siu document an acceleration of technological unemployment after the Great Recession and argue that this acceleration is one reason for the relatively slow postrecession job recovery. Nir Jaimovich and Henry Siu, "The Trend Is the Cycle: Job Polarization and Jobless Recoveries," NBER Working Paper 18334 (Boston: National Bureau of Economic Research, August 2012).

23. U.S. Department of Labor, Bureau of Labor Statistics, "Employment Projections to 2024," *Monthly Labor Review*, December 2015, http://www.bls.gov/news.release/ecopro.toc.htm. One issue is whether the national growth rates should be adjusted upward for North Carolina, since the state has grown more rapidly than the nation in the post–World War II era. However, the positive difference between the North Carolina growth rate (in GDP) and the national growth rate has been narrowing, from 28 percent during the decade 1980–90 to 23 percent during the decade 1990–2000 to 11 percent during the decade 2000–2010. U.S. Department of Commerce, Bureau of Economic Analysis, "GDP by State," https://www.bea.gov/iTable/iTable.cfm?reqid=70&step=1&isuri=1&acrdn=2#reqid=70&step=1&isuri=1. This trend is in line with the theory of growth convergence between states and regions. Matthew Higgins, Daniel Levy, and Andrew Young, "Growth and Convergence across the U.S.: Evidence from County-Level Data," *Review of Economics and Statistics* 88, no. 4 (November 2006): 671–81. The national growth rates for occupations were therefore directly applied to North Carolina.

24. U.S. Department of Labor, Bureau of Labor Statistics, "Employment Projections to 2024." Following the logic of note 23, above, the same national industry growth rates were applied to North Carolina. The rate at which employment changes when economic output changes is from William Seyfried, "Examining the Relationship between Employment and Economic Growth in the Ten Largest States," *Southwestern Economic Review* 32, no. 1 (Spring 2005): 13–24.

25. Total population and working age population growth rates are from the U.S. Department of Labor, Bureau of Labor Statistics, "Employment Projections to 2024" and table 1.2.

26. To demonstrate the difficulty in achieving consensus on job forecasts, some analysts see the problem being too few workers (as a result of declining birth rates) for the number of available jobs—that is, a labor shortage. Gad Levanon et al., *Not Enough Workers* (Conference Board, September 2014). Conversely, some analysts even see an oversupply of STEM workers in the future. Michael S. Teitelbaum, *Falling Behind? Boom, Bust, and the Global Race for Scientific Talent* (Princeton, N.J.: Princeton University Press, 2014).

27. An even bolder argument states that all past, present, and future knowledge will be able to be produced by computers. Pedro Domingos, *The Master Algorithm: How*

the Quest for the Ultimate Learning Machine Will Remake Our World (New York: Basic Books, 2015). For a discussion of life under a robot- and technologically controlled world, see Robin Hanson, *The Age of Em: Work, Love, and Life When Robots Rule the Earth* (Oxford: Oxford University Press, 2016).

28. See Guy Standing, *The Precariat: The New Dangerous Class* (London: Blooms-bury, 2014); and Ulrich Beck, *The Brave New World of Work* (Cambridge, Mass.: Pol-ity, 2000). The word "precariat" is derived by merging precarious with proletariat and connotes a permanent situation of job insecurity and underemployment. It might be expected that precariats would exhibit negative social indicators, such as higher mortal-ity rates. Indeed, research has documented a recent rise in mortality rates among some middle-age households with low levels of educational attainment, precisely the house-holds who would be expected to have been adversely impacted by current labor mar-ket trends. Anne Case and Angus Deaton, "Rising Morbidity and Mortality in Midlife among White Non-Hispanic Americans in the 21st Century," *Proceedings of the National Academy of Sciences* 112, no. 49 (2015): 15078–83. For a discussion of the broad social issues related to the impact of technological advances on human life and values, see John Markoff, *Machines of Loving Grace: The Quest for Common Ground between Humans and Robots* (New York: HarperCollins, 2015).

29. Nicholas Eberstadt, *Men without Work: America's Invisible Crisis* (West Consho-hocken, Pa.: Templeton, 2016), 108.

30. Tyler Cowen, *Average Is Over: Powering America beyond the Age of the Great Stag-nation* (New York: Dutton, 2013); Derek Thompson, "A World without Work," *Atlantic*, July–August 2015, 50–61; David Colander, "A Minimum Guaranteed Jobs Proposal," *Eastern Economic Journal* 42, no. 6 (September 2016): 666–69.

31. For a gloomy economic and social outlook of a future dominated by technology and machines, see Yuval Harari, *Homo Deus: A Brief History of Tomorrow* (New York: Harper, 2016).

32. For an analysis of the impact of technological advancement on consumer prices, see Ben Miller and Robert D. Atkinson, *Are Robots Taking Our Jobs, or Making Them?* (Washington, D.C.: Information and Technology Foundation, September 2013). Opti-mists also think that the two forces of technology and economic liberalization will make it easier for business start-ups to develop and new industries to take hold. John Hagel, "The Disruption Debate—What's Missing?," *Edge Perspectives*, June 30, 2014, http:// edgeperspectives.typepad.com/edge_perspectives/2014/06/the-disruption-debate .html. This, they argue, will likely result in a society that is richer and happier. Ryan Avent, *The Wealth of Humans: Work, Power, and Status in the Twenty-First Century* (New York: St. Martin's, 2016). Others see a rise of self-employment in the future workforce, which—they argue—could increase worker happiness. Carl Benedikt Frey and Michael Osborne, *Technology at Work: The Future of Innovation and Employment*, Citi GPS: Global Perspectives and Solutions (Oxford: Citi and Oxford University, February 2015). There is also the theoretical argument over whether labor and capital (technology) are substitutes or complements. If the latter, then technological improvements would increase the value of labor and lead to greater labor usage. Robert Lawrence, "Recent Declines in Labor's Share in U.S. Income: A Preliminary Neoclassical Account," NBER Working Paper 21296 (Boston: National Bureau of Economic Research, June 2015);

David Autor, "Why Are There Still So Many Jobs? The History and Future of Workplace Automation," *Journal of Economic Perspectives* 29, no. 3 (Summer 2015): 3–30.

33. Geoffrey Fowler, "The Uber of Everything: Build a Staff with Apps," *WSJ*, May 6, 2015; Ryan Lawler, "Meet Hello Alfred, a Single Portal for Your Home Service Needs," May 10, 2015, https://techcrunch.com/2015/05/10/meet-hello-alfred-a-single-portal-for-your-home-service-needs/.

34. The "internet of everything" is a term describing the emerging ability to monitor an increasing number of processes and actions, from human health conditions and sleeping patterns to the structural integrity of buildings and infrastructure. Samuel Greengard, *The Internet of Things* (Cambridge, Mass.: MIT Press, 2015).

35. The ability of information technology to link countries and world regions and move information and data as well as facilitate trade and international relations is documented in Richard Dobbs, James Manyika, and Jonathan Woetzel, *Digital Globalization: The New Era of Global Flows* (London: McKinsey Global Institute, March 2016).

36. For a detailed look at this future industry, see Steve Lohr, *Data-ism: The Revolution Transforming Decision Making, Consumer Behavior, and Almost Everything Else* (New York: HarperCollins, 2015); Shawn DuBravac, *Digital Destiny: How the New Age of Data Will Transform the Way We Work, Live, and Communicate* (Washington, D.C.: Regnery, 2015); and Michael Malone, "The Big-Data Future Has Arrived," *WSJ*, February 23, 2016.

37. Geoff Colvin, *Humans Are Underrated: What High Achievers Know That Brilliant Machines Never Will* (New York: Portfolio/Penguin, 2015).

38. Indeed, Claire Miller estimates that jobs requiring social skills increased by 24 percent between 1980 and 2014, whereas routine task jobs and even analytical jobs not requiring teamwork declined. Claire Cain Miller. "The Best Jobs Require Social Skills," *NYT*, October 18, 2015.

39. David Deming, "The Growing Importance of Social Skills in the Labor Market," NBER Working Paper 21473 (Boston: National Bureau of Economic Research, August 2015); George Anders, "Good News, Liberal-Arts Majors: You Do Just Fine," *WSJ*, September 12, 2016.

40. Justin Bowles, "Hiding from the Computers Part 4: Time to get Skeptical on Lump of Labour Skeptics," *Risk and Well-Being*, June 11, 2014, https://therationalpessimist.com/2014/01/11/hiding-from-the-computers-part-4-time-to-get-skeptical-on-lump-of-labour-skeptics/.

41. Gerd Leonhard, *Technology vs. Humanity: The Coming Clash between Man and Machine* (London: Fast Future, 2016).

42. Steve Lohr, "Don't Fear the Robots," *NYT*, October 25, 2015.

43. Noah Smith, "The End of Labor: How to Protect Workers from the Rise in Robots," *Atlantic*, January 14, 2013, www.theatlantic.com/business/archive/2013/01/the-end-of-labor-how-to-protect-workers-from-the-rise-of-robots/267135/.

44. James Fallows, "Made in America, Again," *Atlantic*, October 2014, www.theatlantic.com/magazine/archive/2014/10/made-in-america-again/379343/; James Hagerty, "Meet the New Robots," *WSJ*, June 3, 2015; Markus Lorenz et al., *Man and Machine in Industry, 4.0* (Boston: Boston Consulting Group, September 2015). For a look at relatively small manufacturing firms that have developed in recent years, see Nelson Schwartz, "The Power of Small Factories," *NYT*, October 30, 2016.

45. Clermont Ripley and Allan Freyer, *The Age of Contingent Employment* (Raleigh: North Carolina Justice Center, 2015). One estimate suggests that between 20 percent and 30 percent of the U.S. working age population is engaged in independent, or gig, work. James Manyika et al., *Independent Work: Choice, Necessity, and the Gig Economy* (Washington, D.C.: McKinsey Global Institute, October 2016).

46. Ronald Coase, "The Nature of the Firm," *Economica* 4, no. 16 (November 1937): 386–405. The latest technology that might reduce the value of the firm and increase the value of freelance workers is "blockchain," an open-source system of recording financial and business transactions. Don Tapscott and Alex Tapscott, *Blockchain Revolution: How the Technology behind Bitcoin Is Changing Money, Business, and the World* (New York: Portfolio, 2016).

47. Allan Freyer et al., *The Future of Work and Ensuring Job Quality in North Carolina* (Raleigh: North Carolina Justice Center, 2015). Seth Harris and Alan Krueger argue for a new classification of independent workers that allows them to qualify for some, but not all, of the benefits of standard employees. Seth Harris and Alan Krueger, "A Proposal for Modernizing Labor Laws for Twenty-First-Century Work: The 'Independent Worker,'" Discussion Paper 2015-10 (Washington, D.C.: Hamilton Project of the Brookings Institute, December 2015).

48. Don Fullerton and Gilbert Metcalf, "Tax Incidence," NBER Working Paper 8829 (Boston: National Bureau of Economic Research, 2002).

49. Freyer et al., *Future of Work*.

50. See Robert Reich, *Saving Capitalism: For the Many, not the Few* (New York: Alfred A. Knopf, 2015); Paul Mason, *Postcapitalism: A Guide to Our Future* (New York: Farrar, Straus and Giroux, 2015); and Joseph E. Stiglitz, *Rewriting the Rules of the American Economy: An Agenda for Growth and Shared Prosperity* (New York: W. W. Norton, 2016). Reich, Mason, and Stiglitz each recommend major institutional and political changes to the U.S. economic system in order to address modern issues in the labor market and with the distribution of income.

51. "The World Economy," *Economist*, October 4, 2014, 7–11.

52. For excellent summaries of the debate over trends in worker compensation and worker productivity, see James Sherk, *Productivity and Compensation: Growing Together*, Backgrounder 2825 (Washington, D.C.: Heritage Foundation, July 17, 2013); and Robert Z. Lawrence, "The Growing Gap between Real Wages and Labor Productivity," *Realtime Economic Issues Watch* (Washington, D.C.: Peterson Institute for International Economics, July 21, 2015).

53. Rakesh Kochhar, Richard Fry, and Molly Rohal, *The American Middle Class Is Losing Ground* (Washington, D.C.: Pew Research Center, December 2015). Research shows that three metropolitan areas in North Carolina—Rocky Mount, Hickory, and Goldsboro—were among the top ten of regions in the country in widening income inequality between 2000 and 2014. Rakesh Kochhar, Richard Fry, and Molly Rohal, *America's Shrinking Middle Class: A Close Look at Changes within Metropolitan Areas* (Washington, D.C.: Pew Research Center, May 2016). A Brookings Institute study showed income inequality widening in Charlotte and Raleigh between 2007 and 2014. Alan Berube and Natalie Holmes, *City and Metropolitan Inequality on the Rise, Driven*

by Declining Incomes, Brookings Research Papers (Washington, D.C.: Brookings Institute, January 14, 2016). Part of the reason for the income inequality trends in North Carolina may be the greater relative importance in the state of manufacturing, an industry that has had large employment declines—declines that have been shown to be related to increases in income inequality. John Dunn Jr. and Robert Morris, "The Decline in Manufacturing in the United States and Its Impact on Income Inequality," *Journal of Applied Business Research* 28, no. 5 (September–October 2012): 995–1000. Although most studies show widening income inequality using snapshots of households at particular years, studies tracing income mobility of specific households over their lifetime still show substantial movement—both up and down—through income levels. U.S. Department of the Treasury, *Income Mobility in the U.S. from 1996 to 2005* (Washington, D.C.: Government Printing Office, November 13, 2007). Growing income inequality is also an international issue, although some research shows that it is more of an issue in the United States. Branko Milanovic, *Global Inequality: A New Approach for the Age of Globalization* (Cambridge, Mass.: Belknap Press of Harvard University Press, 2016).

54. Daron Acemoglu, "The World Our Grandchildren Will Inherit," in *In 100 Years: Leading Economists Predict the Future*, ed. Ignacio Palacios-Huerta (Cambridge, Mass.: MIT Press, 2013), 1–36. Also, there is evidence that within the broadly defined middle class, the proportion in the upper range ("upper middle class") has been increasing, whereas the proportions in the middle and low ranges ("middle middle class" and "lower middle class") have been decreasing. Stephen Rose, *The Growing Size and Incomes of the Upper Middle Class*, Research Report (Washington, D.C.: Urban Institute, June 2016). For a view that income inequality benefits the economy, see Edward Conard, *The Upside of Inequality: How Good Intentions Undermine the Middle Class* (New York: Portfolio, 2016).

55. The labor force participation rate of women has actually declined slightly in the twenty-first century. One reason may be the rising cost of child care, which reduces the financial benefits of working outside the home. So Kubota, "Child Care Costs and Stagnating Female Labor Force in the U.S.," Working Paper (Princeton University, November 17, 2016).

56. Heather Boushey, *Finding Time: The Economics of Work-Life Conflict* (Cambridge, Mass.: Harvard University Press, 2016). Universal family-leave mandates in the United States would still leave U.S. firms at a competitive disadvantage to foreign firms without such mandates.

57. Home-work time tensions could also be eased by new technology performing household chores, such as 3D home manufacturing of food and home robots preparing meals Jayson Lusk, *Unnaturally Delicious: How Science and Technology Are Serving Up Super Foods to Save the World* (New York: St. Martin's, 2016).

58. Board of Trustees of the Federal Old-Age and Survivors Insurance and Federal Disability Trust Funds, *The 2015 Annual Report* (Washington, D.C.: General Accounting Office, 2015).

59. Lynda Gratton and Andrew Scott, *The 100-Year Life: Living and Working in an Age of Longevity* (London: Bloomsbury, 2016, 39).

Chapter 5

1. David Autor argues that making the necessary improvements in the educational system may be the biggest challenge in coping with technological unemployment. David H. Autor, "Why Are There Still So Many Jobs? The History and Future of Workplace Automation," *Journal of Economic Perspectives* 29, no. 3 (Summer 2015): 3–30.

2. The same pattern is seen for the nation. Although aggregate gains slowed in the early twenty-first century, there were significant differences among subgroups. Between 2003 and 2015, NAEP test score gains for African American and Hispanic students were generally much greater than for non-Hispanic white students. U.S. Department of Education, "Digest of Education Statistics," https://nces.ed.gov/programs/digest/.

3. There has also been a comparable improvement in the percentage of entering high school freshmen who graduate within four years. The rate has improved from 72.6 percent in 2005 to 85.6 percent in 2015. U.S. Department of Education, "Digest of Education Statistics"; Public Schools of North Carolina, "2015 North Carolina Cohort Graduation Rate," http://www.ncpublicschools.org/accountability/reporting/cohortgradrate.

4. In 2010, forty-one North Carolina counties had less than 15 percent of their adult (twenty-five years and older) population holding a college degree. The state average was 25 percent. Also, thirty-nine counties had more than 8 percent of their adult population without a high school degree. The state average was 5.9 percent. Twenty-eight counties had less than 15 percent of their adult population with a college degree *and* 8 percent or more of their adult population without a high school degree. North Carolina Department of Budget and Management, "Log into North Carolina: NCLINC," http://data.osbm.state.nc.us/pls/linc/dyn_linc_main.show.

5. See, e.g., the findings and references cited in P. Aghion et al., "The Causal Impact of Education on Economic Growth: Evidence from the U.S.," Working Paper (Harvard University, March 2009).

6. Calculated by multiplying the number of dropouts by the difference in the annual earnings between the median earnings with a high school degree and the median earnings without a high school degree, and adding to this total the result of multiplying the number of incarcerated individuals with various levels of educational attainment by the median earnings associated with that level of educational attainment. Earnings data are from the U.S. Census, "American Community Survey," for North Carolina in 2014, https://www.census.gov/programs-surveys/acs/. Educational attainments of incarcerated individuals are from Caroline Wolf Harlow, *Education and Correctional Profiles*, Bureau of Justice Statistics, Special Report 195670 (Washington, D.C., January 2003), https://www.bjs.gov/content/pub/pdf/ecp.pdf.

7. The finding was first publicized by the famous "Coleman Report." James S. Coleman, *Equality of Educational Opportunity* (Washington, D.C.: U.S. Department of Education, 1966), http://dx.doi.org/10.1080/0020486680060504. For a more recent review of the impacts of family characteristics on educational performance, see Toby L. Parcel, Mikaela J. Dufur, and Rena Cornell Zito, "Capital at Home and at School: A Review and Synthesis," *Journal of Marriage and the Family* 72, no. 4 (August 2010): 828–46. Eric Hanushek reviewed subsequent literature and supported the Coleman conclusions. Eric A. Hanushek, "The Economics of Schooling: Production

and Efficiency in Public Schools," *Journal of Economic Literature* 23, no. 3 (September 1986): 1141–77. The current debate centers on whether school inputs can affect student achievement in any meaningful way. Recent research indicates that school inputs can still have positive effects on student learning even in the presence of challenging environmental conditions. C. Kirabo Jackson, Rucker C. Johnson, and Claudia Persico, "The Effects of School Spending on Educational and Economic Outcomes: Evidence from School Finance Reforms," NBER Working Paper 20847 (Boston: National Bureau of Economic Research, January 2015).

8. Patrick Sharkey, *Stuck in Place: Urban Neighborhoods and the End of Progress toward Racial Equality* (Chicago: University of Chicago Press, 2013).

9. David Austen-Smith and Roland Fryer Jr., "An Economic Analysis of 'Acting White,'" *Quarterly Journal of Economics* 120, no. 2 (May 2005): 551–83.

10. Charlotte was ranked last in intergenerational economic mobility in a recent study of the fifty largest U.S. metropolitan areas. Raj Chetty et al., "Where Is the Land of Opportunity? The Geography of Intergenerational Mobility in the United States," *Quarterly Journal of Economics* 129, no. 4 (November 2014): 1553–623. Estimations based on the data in Chetty and colleagues suggest intergenerational economic mobility is relatively low across most of North Carolina. MDC, *North Carolina's Economic Imperative: Building an Infrastructure of Opportunity* (Durham, N.C., 2016).

11. Richard Arum and Josipa Roksa, *Academically Adrift: Limited Learning on College Campuses* (Chicago: University of Chicago Press, 2011); Philip Babcock and Mindy Marks, "The Falling Time Cost of College: Evidence from Half a Century of Time Use Data," *Review of Economics and Statistics* 93, no. 2 (May 2011): 468–78. Some studies show that a quarter of students arrive at college thinking "having fun" is their main priority. Jackson Toby, *The Lowering of Higher Education in America: Why Financial Aid Should Be Based on Student Performance* (Santa Barbara, Calif.: Praeger, 2010). A new concern is the impact of student texting during classroom time. Some studies have found an adverse impact of texting activity on academic performance. Amanda Banks, H. Russell Searight, and Susan Ratwik, "Effects of Text Messaging on Academic Performance," *Journal of Pedagogy and Psychology* 4, no. 1 (February 2013): 4–9; Brian Wardygo, "The Relationship between Text Message Volume and Formal Writing Performance among Upper Level High School Students and College Freshman" (Ph.D. diss., Liberty University, 2012). For a contrary view, that use of social media and web-surfing enhances creativity and intelligence, see Kenneth Goldsmith, *Wasting Time on the Internet* (New York: Harper Perennial, 2016).

12. University of North Carolina General Administration, *Retention and Graduation Report, 2014–2015* (Chapel Hill, February 2015). The graduation rate does increase slightly (from 63 percent to 67 percent) if graduation from any institution is included, rather than graduation only from the entering institution. The UNC system rate is higher (by four percentage points) than the national rate. However, there is a wide variation in the six-year graduation rate among UNC system campuses, ranging from 31 percent to 90 percent for the 2009 cohort. An analysis of national data suggests lack of academic preparation by students entering the least selective colleges and universities and increased labor force participation by students as the main factors behind not graduating within a given time. John Bound, Michael Lovenheim, and Sarah Turner, "Why Have

College Completion Rates Declined?," NBER Working Paper 15566 (Boston: National Bureau of Economic Research, December 2009); Sara Goldrick-Rab, *Paying the Price: College Costs, Financial Aid, and the Betrayal of the American Dream* (Chicago: University of Chicago Press, 2016). The North Carolina Community College System has calculated a comparable six-year graduation rate. For students entering in 2004, 41 percent graduated within six years, implying that 59 percent did not. Jane Stancill, "N.C. Community Colleges Sharpen Focus on Graduating More Students," *N&O*, January 21, 2015.

13. Jordan Weissmann, "America's Awful Dropout Rates, in Four Charts," *Moneybox* (blog), November 19, 2014, http://www.slate.com/blogs/moneybox/2014/11/19/u_s_college_dropouts_rates_explained_in_4_charts.html. One study estimated the public cost of nongraduates in the public universities of the UNC system at $446 million annually. Stephanie Keaveney, "College Dropouts Cost N.C. Taxpayers $446 Million per Year," *Carolina Journal* 25, no. 7 (July 2016): 16.

14. Michael Greenstone and Adam Looney, The Hamilton Project, *Is Starting College and Not Finishing Really That Bad?* (Washington, D.C.: Brookings Institute, June 7, 2013). Using census data for 2008–12, the authors find that workers who attended either a two- or four-year college without receiving a degree earned $8,000 more annually than workers with only a high school degree (but still far less than the $30,000 annual salary premium for college graduates with a bachelor's degree compared to workers with a high school diploma). Seth Zimmerman also finds earnings gains for academically marginal students merely attending college. Seth Zimmerman, "The Returns to College Admission for Academically Marginal Students," *Journal of Labor Economics* 32, no. 4 (October 2014): 711–54.

15. This is the "screening" explanation for why college graduates earn more: because they learn valuable soft skills (showing up for class, preparing for tests, working with others) important to employers. Peter Cappelli, *Will College Pay Off?* (New York: Public Affairs, 2015).

16. Clare Kaufman, "Why Employers Don't Care about Your College Major," *Glassdoor* (blog), January 30, 2012, https://www.glassdoor.com/blog/employers-care-college-major/; Karin Fischer, "The Employment Mismatch," *Chronicle of Higher Education Special Reports*, March 4, 201, www.chronicle.com; Hart Research Associates, *Falling Short: College Learning and Career Success* (Washington, D.C., January 2015); Jerry Gray and Richard Chapman, "Conflicting Signals: The Labor Market for College-Educated Workers," *Journal of Economic Issues* 33, no. 3 (September 1999): 661–75. Still, a common complaint of employers is the lack of applied knowledge, critical thinking, and communication skills among college graduates. Hart Research Associates, "It Takes More than a Major: Employer Priorities for College Learning and Student Success" (Paper presented at the meeting of the Association of American Colleges and Universities, Washington, D.C., April 10, 2013).

17. The Federal Reserve Bank of New York reported in 2016 that 44 percent of recent college graduates (ages twenty-two to twenty-seven with a bachelor's degree or higher) and 34 percent of all college graduates (ages twenty-two to sixty-five with a bachelor's degree or higher) had degrees that did not apply to their current job. Furthermore, these rates had been little changed for twenty-five years. Josh Mitchell, "Students to Get Aid for Alternative Training," *WSJ*, August 17, 2016.

18. State nongrants include loans, work-study, and tuition waivers.

19. North Carolina is not alone in these trends—tuition and fees have been rising in all states. However, North Carolina did have the sixth highest increase in gross average tuition and fees at public institutions for the period 2010–15. Still, in 2015 the state ranked sixth among all states in public funding per FTE (full-time equivalent) students at higher education public institutions. College Board, *Trends in College Pricing* (New York, 2014).

20. Even with the increases, North Carolina maintained its position among the states as a low-tuition state. In 2004, North Carolina had the twelfth lowest four-year public institutions undergraduate annual tuition and fees rate; in 2015, it had the eleventh lowest rate. For two-year public institutions, North Carolina had the fifth lowest annual tuition and fees rate in both 2004 and 2015. U.S. Department of Education, *Digest of Education Statistics*.

21. Trends in Higher Education, "Maximum Average Pell Grants over Time," https://trends.collegeboard.org/student-aid/figures-tables/maximum-and-average-pell-grants-over-time. The average grant amount is for all (national) Pell Grant recipients. The percentage change is in inflation-adjusted dollars.

22. U.S. Department of Education, "Digest of Educational Statistics"; U.S. Department of Commerce, Bureau of Economic Analysis, "Regional Economic Accounts," https://www.bea.gov/regional/; University of North Carolina General Administration, *"Finance and Budget,"* www.northcarolina.edu/node/244. Even with the funding changes, higher education spending in North Carolina from all sources averaged 2 percent of GDP from 2000 to 2013, higher than the 1.7 percent average in the 1990s.

23. For a discussion of these potential explanations, see Robert B. Archibald and David H. Feldman, *Why Does College Cost So Much?* (New York: Oxford University Press, 2011); William Bennett and David Wilezol, *Is College Worth It? A Former United States Secretary of Education and a Liberal Arts Graduate Expose the Broken Promise of Higher Education* (Nashville, Tenn.: Thomas Edison, 2013); Ronald Ehrenberg, ed., *What's Happening to Public Higher Education? The Shifting Financial Burden* (Baltimore: Johns Hopkins University Press, 2006); David O. Lucca, Taylor Nadauld, and Karen Shen, *Credit Supply and the Rise in College Tuition: Evidence from the Expansion in Federal Student Aid Programs*, Staff Report 733 (New York: Federal Reserve Bank of New York, July 2015); Grey Gordon and Aaron Hedlund, "Accounting for the Rise in College Tuition," NBER Working Paper 21967 (Boston: National Bureau of Economic Research, February 2016); and Richard Vedder, *Going Broke by Degree: Why College Costs So Much* (Washington, D.C.: AEI, 2004). Vedder argues that higher education institutions also use the widely applied private business technique of market segmentation in their tuition and fee pricing structure. Students and parents who are less sensitive to tuition and fee levels (typically those with higher incomes) pay the advertised tuition and fees, while students and parents who are more sensitive to tuition and fee levels (typically those with lower incomes) receive grants or loans and thus pay lower tuition and fees.

24. Geographic Solutions (www.geographicsolutions.com) is a private-sector firm that has developed software to address this goal. Some researchers have used LinkedIn data to trace the changing demand for skills. Bogdan State et al., "Migration of Professionals to the U.S.: Evidence from LinkedIn Data," in *Social Informatics: 6th*

International Conference, SocInfo 2014, Barcelona, Spain, November 11-13, 2014, Proceedings, ed. Luca Aiello and David McFarland (New York: Springer), 531–43. Some community colleges are also using job postings to develop data about workplace skill needs. Anna Louie Sussman and Melissa Korn, "Colleges Mine Job Listings to Parse Employers' Needs," *WSJ,* April 4, 2016.

25. See, e.g., Eric A. Hanushek and Alfred A. Lindseth, *Schoolhouses, Courthouses, and Statehouses: Solving the Funding-Achievement Puzzle in America's Public Schools* (Princeton, N.J.: Princeton University Press, 2009).

26. Jackson, Johnson, and Persico, "Effects of School Spending on Educational and Economic Outcomes"; David Deming, "Early Childhood Intervention and Life-Cycle Skill Development: Evidence from Head Start," *American Economics Journal: Applied Economics* 1, no. 3 (July 2009): 111–34; Peter Fredriksson, Björn Öckert, and Hessel Oosterbeek, "Long-Term Effects of Class Size," *Quarterly Journal of Economics* 128, no. 1 (February 2013): 249–85; Vilsa E. Curto and Roland G. Fryer Jr., "The Potential of Urban Boarding Schools for the Poor: Evidence from SEED," *Journal of Labor Economics* 32, no. 1 (January 2014): 65–93; Raj Chetty, John N. Friedman, and Jonah E. Rockoff, "Measuring the Impacts of Teachers II: Teacher Value-Added and Student Outcomes in Adulthood," *American Economic Review* 104, no. 9 (September 2014): 2633–79. Improving teacher quality could be achieved in several ways, including attracting more qualified teachers through higher salaries and advanced academic training for teachers. For an excellent review of the literature examining educational inputs and student achievement, see Simon M. Burgess, *Human Capital and Education: The State of the Art in the Economics of Education* (Bonn: Institute for the Study of Labor, April 2016).

27. There is a large literature and detailed discussion and debate about each of the techniques. See, e.g., Timothy J. Bartik, *Investing in Kids: Early Childhood Programs and Local Economic Development* (Kalamazoo, Mich.: W. E. Upjohn Institute for Employment Research, 2011); Douglas Almond and Janet Currie, *"Human Capital Development before Age 5,"* NBER Working Paper 15827 (Boston: National Bureau of Economic Research, March 2010); James J. Heckman, *Giving Kids a Fair Chance* (Cambridge, Mass.: MIT Press, 2013); Joseph P. McDonald. *American School Reform: What Works, What Fails, and Why* (Chicago: University of Chicago Press, 2014); Lawrence Mishel and Richard Rothstein, eds., *The Class Size Debate* (Washington, D.C.: Economic Policy Institute, 2002); Terry M. Moe, ed., *A Primer on America's Schools* (Stanford, Calif.: Hoover Institution Press, 2001); and Abigail Thernstrom and Stephan Thernstrom, *No Excuses: Closing the Racial Gap in Learning* (New York: Simon and Schuster, 2003).

28. Curto and Fryer, "Potential of Urban Boarding Schools for the Poor." A concept similar to boarding schools is the "No Excuses" approach to education. These schools have a long school day, an extended school year, and strict behavioral norms and stress reading and math skills. Studies have shown significant student achievement gains in this educational environment. Joshua Angrist et al., "Who Benefits from KIPP?," *Journal of Policy Analysis and Management* 31, no. 4 (Fall 2012): 837–60. For a discussion of some of the educational challenges associated with students coming from nonsupportive environments, see Richard V. Reeves and Kimberly Howard, Center on Children and Families, *The Parenting Gap* (Washington, D.C.: Brookings Institute, September 8, 2013); Annette Lareau, *Unequal Childhoods: Class, Race, and Family Life,* 2nd ed.

(Berkeley: University of California Press, 2011); and Raj Chetty, Nathaniel Hendren, and Lawrence F. Katz, "The Effects of Exposure to Better Neighborhoods on Children: New Evidence from the Moving to Opportunity Experiment," *American Economic Review* 106, no. 4 (April 2016): 855–902.

29. James A. Kulik, *Effects of Using Instructional Technology in Elementary and Secondary Schools: What Controlled Evaluation Studies Say* (Arlington, Va.: SRI International, May 2003); Ulrich Boser, *Are Schools Getting a Big Enough Bang for Their Education Technology Buck?* (Washington, D.C.: Center for American Progress, June 2013); Michael Trucano, "Two New Rigorous Evaluations of Technology Use in Education," *EduTech* (blog), March 18, 2014, World Bank, http://blogs.worldbank.org/edutech/IDB-research.

30. See Peter Dolton and Oscar Gutierrez, "Teachers' Pay and Pupil Performance," *CentrePiece: The Magazine for Economic Performance* 16, no. 2 (Autumn 2011): 20–22, for the potential connection between teacher pay and performance. Also, North Carolina teacher pay could be falling if a larger percentage of younger teachers starting at the lowest pay scale were being hired in the state. However, between 2000 and 2012, the percentage of the state's teachers with less than three years of experience was halved, from 17.2 percent to 8.4 percent, while the percentage with more than ten years of experience rose from 54.3 percent to 55.9 percent. U.S. Department of Education, "Digest of Education Statistics." Although North Carolina lags the nation in the proportion of teachers with a master's degree, the percentage of master's degree teachers in the state rose 21 percent between 2008 and 2012, almost three times faster than in the nation overall.

31. The changes for each of the three educational inputs were in the same direction for the nation as for North Carolina, but to a much smaller degree. The pupil-teacher ratio increased 19 percent for North Carolina between 2006 and 2013; for the nation the increase was 3 percent. Average inflation-adjusted teacher salaries fell 20 percent in North Carolina between 2002 and 2014; in the nation the drop was 4 percent. Current expenditures (inflation-adjusted) per pupil were reduced by 10 percent in North Carolina from 2009 to 2012; the reduction was 5 percent for the nation. U.S. Department of Education, "Digest of Education Statistics."

32. James J. Heckman, John Eric Humphries, and Tim Kautz, eds., *The Myth of Achievement Tests: The GED and the Role of Character in American Life* (Chicago: University of Chicago Press, 2014); C. Kirabo Jackson, "Non-Cognitive Ability, Test Scores, and Teacher Quality: Evidence from 9th Grade Teachers in North Carolina," NBER Working Paper 18624 (Boston: National Bureau of Economic Research, December 2012).

33. For a superb journalistic summary of the importance of noncognitive characteristics in learning—and ways to develop those characteristics—see Paul Tough, *Helping Children Succeed: What Works and Why* (Boston: Houghton Mifflin Harcourt, 2016). Also see Laura Hanby Hudgens, "How to Fix the Apathy Problem in Schools," *N&O*, June 6, 2016; and Angela Duckworth, *Grit: The Power of Passion and Perseverance* (New York: Scribner, 2016).

34. For a sobering discussion of the challenges of addressing the social, demographic, and political factors involved in improving K–12 schools, see Dale Russakoff,

The Prize: Who's in Charge of America's Schools? (Boston: Houghton Mifflin, 2015), an account of recent reforms attempted in the Newark, New Jersey, city schools.

35. Derived by applying the results from Clive R. Belfield, Henry M. Levin, and Rachel Rosen, *The Economic Value of Opportunity Youth* (Washington, D.C.: Corporation for National and Community Service, January 2012), to North Carolina.

36. Eric A. Hanushek and Ludger Woessmann, "How Much Do Educational Outcomes Matter in OECD Countries?," *Economic Policy* 26, no. 67 (July 2011): 427–91. The result for the United States is used.

37. For an intriguing discussion of new approaches to teaching and learning, see Tony Wagner and Ted Dintersmith, *Most Likely to Succeed: Preparing Our Kids for the Innovation Era* (New York: Scribner, 2015). For a discussion of the tradeoffs between teaching methods, see Harold W. Stevenson and James W. Stigler, *The Learning Gap: Why Our Schools Are Failing and What We Can Learn from Japanese and Chinese Education* (New York: Simon and Schuster, 1992); and Lucy Crehan, *Cleverlands: The Secrets behind the Success of the World's Education Superpowers* (London: Unbound, 2016). For a discussion of the role of practice and repetition in achieving success, see Geoff Colvin, *Talent Is Overrated: What Really Separates World-Class Performers from Everybody Else* (New York: Portfolio, 2010). Another issue is the economic concept of "diminishing marginal returns," meaning that the more a technique is used, the lower is the payoff in effectiveness. For example, reducing class size from twenty to fifteen students might improve test scores by 20 percent, but then further reducing class size from fifteen to ten students may result in a test score improvement of only 12 percent. For an analysis of the results from a school choice program in North Carolina, see David J. Deming et al., "School Choice, School Quality, and Postsecondary Attainment," *American Economic Review* 104, no. 3 (March 2014): 991–1013. For a cautionary analysis of the benefits from teaching improvement programs, see the New Teacher Project, *The Mirage: Confronting the Hard Truth about Our Quest for Teacher Development* (Brooklyn, N.Y.: TNTP, August 4, 2015). Some have argued for a special role of historically black colleges and universities (HBCUs) in improving the college readiness of minority high school students. Arne Duncan, "The Enduring and Evolving Role of HBCUs" (Remarks of the U.S. secretary of education to the National HBCU Week Conference, September 26, 2013), https://www.ed.gov/news/speeches/enduring-and-evolving-role-hbcus.

38. The comparable rates for the nation were 54.3 percent in 1992 and 62.5 percent in 2010. NCHEMS Information Center for Higher Education Policymaking and Analysis, www.higheredinfo.org.

39. For a discussion of this shift as well as a history of vocational and technical education, see Howard Gordon. *The History and Growth of Career and Technical Education in America*, 4th ed. (Long Grove, Ill.: Waveland, 2014).

40. NEA Research, *Reality Check: The U.S. Job Market and Students' Academic and Career Paths Necessitate Enhanced Vocational Education in High Schools* (National Education Association, March 2012), http://www.nea.org/assets/docs/Vocational_Education_final.pdf.

41. Alexandra Pannoni, "Vocational High School Programs an Option for Teens," *U.S. News and World Report*, October 20, 2014; Allie Bidwell, "Vocational High Schools: Career Path or Kiss of Death?," *U.S. News and World Report*, May 2, 2014;

James E. Rosenbaum, *Beyond College for All: Career Paths for the Forgotten Half* (New York: Russell Sage Foundation, 2001).

42. Based on Howard Gardner's seven intelligences of bodily kinesthetic intelligence (what I term physical intelligence), musical intelligence, interpersonal intelligence, intrapersonal intelligence, spatial intelligence, logical-mathematical intelligence, and linguistic intelligence. Howard Gardner, *Frames of Mind: The Theory of Multiple Intelligences* (New York: Basic Books, 1983). Maria Prada and Sergio Urzua found that individuals with mechanical capabilities actually experienced reductions in earnings by attending a four-year college. Maria Prada and Sergio Urzua, "One Size Does Not Fit All: Multiple Dimensions of Ability, College Attendance, and Wages," NBER Working Paper 20752 (Boston: National Bureau of Economic Research, 2014).

43. For a discussion of the "male economic problem," see Mitchell Hartman, "The Employment Problem of Prime-Age Men," *Marketplace*, April 18, 2014, https://www.marketplace.org/2014/04/18/economy/employment-problem-prime-age-men; and "Men Adrift," *Economist*, May 30, 2015, 21–26.

44. Rework America, *America's Moment: Creating Opportunity in the Connected Age* (New York: W. W. Norton, 2015). However, other analysis suggests that the alleged skills gap has been overstated. Boston Consulting Group, *Skills Gap in U.S. Manufacturing Is Less Pervasive Than Many Believe* (Boston, October 15, 2012); Peter Cappelli, *Why Good People Can't Get Jobs: The Skills Gap and What Companies Can Do about It* (Philadelphia: Wharton Digital Press, 2012); Andrew Hacker, *The Math Myth: And Other STEM Delusions* (New York: New Press, 2016).

45. See the North Carolina High School to Community College Articulation Agreement, www.ncperkins.org/course/view.php?id=4; the Learn and Earn program, http://www.elearningnc.gov/k-12_elearning/college_classes_for_hs_students/; and the Apprenticeship2000programinCharlotte,http://charlotteusa.com/news-media/monday-memo/apprenticeship-2000-addresses-high-tech-needs-with-old-world-model/.In2015,North Carolina began a pilot program called the North Carolina Career Coach Program, which places community college career coaches in high schools. Jane Stancil, "UNC Faces Cuts; Community Colleges, Raises," *N&O*, September 16, 2015.

46. The tech high school is Vernon Malone College and Career Academy, www.wcpss.net/vernonmalonecca.

47. Katherine Peralta, "Apprenticeships Could Be Gateway to Middle Class," *U.S. News and World Report*, January 1, 2015; Katherine S. Newman and Hella Winston, *Reskilling America: Learning to Labor in the Twenty-First Century* (New York: Henry Holt, 2016); Jeffrey Selingo "College Isn't Always the Answer," *WSJ*, May 27, 2016.

48. For a discussion of technology in bricklaying, see Steve Castle, "Forget 3D Printed Houses—This Brick-Laying Robot Can Build an Entire House in 2 Days," *Digital Trends* (blog), June 30, 2015, http://www.foxnews.com/tech/2015/06/30/forget-3d-printed-houses-this-brick-laying-robot-can-build-entire-house-in-2.html.

49. This was greater than the 46 percent rise in college enrollment in the nation. U.S. Department of Education, "Digest of Education Statistics."

50. Yasima Blackburn, "Employers Care about Soft Skills (You Should Too)," *Huffington Post*, January 9, 2015, http://www.huffingtonpost.com/yasmina-blackburn/employers-care-about-soft_b_6440656.html.

51. The percentage is for undergraduate degree holders and is based on 2010 data from the U.S. Census. Jaison R. Abel and Richard Deitz, "Do Big Cities Help College Graduates Find Better Jobs?," *Liberty Street Economics* (blog), Federal Reserve Bank of New York, May 20, 2013, http://libertystreeteconomics.newyorkfed.org/2013/05/do-big-cities-help-college-graduates-find-better-jobs.html. The percentage varied by major, being lowest (meaning that a low percentage of graduates work outside their field) for accounting, architecture, and elementary education and highest (indicating that a high percentage of graduates work outside their field) for liberal arts, mathematics, philosophy, and history. The authors also found that 62 percent of the college graduates had a job that required a college degree. See also note 17, above.

52. For this point of view, see Kevin Carey, *The End of College: Creating the Future of Learning and the University of Everywhere* (New York: Riverhead Books, 2015); and Richard A. DeMillo, *Revolution in Higher Education: How a Small Band of Innovators Will Make College Accessible and Affordable* (Cambridge, Mass.: MIT Press, 2015). For a discussion of alternative college teaching methods not relying on the traditional lecture format, see "Flying High," *Economist*, June 25, 2016, 53–54.

53. Tom Vanderbilt, "How Artificial Intelligence Can Change Higher Education," *Smithsonian Magazine*, December 2012, http://www.smithsonianmag.com/people-places/how-artificial-intelligence-can-change-higher-education-136983766/.

54. This will require a major improvement in high school accomplishment. It is estimated that two out of three high school graduates in North Carolina who enroll in a community college must take remedial courses in English, reading, and/or math. Terry Stoops, *High School Graduation in NC: Quantity over Quality?*, Spotlight 413 (John Locke Foundation, September 20, 2011). Even the University of North Carolina System spends a nontrivial amount on remedial education. In the 2011–12 schoolyear, 3,900 students received instruction in remedial education at a cost of $1.8 million. However, both the number of students and the cost have been trending downward. University of North Carolina General Administration, *The University of North Carolina Remedial/Developmental Activities Report, 2011–12* (Chapel Hill, February 2013).

55. This model of technical colleges is presented in James Rosenbaum, Regina Deil-Amen, and Ann. E. Person, *After Admission: From College Access to College Success* (New York: Russell Sage Foundation, 2006). The difference between technical college training and analytical college training is illustrated by the field of logistics. Technical colleges train students to use logistics systems—for example—in transportation. Analytical colleges train students to design, modify, and improve logistics systems. North Carolina has actually moved in the opposite direction of this recommendation by establishing a program for academically weak enrollees in the UNC system campuses to spend their first two years obtaining an associate's degree at a community college campus. Research performed to date indicates, however, that the program has not improved the rate of baccalaureate degree completion of the students. Board of Governors of the University of North Carolina and the State Board of Community Colleges, *Report to the Joint Legislative Education Oversight Committee, Fiscal Division, and the Office of State Budget and Management* (Raleigh, March 6, 2016).

56. Jeffrey Selingo and Charles Sykes also discuss the idea of a shorter time for achieving an undergraduate degree. Jeffrey Selingo, *There Is Life after College* (New

York: William Morrow, 2016); Charles Sykes, *Fail U.: The False Promise of Higher Education* (New York: St. Martin's, 2016). In addition, some observers think that courses will be shorter, focusing on core content and how students can then augment that content with self-learning as knowledge changes. Marilyn Achiron, "Future Shock: Teaching Yourself to Learn," *Education and Skills Today* (blog), July 29, 2015, http:// oecdeducationtoday.blogspot.com/2015/07/future-shock.html.

57. "The Digital Degree," *Economist*, June 28, 2014. For a summary discussion of the pros and cons of cyber education tools at the college level, see Michael McPherson and Lawrence Bacow, "Online Higher Education: Beyond the Hype Cycle," *Journal of Economic Perspectives* 29, no. 4 (Fall 2015): 135–54; and William Alpert, Kenneth Couch, and Oskar Harmon, "A Randomized Assessment of Online Learning," *American Economic Review: Papers and Proceedings* 106, no. 5 (May 2016): 378–82. Alpert and colleagues conclude that a blended structure including both online and face-to-face instruction may be the most effective for learning and cost minimization.

58. Gary Fethke and Andrew Policano, *Public No More: A New Path to Excellence for America's Public Universities* (Stanford, Calif.: Stanford University Press, 2012). Fethke and Policano argue that the implicit "contract" between taxpayers and public universities, in which state taxpayers provided financial support in return for public universities giving up control of access criteria and tuition rates, will be increasingly eroded by international competition, technological alternatives for learning, and increased mobility of college graduates among states. These trends will reduce public support for universities and motivate the institutions to seek more private support, including tuition rates that more closely reflect the marginal cost of educating a student. There is the corollary debate about the degree to which the benefits of a college education are shared by the student and the public. The more the benefits accrue to the student, the more the justification for public subsidies diminishes. Jane S. Shaw, "Education—A Bad Public Good?," *Independent Review* 15, no. 2 (Fall 2010): 241–56; Simon Marginson, "The Problem of Public Good(s) in Higher Education" (Paper presented at the 41st Australian Conference of Economists, Melbourne, July 8–12, 2012).

59. Thomas Frey, "The Future of Colleges and Universities: Blueprint for a Revolution," DaVinci Institute, http://www.futuristspeaker.com/extended-bio/ future-of-colleges-universities-futurist-thomas-frey/.

60. The EPIC (Energy Production and Infrastructure Center) at UNC-Charlotte is another example of private sector–public sector collaboration in a specific industry.

61. Ryan Craig, *College Disrupted: The Great Unbundling of Higher Education* (New York: Palgrave Macmillan, 2015). Another potential change may come to the work environment of higher education faculty. Rather than being tenured at a specific institution, faculty may become freelance workers, taking contracted positions with public and private core and analytical higher education institutions. Frey, "Future of Colleges and Universities."

62. Charles Murray, *Real Education: Four Simple Truths for Bringing America's Schools Back to Reality* (New York: Crown Forum, 2008).

63. Education is a sector that has been thought to suffer from "Baumol's cost disease," meaning an economic activity for which it is difficult to substitute technology for labor and therefore take advantage of labor-saving devices. William J. Baumol, *The Cost*

Disease: Why Computers Get Cheaper and Health Care Doesn't (New Haven, Conn.: Yale University Press, 2012).

64. N.C. Gen. Stat. § 116-143.7, Tuition Surcharges. Conditions under which the tuition surcharge is waived include a military service obligation, serous medical debilitation, disability, or other extraordinary hardship.

65. Bryan Anderson, "N.C. Legislature's Plan to Freeze, Lower Tuition Raises Concerns," *N&O*, July 10, 2016.

66. University of North Carolina General Administration, *The University of North Carolina Retention and Graduation Report, 2013–2014* (Chapel Hill, February 2015).

67. Stacy Cowley, "Getting a Student Loan with Collateral from a Future Job," *NYT*, April 9, 2016. For an excellent review and analysis of the student debt issue, see Sandy Baum, *Student Debt: Rhetoric and Realties of Higher Education Financing* (New York: Palgrave, 2016).

68. Timothy Ferguson and Mark Kurt, "Adding 'Invest' to Loan Language," *N&O*, June 18, 2016.

69. Claudia Goldin and Lawrence F. Katz, *The Race between Education and Technology* (Cambridge, Mass.: Harvard University Press, 2008).

Chapter 6

1. For a balanced view of the climate change debate, including an extensive set of references on both sides of the argument, see Melissa Dell, Benjamin F. Jones, and Benjamin A. Olken, "What Do We Learn from the Weather? The New Climate-Economy Literature," *Journal of Economic Literature* 52, no. 3 (September 2014): 740–98.

2. The seven coastal counties are Brunswick, Carteret, Currituck, Dare, New Hanover, Onslow, and Pender. Data are from the North Carolina State Data Center, the U.S. Department of Commerce, and *IMPLAN* for North Carolina.

3. Some will say the funds spent and jobs created by replacing the infrastructure and buildings are beneficial to the economy by creating additional activity and earnings. This thinking is fallacious, however, because the funds spent replacing what had already existed results in less spending on other products and services. In the economic literature, the mistake is termed the "broken window fallacy." Frédéric Bastiat, *Selected Essays on Political Economy* (1848), trans. Seymour Cain, ed. George B. de Huszar, introduction by F. A. Hayek (Irving-on-Hudson, N.Y.: Foundation for Economic Education, 1995).

4. Edward Martin, "Land's End," *Business North Carolina* 34, no. 11 (November 2014): 44–53.

5. Okmyung Bin et al., *Measuring the Impacts of Climate Change on North Carolina Coastal Resources*, Final Report (Washington, D.C.: National Commission on Energy Policy, March 15, 2007). Dollar values have been converted from 2007 to 2015.

6. U.S. Department of Agriculture, "Climate Change and Agriculture in the United States: Effects and Adaptation," Technical Bulletin 1985 (Washington, D.C.: Agricultural Research Service, February 2013); William Nordhaus, *The Climate Casino: Risk, Uncertainty, and Economics for a Warming World* (New Haven, Conn.: Yale University Press, 2013), 78–90.

7. Melissa Dell, Benjamin F. Jones, and Benjamin A. Olken, "What Do We Learn from the Weather? The New Climate-Economy Literature," *Journal of Economic Literature* 52, no. 3 (September 2014): 740–98.

8. North Carolina Department of Agriculture and Consumer Services, *North Carolina Agricultural Statistics* (Raleigh, 2013), 18.

9. Ibid., 15.

10. Ibid., 61–75; Matthew Vann, Ph.D. (tobacco extension specialist, North Carolina State University), pers. comm., August 11, 2015. Burke and Emerick estimate that the adverse effect of climate change on corn and soybean yields is the same over both shorter and longer periods. Marshall Burke and Kyle Emerick, "Adaptation to Climate Change: Evidence from U.S. Agriculture," *American Economic Journal: Economic Policy* 8, no. 3 (August 2016): 106–40.

11. Research indicates that specialty crops can tolerate increased temperatures with only moderate reduction in yields. U.S. Department of Agriculture, "Climate Change and Agriculture in the United States," 75–88.

12. Ibid., table 6.1, 102; Olivier Deschênes and Michael Greenstone, "Climate Change, Mortality, and Adaptation: Evidence from Annual Fluctuations in Weather in the U.S.," *American Economic Journal: Applied Economics* 3, no. 4 (October 2011): 152–85. The 80 percent reduction in yields is for crops (corn, soybeans, cotton) but does not account for the potential positive impacts on yields of increased levels of carbon dioxide. Wolfram Schlenker and Michael J. Roberts, "Nonlinear Temperature Effects Indicate Severe Damages to U.S. Crop Yields under Climate Change," *Proceedings of the National Academy of Sciences* 106, no. 37 (September 2009): 15594–98.

13. Dan Charles, "Big Data Companies Agree: Farmers Should Own Their Information," *The Salt* (blog), November 16, 2014, *NPR*, www.npr.org/blogs/thesalt/2014/11/16/364115200/big-data-companies-agree-farmers-should-own-their-information.

14. Daily consumption rate is for all uses (residential, nonresidential, and industrial) in 2010 and from the North Carolina State Data Center, http://www.osbm.nc.gov/facts-figures/linc.

15. IPCC, *Climate Change 2007: The Physical Science Basis Contribution of Working Group I to the Fourth Assessment Report of the Intergovernmental Panel on Climate Change* (Cambridge: Cambridge University Press, 2007), "Frequently Asked Question 10.1: Are Extreme Events, Like Heat Waves, Droughts or Floods, Expected to Change as the Earth's Climate Changes?," http://oceanservice.noaa.gov/education/pd/climate/factsheets/areextreme.pdf.

16. Based on data from Georgia in MACTEC Engineering and Consulting, *Georgia Inventory and Survey of Feasible Sites for Water Supply Reservoirs*, Project 6110-08-0257 (Georgia Environmental Facilities Authority, October 2008), https://gefa.georgia.gov/sites/gefa.georgia.gov/files/related_files/document/GEFA-MACTEC-Inventory-Survey-Feasible-Reservoir-Sites.pdf. Costs have been updated to 2015 dollars.

17. "Fayetteville Upset about Raleigh Area Water Plans," January 15, 2015, *Washington Times*, http://www.washingtontimes.com/news/2015/jan/15/fayetteville-upset-about-raleigh-area-water-plans/.

18. WRAL-TV, "Water Plans Could Mean Water War over Kerr Lake," March 13, 2008, http://www.wral.com/news/local/story/2574842/.

19. The usage savings are greater in multiunit residential structures than in single-unit residential structures. L.T. Zita et al., "Cost-Benefit Analysis of Onsite Residential Graywater Recycling—A Case Study of Los Angeles," Working Paper (University of California, 2014); Michael Brennan and Robert Patterson, "Economic Analysis of Greywater Recycling," in *Proceedings of the 1st International Conference on Onsite Wastewater Treatment and Recycling Organized by Environmental Technology Centre* (Murdoch University, Perth, February 11–13, 2004); and U.S. Environmental Protection Agency, Office of Water, *Case Studies of Sustainable Water and Wastewater Pricing*, EPA 816-R-05-007 (Washington, D.C., December 2005).

20. Technically the example is an illustration of "increasing block rate pricing."

21. Kenneth A. Baerenklau, Kurt A. Schwabe, and Ariel Dinar, "The Residential Water Demand Effect of Increasing Block Rate Water Budgets," *Land Economics* 90, no. 4 (November 2014): 683–99; Nelson D. Schwartz, "Water Pricing in Two Thirsty Cities: In One, Guzzlers Pay More, and Use Less," *NYT*, May 7, 2015; Sheila M. Olmstead and Robert N. Stavins, *Managing Water Demand: Price vs. Non-Price Conservation Programs*, Public Policy Research 39 (Boston: Pioneer Institute, July 2007). The research by Baerenklau, Schwabe, and Dinar, found the 17 percent reduction.

22. Kenneth Waldroup et al., "2013 City of Raleigh Water Resources Assessment and Plan" (Raleigh, 2013), https://www.raleighnc.gov/content/PubUtilAdmin/Documents/WaterResourceAssessment/2013WaterResourceAssessmentandPlan.pdf..

23. The results cited in Baerenklau, Schwabe, and Dinar, "Residential Water Demand of Increasing Block Rate Pricing," were achieved with only a 4 percent increase in average water rates.

24. David Tucker, Shadi Eskaf, and Alex Clegg, *Water and Wastewater Rates and Rate Structures in North Carolina* (North Carolina League of Municipalities and UNC Environmental Finance Center, Raleigh, February 2015).

25. Found by using the 2010 total water use consumption rate, a 17 percent reduction in the consumption rate for implementing tiered pricing, and a 32.5 percent (average of the low and high range from studies) reduction in the consumption rate for implementing wastewater recycling.

26. U.S. Department of Energy, Energy Information Agency, http://www.eia.gov/state/seds/data.php?incfile=/state/seds/sep_use/tx/use_tx_NC.html&sid=NC. The decline in total energy consumption was likely influenced by the severity of the 2007–9 recession and subsequent slow recovery.

27. Brad Plumer, "Cars in the U.S. Are More Fuel Efficient Than Ever: Here's How It Happened," *Washington Post*, December 13, 2013; U.S. Environmental Protection Agency, *Light-Duty Automotive Technology, Carbon Dioxide Emissions, and Fuel Economy Trends, 1975–2014*, EPA-420-S-14-001 (Washington, D.C., October 2014).

28. U.S. Department of Labor, Bureau of Labor Statistics, "Consumer Price Index," www.bls.gov/cpi/.

29. U.S. Department of Transportation, National Highway Transportation Safety Administration, *Summary of Fuel Efficiency Performance* (Washington, D.C., April 2011).

30. American Physical Society, *Energy = Future: Think Efficiency*, September 16, 2008, www.aps.org/energyefficiencyreport; Hannah Granade et al., *Unlocking Energy Efficiency in the U.S. Economy* (Washington, D.C.: McKinsey, July 2009).

31. An example of a company engaged in these activities is PowerShare, headquartered in Wake Forest, North Carolina. Jeff Jeffrey, "Flipping the Switch to Lower Energy Bills," *Triangle Business Journal*, October 9, 2015, 15.

32. For example, federal fuel efficiency standards for passenger vehicles are set to increase 67 percent between 2012 and 2025, with possible revisions. U.S. Department of Transportation, National Highway Transportation Safety Administration, *2017–2025 Model Year Light-Duty Vehicle GHG CAFE Standards: Supplemental* (Washington, D.C., July 2011). From 2013 to 2040, electricity prices are forecasted to increase 0.6 percent annually, motor fuel prices are projected to rise 0.4 percent annually, and natural gas prices are expected to increase 1.6 percent annually (all inflation-adjusted dollars and per million BTU). U.S. Department of Energy, Energy Information Administration, *Annual Energy Outlook, 2015* (Washington, D.C., April 2015).

33. Based on assumptions of a state population of 13.4 million in 2050 and an annual growth rate in real state GDP of 1.6 percent.

34. Other sources such as hydropower and renewables bring the totals to 100 percent. U.S. Department of Energy, Energy Information Agency, http://www.eia.gov/state/seds/seds-data-fuel.php?sid=NC.

35. In August 2015, the EPA announced new requirements for reducing carbon dioxide emissions from coal fueled plants by 30 percent by 2030 compared to 2005 levels. U.S. Environmental Protection Agency, "Clean Power Plan for Existing Power Plants," https://www.epa.gov/cleanpowerplan/carbon-pollution-standards-new-modified-and-reconstructed-power-plants. In 2017 the Trump administration nullified the regulations. Coral Davenport and Alissa Rubin, "Trump Signs Executive Order Unwinding Obama Climate Policies," *NYT*, March 28, 2017.

36. See https://www.duke-energy.com/our-company/about-us/coal-plant-decommissioning-program.

37. Derek Medlin, "Duke Suspends Plans for Shearon Harris Expansion," WRAL-TV, May 3, 2013, www.wral.com/duke-suspends-plans-for-shearon-harris-expansion/12408113/.

38. Sonya Reinhardt, "Economic Barriers to the Expansion of Nuclear Power in the U.S." (Master's Degree Project, Duke University, 2008).

39. See chapter 3.

40. The existing gas pipeline runs through the western piedmont of the state and importantly provides service to the metropolitan areas of Charlotte, the Triad (Winston-Salem, Greensboro, and High Point), and the Triangle. The new eastern natural gas pipeline would enter the eastern section of the state at Northampton County and run south to Robeson County. John Murawski, "New Natural Gas Pipeline to NC Could Dampen Interest in Fracking," *Charlotte Observer*, June 13, 2014. However, the proposed new eastern pipeline is not without opposition. Paul Specht, "Pipeline Plans Draw Protest," *N&O*, November 20, 2016.

41. National Oceanic and Atmospheric Administration, National Centers for Environmental Information, https://www.ncei.noaa.gov/. Solar power installations in North Carolina rose 2,100 percent between 2011 and 2015, corresponding to an expanded renewable energy credit program offered by the state. Lauren Ohnesorge, "When It Comes to Solar, Markus Wilhelm Says He'll Go Big or Go Home," *Triangle Business Journal*, March 4, 2016, 10–12.

42. The cost comparisons are without any subsidy for solar power. For coal power using a carbon capture system, solar power is 13 percent *less* expensive, and including current solar subsidies, solar power is only 19 percent costlier than natural gas power. U.S. Energy Information Administration, *Levelized Cost and Levelized Avoided Cost of New Generation Resources in the Annual Energy Outlook 2015* (Washington, D.C., April 14, 2015), http://www.eia.gov/outlooks/aeo/pdf/electricity_generation_2015.pdf. However, there is a wide range of comparative cost estimates for solar power (much more than for other fuels), and in some comparisons solar power is currently much more competitive. Severin Borenstein, "The Private and Public Economics of Renewable Electricity Generation," *Journal of Economic Perspectives* 26, no. 1 (Winter 2012): 67–92. Another concern expressed by agricultural interests is that the potential toxicity of solar panels may damage the underlying value of the land. These groups have proposed requiring guarantees from solar power operators to compensate landowners financially for any damage when solar panels are removed at the end of their lifetime. John Murawski, "Peak Solar: NC's Frenetic Pace of Solar Development Faces Hurtles," *N&O*, June 18, 2016.

43. The comparisons are based on "levelized costs" of generating power from a large utility. Stefan Reichelstein and Michael Yorston, "The Prospects for Cost Competitive Solar PV Power," *Energy Policy* 55 (April 2013): 117–27. Levelized cost is the real (inflation-adjusted) price of power that equates the net present value of revenue from the power output with the net present value of production. Borenstein, "Private and Public Economics of Renewable Electricity Generation."

44. Anastasia Pantsios, "Solar Energy: Grid vs. Battery Storage," *EcoWatch*, April 7, 2015, http://ecowatch.com/2015/04/07/solar-energy-grid-battery-storage/; Gautam Gowrisankaran, Stanley S. Reynolds, and Mario Samano, "Intermittency and the Value of Renewable Energy," *Journal of Political Economy* 124, no. 4 (August 2016): 1187–234; "Lithium-Air Batteries: Their Time Has Come," *Economist*, August 6, 2016, 64. An interesting related issue is whether the growth of solar power—as well as wind and biomass power—could reduce peak loads at existing power plants enough to create significant excess capacity and economic losses for the utilities. Also, creating a national grid for regional transfer of solar and wind power is another way of addressing the irregular availability of these renewable energy sources. Vauhini Vara, "The Energy Interstate," *Atlantic*, June 2016, 24–26.

45. The facility is on twenty-two thousand acres in the eastern coastal counties of Pasquotank and Perquimans. The capital cost is between $400 million and $500 million with major financing from Amazon. Construction was expected to be completed by the end of 2016 ("Amazon to the Rescue," *Business North Carolina*, September 2015, 40), but the project faces continued opposition and possible legislative hurtles. Christopher Thomas, "Wind Energy's Future in NC Still Up in the Air," *Public Radio East*, July 26, 2016, www.publicradioeast.org/post/wind-energys-future-nc-air.

46. U.S. Department of Energy, WINDExchange, "North Carolina Wind Resource Map and Potential Wind Capacity," http://apps2.eere.energy.gov/wind/windexchange/wind_resource_maps.asp?stateab=nc; Carolyn Elfland, *Coastal Wind: Energy for North Carolina's Future*, Report Prepared for the North Carolina General Assembly (Chapel Hill: University of North Carolina, 2009). In 2016, the U.S. Department of the

Interior announced plans to offer leases on 122,000 acres in the coastal waters of North Carolina for offshore wind turbines. Bruce Henderson, "Feds to Offer Wind-Energy Leases off N.C. Shore," *N&O*, August 13, 2016.

47. U.S. Department of Energy, Energy Information Administration, *Levelized Cost and Levelized Avoided Cost of New Generation Resources in the Annual Energy Outlook 2015*.

48. U.S. Department of Energy, Office of Energy Efficiency and Renewable Energy, "Environmental Impacts and Siting of Wind Projects," https://energy.gov/eere/wind/environmental-impacts-and-siting-wind-projects. There have also been efforts in North Carolina to restrict the location of wind-power facilities due to concerns about interference with military flight paths as well as worries over potential health issues (from the strobelike effect of shadows cast by blades and low-frequency sounds disrupting sleep) and adverse effects on surrounding property values. John Murawski, "Wind Farms Are Feeling Blowback," *N&O*, June 24, 2016. Research by North Carolina State University revealed that a substantial number of vacation renters at North Carolina's coast would have to be compensated by a lower rent—hence reducing revenues to the state coastal tourist industry—if offshore windfarms were visible. Sanja Lutzeyer, Daniel Phaneuf, and Laura Taylor, "The Amenity Costs of Offshore Wind Farms: Evidence from a Choice Experiment," Working Paper (North Carolina State University, Center for Environmental and Resource Economic Policy, April 2016).

49. U.S. Department of Energy, Energy Information Administration, www.eia.gov/state/?sid=NC. Data are for 2014.

50. The cost comparisons are based on levelized costs. U.S. Department of Energy, Energy Information Administration, *Levelized Cost and Levelized Avoided Cost of New Generation Resources in the Annual Energy Outlook 2015*.

51. Biomass power plants emit nitrogen oxide, carbon dioxide, and a small amount of sulfur dioxide. Partnership for Policy Integrity, "Carbon Emissions from Burning Biomass for Energy," www.pfpi.net/carbon-emissions.

52. Using pine trees as the biomass source with a conversion rate of one acre of pine trees annually providing 25.5 million BTUs of energy annually (National Association of Conservation Districts, *Woody Biomass Desk Guide and Tool Kit, Appendix*, http://www.nacdnet.org/wp-content/uploads/2016/06/Woody-Biomass-Desk-Guide-and-Toolkit.compressed.pdf, and annual energy consumption in North Carolina of 2554.8 trillion BTUs. U.S. Department of Energy, Energy Information Administration, www.eia.gov/state/?sid=NC. Data are for 2014.

53. U.S. Energy Information Administration, *Annual Energy Outlook 2015: With Projections to 2040*, DOE/EIA-0383 (2015) (Washington, D.C., April 2015). The implied annual rate of change between 2014 and 2040 is used to project forecasts to 2050.

54. North Carolina has a mandate to derive 12.5 percent of retail electricity sales from renewable sources by 2021. David Tuerck, Michael Head, and Paul Bachman, *The Economic Impact of North Carolina's Energy and Energy Efficiency Portfolio Standard*, Working Paper (Boston: Suffolk University, Beacon Hill Institute, August 2009). Hastening the state's movement to renewable sources and away from coal would be implementation of the federal Clean Power Plan, which would mandate a reduction in state carbon emissions by 13 percent between 2012 and 2030. U.S. Environmental Protection Agency,

"Clean Power Plan, North Carolina Fact Sheet," https://www.epa.gov/sites/production/files/2016-09/documents/north-carolina.pdf. However, several states, including North Carolina, have joined in a lawsuit challenging the plan. Amy Harder and Brent Kendall, "Battle over EPA Rules Fires Up," *WSJ*, October 24–25, 2015. For the broader economic impact from expansion of North Carolina's renewable energy sources, see Keith Debbage, "Renewable Energy in North Carolina: The Potential Supply Chain," Working Paper (North Carolina State University, Institute for Emerging Issues, August 2008).

55. U.S. Energy Information Administration, *Energy-Related Carbon Dioxide Emissions at the State Level, 2000–2014*, January 2017, http://www.eia.gov/environment/emissions/state/analysis/.

56. American Lung Association, *State of the Air, 2016*, http://www.lung.org/assets/documents/healthy-air/state-of-the-air/sota-2016-full.pdf; American Lung Association, *State of the Air, 2000*, released May 1, 2002.

57. Ken Gwilliam, Masami Kojima, and Todd Johnson, "Reducing Air Pollution from Urban Transport," (Washington, D.C.: The World Bank, June 2004), http://documents.worldbank.org/curated/en/989711468328204490/pdf/304250PAPER0Reducingoairopollution.pdf.

58. Between 2000 and 2013, county vehicle registrations increased 13 percent in Forsyth, 12 percent in Guilford, 27 percent in Mecklenburg, and 43 percent in Wake. North Carolina State Data Center, log into North Carolina, data.osbm.state.nc.us.

59. Arjun Sreekumar, "Two Challenges Holding Back Natural Gas Vehicles," *Motley Fool*, March 4, 2013, www.fool.com/investing/general/2013/03/04/the-biggest-challenges-for-natural-gas-vehicles.aspx.

60. Promoters of using electric-powered vehicles as a way of reducing air pollution need to be aware of how the electric power is generated. If generated from highly polluting sources such as traditional coal, then the reductions in pollution may be minimal. David Biello, "If the Fuel Source Ain't Clean, Your Electric Car Ain't Green," *Scientific American*, January 26, 2014, www.scientificamerican.com/podcast/episode/coal-powered-electric-cars-pollute/.

61. "From Horseless to Driverless," *Economist*, August 1, 2015, 15–16. Some also see driverless vehicles changing the physical structure of retailers, with outlets and distribution centers built to accommodate driverless vehicles, thereby replacing structures built around on-site shoppers. Lauren Ohnesorge, "NCSU Researcher: How Driverless Cars Could Deliver Your Groceries," *Triangle Business Journal*, December 11, 2015, 6. It is also argued that privately owned vehicles are extremely inefficient, with inactivity (being parked) accounting for 95 percent of their use. Dan Neil, "Could Self-Driving Cars Spell the End of Ownership?," *WSJ*, December 1, 2015. Chauffeured or driverless commuting vans, already operating in some metropolitan areas, are another way to reduce air pollution related to daily work commutes. Taylor Soper, "Meet SnapTransit: A Private Shuttle Bus That Wants to Make Your Commute More Productive," Geekwire.com, December 23, 2015, www.geekwire.com/2015/meet-snaptransit-private-shuttle-bus-wants-make-commute-productive/. Some housing developments in high-density areas are already offering financial incentives to tenants using ride-sharing vehicles rather than private vehicles, thereby reducing the need to construct garage facilities. Ester Fung, "Dear Tenant: Your Uber Car is Here," *WSJ*, November 23, 2016.

62. In economic theory, pollution is termed a "negative externality," implying that it is an unintended consequence from a user pursuing another objective (such as driving to work) and for which the user does not pay the cost of the associated pollution. Therefore, the solution is for the user to pay the cost and likely alter (reduce) the behavior that is creating the adverse unintended consequence. Christoher R. Knittel and Ryan Sandler, "The Welfare Impact of Indirect Pigouvian Taxation: Evidence from Transportation," NBER Working Paper 18849 (Boston: National Bureau of Economic Research, February 2013).

63. The per-gallon fee would need to be near one dollar to achieve a 15 percent reduction in carbon emissions. Lucas Davis and Lutz Kilian, "Estimating the Effect of a Gasoline Tax on Carbon Emissions," NBER Working Paper 14685 (Boston: National Bureau of Economic Research, January 2009). One issue with this approach is the impact of such taxes on low-income households, which typically pay a larger proportion of their income on gasoline and other fuels. A solution is to use some of the resulting tax revenues to reduce other taxes (income, sales) for these households, but this approach has not been universally accepted. N. Gregory Mankiw, "Shifting the Tax Burden to Cut Carbon," *NYT*, September 6, 2015.

64. The energy intensities of passenger modes (BTU per passenger mile) is 2,898 for passenger car, 5,472 for a truck, 823 for a passenger bus, and 1,629 for a passenger train (all data are for 2014, except 2006 for passenger car). U.S. Department of Transportation, Bureau of Transportation Statistics, www.rita.dot.gov/bts/files/publications/transportation-statistical/html/table_04_20.html.

65. There is in fact a debate over whether mass transit reduces emissions and improves the environment, with the disagreement centered on the degree of use of mass transit options. Thomas Rubin et al., "Does Bus Transit Reduce Greenhouse Gas Emissions?," *Reason Foundation*, April 5, 2010, www.reason.org/news/show/does-bus-transit-reduce-greenhouse.

66. The Public Purpose, "U.S. Light Rail Costs Near $70 Million per Mile," *Urban Transit Fact Book*, 2004, www.publicpurpose.com/ut-lrtoocapcost.htm.

67. Thomas A. Garrett, "The Costs and Benefits of Light Rail, *Federal Reserve Bank of St. Louis*, Fall 2004, www.stlouisfed.org/publications/central-banker/fall-2004/the-costs-and-benefits-of-light-rail.

68. Christopher Zegras and Shan Jiang, "Sustaining Mass Transit through Land Value Taxation? Prospects for Chicago," Working Paper (MIT, May 2013).

69. TetraTech and Andrew Stoddard and Associates, *Progress in Water Quality: An Evaluation of the National Investment in Municipal Wastewater Treatment*, 832-R-00-008, (U.S. Environmental Protection Agency, Office of Wastewater Management, June 2000), https://semspub.epa.gov/work/10/100003841.pdf. U.S. Environment Protection Agency, "WATERS (Watershed Assessment, Tracking, and Environmental Results System," https://www.epa.gov/waterdata/waters-watershed-assessment-tracking-environmental-results-system.

70. Statistics are for the annual number of broilers produced. North Carolina Department of Agriculture and Consumer Services, *North Carolina Agricultural Statistics* (Raleigh, 2013).

71. Statistics are for annual hog inventory measured in numbers of animals. Ibid.

72. "In the Aftermath of Floyd," *North Carolina River Keepers and Waterkeeper Alliance*, 2003, www.riverlaw.us/hurricanefloyd.html.

73. Mark Drajem, "What a Load of (Pig) Crap!," *Bloomberg Business*, September 1, 2015, 27–29; Rose Rimler, "Study Finds Hog Waste in N.C. Waters," *N&O*, August 31, 2015.

74. The cap was made permanent in 2007. The limitation is actually a quasi-cap in that new hog farms are permitted as long as they meet state environmental standards. However, the number of hogs in North Carolina declined from 10.6 million in 1997 to 8.5 million in 2014. U.S. Department of Agriculture, National Agricultural Statistics Service, www.quickstats.nass.usda.gov.

75. A waste management research center has been charged with developing and testing both the environmental and economic impacts of alternative hog waste disposal technologies. Their major benchmark for the development of a successful technology is that its implementation *not* result in more than a 10 percent reduction in the inventory of hogs. As of 2015, no technologies had been found to meet this criterion. C. M. Williams, "Evaluation of Generation 3 Treatment Technology for Swine Waste," Working Paper (North Carolina State University, Animal and Poultry Waste Management Center, August 19, 2013); C. M. Williams, "Development of Environmentally Superior Technologies," Working Paper (North Carolina State University, Animal and Poultry Waste Management Center, March 8, 2006).

76. Another "capitalist" answer is the development of profitable new markets that reduce environmental harm. One example is for-profit companies that convert food waste to fertilizer and that match food suppliers, such as farmers, having surplus stocks to be discarded with buyers desiring the commodities. Stephanie Strom, "Leftovers, Scraps, Profit," *NYT*, May 27, 2016.

Chapter 7

1. Roby Sawyers, "The History of State and Local Taxes in North Carolina—Changes in Sources and Burdens," Working Paper (North Carolina State University, Institute for Emerging Issues, November 28, 2006).

2. In 2013, the North Carolina General Assembly added movie and other admission tickets and manufactured home sales to the sales tax base, and in 2015, it added car repairs, oil changes, flooring installations, appliance installations, kitchen remodeling, and some service contracts—such as on computers—to the sales tax base. Colin Campbell, "More Sales Taxes in 2016, Income Tax Cuts in 2017," *N&O*, September 20, 2015.

3. There is also a debate about the volatility of consumption versus income taxes. The traditional view was that consumption taxes were more stable—with revenues falling less than those from income taxation during recessions but also rising less during economic recoveries. However, recent research for the business cycle including the Great Recession does not find greater stability for consumption taxes. Howard Chernick and Cordelia Reimers, "Consumption Taxes, Income Taxes, and Revenue Stability: States and the Great Recession," Working Paper (Hunter College, City University of New York, December 2014); Elizabeth McNichol, *Strategies to Address the State Tax Volatility Problem: Eliminating the State Income Tax Not a Solution* (Washington, D.C.: Center on Budget and Policy Priorities, April 18, 2013).

4. There is a federal EITC, and many states have a state version. North Carolina instituted a state EITC in 2007 but removed it in 2014. Leoneda Inge, "N.C. Says Good-Bye to Earned Income Tax Credit, Only State to Do So in 30 Years,"*North Carolina Public Radio*, March 15, 2014, wunc.unc.org/post/nc-says-good-bye-earned-income-tax-credit-only-state-to-do-so-30-years#stream/0.

5. A generous EITC would also allow North Carolina to reduce expenditures on other programs designed to assist limited resource households. For example, North Carolina spent $567 million of state funds on TANF (Temporary Aid to Needy Families) in 2015. Center on Budget and Policy Priorities, North Carolina TANF Spending (Washington, D.C., January 2017), http://www.cbpp.org/sites/default/files/atoms/files/tanf_spend-ing_nc.pdf. For an examination of the economic condition of single individuals with no children receiving little public assistance, see Kathryn Edin and Luke Shaefer, *$2.00 a Day: Living on Almost Nothing in America* (Boston: Houghton Mifflin Harcourt, 2015). It should be noted the expanded EITC proposed here differs from the concept of a univer-sal basic income, in which the latter provides a basic income to all citizens regardless of their economic situation. Eduardo Porter, "A Basic Income Is a Poor Tool to Fight Poverty," *NYT*, May 31, 2016; Matt Zwolinski, "The Pragmatic Libertarian Case for a Basic Income," *Cato Unbound*, August 4, 2014, www.cato-unbound.org/2014/08/04/matt-zwolinski/pragmatic-libertarian-case-basic-income-guarantee.

6. For an analysis of this issue, see Michael L. Walden, "Implicit Tax Rates of the Expanded Earned Income Tax Credits for Welfare Recipients in North Carolina," *Jour-nal of Consumer Affairs* 30, no. 2 (Winter 1996): 348–72. Interaction of the withdrawal of EITC support should also be coordinated with the withdrawal of support in other programs, such as the Supplemental Nutrition Assistance Program (Food Stamps) and Medicaid, as recipient households gain earnings.

7. Before 1921 North Carolina had a state property tax. Sawyers, "History of State and Local Taxes in North Carolina."

8. Estimates are from the U.S. Census Bureau, "American Community Survey," https://www.census.gov/programs-surveys/acs/; and the U.S. Department of Labor, Bureau of Labor Statistics, "Consumer Expenditure Survey," https://www.bls.gov/cex/. There can—and likely would—be debates about subtle differences between con-sumption and investment. For example, what portion of spending on a house by a homeowner is consumption versus investment? Also, spending on health care and on education could—at least in part—be considered an investment.

9. The annual costs are $13,850 for children aged zero to five, $16,555 for children aged six to eleven, and $21,173 for children aged twelve to seventeen, all in 2014 dollars. Mark Lino, *Expenditures on Children by Families*, Report 0179-14 (Washington, D.C.: U.S. Department of Agriculture, August 2014).

10. The calculations are based on three census categories of household annual earn-ings: earnings averaging $5,000, earnings averaging $12,500, and earnings averaging $20,000. Households with earnings of $5,000 receive a state supplement of $5,000—bringing their total to $10,000; households with earnings of $12,500 receive a sup-plement of $3,750—bringing their total to $16,250; and households with earnings of $20,000 receive a supplement of $2,500—bringing their total to $22,500. Households with no taxable earnings receive an EITC based on the lowest average earnings level.

11. The total "own tax revenue" excluding the motor vehicle revenues and other public fees, is $34 billion. The local property tax revenue is $9 billion, and adding revenue from a state property tax on industrial and commercial property (see note 12, below) brings total property tax revenue to $11 billion. Taking $34 billion minus $11 billion from the existing local and new state property taxes plus $12 billion for the new EITC yields a total of $35 billion to be funded by either the income or consumption tax. However, to keep the non-transportation total state and local tax revenues (excluding property tax revenues) at the long-run average of 5.6 percent of GDP, a further $9 billion must be subtracted, leaving a "revenue required" amount of $26 billion. Presumably these reductions could be made by downsizing programs that currently address the same issues as the expanded child tax deduction and state EITC.

12. Aggregate property tax revenues to North Carolina local governments was $9 billion. U.S. Census Bureau, "State and Local Government Finance," www.census. gov/govs/local/. Of the total, 26 percent was from industrial and commercial property. North Carolina Department of Revenue, "County Taxable Real Property Valuations," 2014, www.dornc.com/publications/taxable_real_property.html. A new state property tax on industrial and commercial would therefore generate $2 billion (0.26 × $9 billion) in 2014.

13. Assuming a 36 percent investment rate for the household earning $100,000. The investment rate is the average for households with gross income above $70,000. U.S. Department of Labor, Bureau of Labor Statistics, "Consumer Expenditure Survey."

14. Congressional Budget Office, *The 2016 Long-Term Budget Outlook* (Washington, D.C., July 2016). An alternative solution is to increase the relative size of public funding. However, total local and state derived taxes (including transportation funding) as a percent of state GDP has averaged a stable 7.9 percent for two decades (1992–2013), rising only during recession years when the tax base (GDP) falls. It is reasonable therefore to expect the total pool of state and local derived tax revenue to remain constant in future decades.

15. U.S. Census Bureau, "State and Local Government Finance."

16. Spending is based on revenues from all sources, including state, local, and federal funds. To give context, in 2010 public spending (from all sources) in North Carolina for education was $23 billion, $10 billion for health care, $3.4 billion for transportation, and $2.3 billion for public safety (including $2 billion for incarcerations). Ibid.

17. Based on an extension of trends in national public health care spending projections between 2015 and 2040. Congressional Budget Office, *The 2015 Long-Term Budget Outlook* (Washington, D.C., June 16, 2015).

18. William J. Baumol, *The Cost Disease: Why Computers Get Cheaper and Health Care Doesn't* (New Haven, Conn.: Yale University Press, 2012).

19. See Eric Topol, *The Patient Will See You Now: The Future of Medicine is in Your Hands* (New York: Basic Books, 2015), for predictions of technological applications in health care resulting in future efficiency gains. For a cautionary view of potential technological changes in health care and the impacts of those changes, see Robert M. Wachter, *The Digital Doctor: Hope, Hype, and Harm at the Dawn of Medicine's Computer Age* (New York: McGraw-Hill, 2015).

20. In economic terminology, fee-for-service systems motivate providers (doctors, hospitals) to recommend a procedure or service as long as the benefits are positive, not as long as the benefits exceed the costs. Laurence J. Kotlikoff, *The Healthcare Fix: Universal Insurance for All Americans* (Cambridge, Mass.: MIT Press, 2007).

21. Amelia Haviland et al., "Do 'Consumer-Directed' Health Plans Bend the Cost Curve over Time?," NBER Working Paper 21031 (Boston: National Bureau of Economic Research, March 2015).

22. Lynn Bonner, "North Carolina to Privatize Medicaid," *N&O*, September 17, 2015. Since federal Medicaid funds are involved, permission for the change must be granted by federal authorities. There is a complementary funding issue in the state health care program for retirees, where a multi-billion-dollar unfunded liability has been estimated. North Carolina General Assembly, Program Evaluation Division, *Unfunded Actuarial Liability for Retiree Health Is Large, but State Could Save Up to $64 Million Annually by Shifting Costs to Medicare Advantage Plans*, Report 2015-05 (Raleigh, July 2015). Identified potential solutions include increasing retiree contributions, reducing eligibility, or shifting costs to the federal government by requiring retirees to be on federal managed care plans and not providing fee-for-service plans options.

23. Bonner, "North Carolina to Privatize Medicaid."

24. For examples of health-care vouchers, see Kotlikoff, *Healthcare Fix*; and Ezekiel J. Emanuel and Victor R. Fuchs, *A Comprehensive Cure: Universal Health Care Vouchers* (Washington, D.C.: Brookings Institute, July 2007).

25. The voucher amount includes funding from both the federal and North Carolina governments. Medicaid funding in North Carolina is split 55 percent from the federal government and 45 percent from the state government. North Carolina Department of Health and Human Services, Division of Medical Assistance, *Medicaid Annual Report 2008* (Raleigh, 2008). The average price of a health insurance policy for a single person in 2015 was $6,251. Henry J. Kaiser Family Foundation, "2015 Employer Health Benefits Survey," http://kff.org/health-costs/report/2015-employer-health-benefits-survey/.

26. Christoper Koopman, Thomas Stratmann, and Mohamad Elbarasse, "Certificate of Need Laws: Implications for Georgia," *Mercatus on Policy* (George Mason University, Mercatus Center, March 31, 2015).

27. For an excellent review of the debate over CON laws, see Tracy Yee et al., "Health Care Certificate-of-Need (CON) Laws: Policy or Politics?," Research Brief 4 (Washington, D.C.: National Institute of Health Care Reform, May 2011).

28. Tara Siegel Bernard, "Program Links Loans to Future Earnings," *NYT*, July 19, 2003.

29. The U.S. Department of Labor has instituted a modest version of this idea called reemployment services assistance. "U.S. Department of Labor Announces $26.5 Million to Implement and Expand Unemployment Insurance REA Grants," News Release (Washington, D.C.: U.S. Department of Labor, July 30, 2009). One potential impediment of relocation—especially of rural residents to fast-growing urban regions—is the higher cost of housing in metropolitan counties. Public housing subsidies to lower income households is one way to address this issue. Another is to modify housing and land regulations that can significantly increase the price of housing. Daniel Shoag and Peter Ganong, "Why Has Regional Income Convergence in the U.S. Declined?," Working Paper (Harvard University, January 2015).

30. Jerry Kaplan, *Humans Need Not Apply: A Guide to Wealth and Work in the Age of Artificial Intelligence* (New Haven, Conn.: Yale University Press, 2015), 154–58.

31. Taylor Soper, "Meet SnapTransit: A Private Bus that Wants to Make Your Commute More Productive," Geekwire.com, December 23, 2015, www.geekwire.com/2015/meet-snaptransit-private-shuttle-bus-wants-make-commute-productive/.

32. Driverless vehicles could increase the capacity of existing highways by allowing tighter spacing between vehicles. 3-D manufacturing could reduce highway usage by shortening supply chains. Jonathan Woetzel et al., *Bridging Global Infrastructure Gaps* (Washington, D.C.: McKinsey Global Institute, June 2016). For a comprehensive look at twenty-first-century transportation issues, see Rosebeth Kanter, *Move: Putting America's Infrastructure Back in the Lead* (New York: W. W. Norton, 2015).

33. The average annual cost of incarcerating an inmate declined from $32,032 in 2000 to $30,400 in 2015 (both in 2015 dollars and averaged over all security levels). North Carolina Department of Public Safety, "Cost of Corrections," http://www.ncdps.gov/Adult-Corrections/Cost-of-Corrections. The three-year recidivism rate in North Carolina's prison population dropped from 36 percent in 2006 to 29 percent in 2010. Council of State Governments Justice Center, *Reducing Recidivism: States Deliver Results* (New York, 2014).

34. Inmate numbers in North Carolina are for 2015 and are from the North Carolina Department of Public Safety, "Prisons," http://www.ncdps.gov/Adult-Corrections/Prisons; household earnings numbers are from the U.S. Bureau of the Census, "American Community Survey 2014, North Carolina," updated to 2015 dollars, https://www.census.gov/programs-surveys/acs/.

35. For a national perspective on this issue, see Executive Office of the President of the United States, *Economic Perspectives on Incarceration and the Criminal Justice System* (Washington, D.C., April 2016).

36. "Prison Rehabilitation," Politics.co.uk, www.politics.co.uk/reference/prison-rehabilitation. The approach has also been applied in New York City. "Being Good Pays," *Economist*, August 18, 2015, 28. Payments are scaled to the rate of success, thus providing an incentive to the contractor for good results.

37. The growth is based on forecasted trends in Medicaid spending from the Congressional Budget Office, *The 2015 Long-Term Budget Outlook* (Washington, D.C., June 2015).

38. For a strong criticism of the effectiveness of many government programs, as well as suggestions for improvement, see Peter H. Schuck, *Why Government Fails So Often—And How It Can Do Better* (Princeton, N.J.: Princeton University Press, 2014).

39. North Carolina Fiscal Research Division, *North Carolina Economic Development Inventory* (Raleigh, March 2013).

40. Ibid.

41. Using the terminology of economic theory, business incentives can be viewed as targeted cost reductions—thereby reducing the net price of a specific location—for firms whose demand curve for location is very price elastic (meaning very price sensitive).

42. Tyler Dukes, "State Leaders' Job Promises Continue to Come Up Short," WRAL-TV, October 20, 2015, www.wral.com/state-leaders-job-promises-continue-to-come-up-short/14949497/. For academic analyses critical of active state economic

development policies, see Mark D. Partridge, "America's Job Crisis and the Role of Regional Economic Development Policy," *Review of Economic Studies* 43, no. 2/3 (2014): 97–110; and Douglas P. Woodward, "Industry Location, Economic Development Incentives, and Clusters," *Review of Regional Studies* 42, no. 1 (2012): 5–23. On a broader level, recent studies have questioned the ability of states to alter tax and public spending policies in ways that stimulate economic growth. Factors beyond the immediate control of public policy, such as the state's industry mix, have been found to be stronger determinants of economic activity. Jed Kolko, David Neumark, and Marisol Cuellar Mejia, "What Do Business Climate Indexes Teach Us about State Policy and Economic Growth?," *Journal of Regional Science* 53, no. 2 (May 2014): 220–55; Georgeanne Artz et al., "Do State Business Climate Indicators Explain Relative Economic Growth at State Borders?," *Journal of Regional Science* 56, no., 3 (2016): 395–419.

43. North Carolina had an unfortunate experience in picking what looked like a "winner" but resulted in a "loser" when it provided business incentives to Dell to open a manufacturing plant in the Triad region. The plant was never constructed. Matt Evans, "The Failure of Dell—Was It Worth It?," *Triad Business Journal*, October 12, 2009.

44. Alicia Munnell and Jean-Pierre Aubry, "The Funding of State and Local Pensions: 2014–2018," State and Local Pension Plans, no. 45 (Boston College, Center of Retirement Research, June 2015). The ratio is the current value (present value) of assets to the current value (present value) of expected liabilities, where assets are the value of investments held by the pension plan and liabilities are the value of future expected pension payments.

45. Ibid.

46. Congressional Budget Office, *The Underfunding of State and Local Pension Plans*, Economic and Budget Issue Brief (Washington, D.C., May 4, 2011); Pew Charitable Trusts, *The State Pension Funding Gap: 2014* (Washington, D.C., August 2016).

47. Robert Novy-Marx and Joshua Rauh, "The Revenue Demands of Public Employee Pension Promises," *American Economic Journal: Economic Policy* 6, no. 1 (February 2014): 193–229. North Carolina's required tax increase of 9.5 percent to remove the pension deficit is less than average state increase of 13.4 percent. The Novy-Marx and Rauh results are confirmed in an updated study. Joshua Rauh, "Hidden Debt, Hidden Deficits," Hoover Institution Essay (Stanford University, Hoover Institution, April 8, 2016). Eileen Norcross also finds a shortfall in North Carolina's pension system when current interest rates are used. Eileen Norcross, *Ranking the States by Fiscal Condition* (George Mason University, Mercatus Center, July 2015).

48. North Carolina Department of State Treasurer, *Annual Report, Fiscal Year 2011–2012* (Raleigh, 2013). North Carolina's fees—on a percentage basis—were well below the highest paid by some states. Jeff Hooke and John J. Walters, *Wall Street Fees, Investment Returns, Maryland and 49 Other State Pension Funds*, Maryland Policy Report (Rockville: Maryland Public Policy Institute, 2013.

49. Michael L. Walden, "Active versus Passive Investment Management of State Pension Plans: Implications for Personal Finance," *Journal of Financial Planning and Counseling* 26, no. 2 (2015): 1–12; Hooke and Walters, *Wall Street Fees, Investment Returns*.

50. This is the debate between "active investment management" versus "passive investment management." Advocates of passive management include Burton

G. Malkiel, *A Random Walk Down Wall Street: The Time-Tested Strategy for Successful Investing*, 12th ed. (New York: W. W. Norton, 2015). Supporters of active management include Andrew W. Lo and A. Craig MacKinlay, *A Non-Random Walk down Wall Street* (Princeton, N.J.: Princeton University Press, 1999).

51. Walden, "Active versus Passive Investment Management of State Pension Plans."

52. North Carolina Future of Retirement Study Commission, *Final Report to Boards of Trustees of the Teachers' and State Employees' Retirement System and the Local Governmental Employees' Retirement System* (Raleigh, November 16, 2010).

53. Fitzpatrick estimated that public school teachers would be willing to accept a current salary increase of only twenty cents in exchange for a reduction of one dollar (in today's purchasing power value) of promised future retirement benefits. Maria Fitzpatrick, "How Much Are Public School Teachers Willing to Pay for Their Retirement Benefits?," *American Economic Journal: Economic Policy* 7, no. 4 (November 2015): 165–88.

54. Quoted in George Gilder, *The Twenty-First-Century Case for Gold* (Washington, D.C.: American Twenty-First Century Project, 2015).

55. Derek Thompson, "Millennials' Political Views Don't Make Any Sense," *Atlantic*, July 15, 2014, www.theatlantic.com/politics/archive/2014/07/millennials-economics-voting-clueless-kids-these-days/374427/.

Chapter 8

1. Joseph Schumpeter, *Capitalism, Socialism, and Democracy* (London: Routledge, 1942).

INDEX